C90 188254

D0298555

GOD'S WOLF

GOD'S WOLF

The Life of the Most
Notorious of All Crusaders:
Reynald de Chatillon

JEFFREY LEE

Atlantic Books
London

First published in hardback in Great Britain in 2016 by Atlantic Books,
an imprint of Atlantic Books Ltd.

Copyright © Jeffrey Lee 2016

The moral right of Jeffrey Lee to be identified as the author of this work has
been asserted by him in accordance with the Copyright, Designs and Patents Act
of 1988.

All rights reserved. No part of this publication may be reproduced, stored
in a retrieval system, or transmitted in any form or by any means, electronic,
mechanical, photocopying, recording, or otherwise, without the prior permission
of both the copyright owner and the above publisher of this book.

1 2 3 4 5 6 7 8 9

A CIP catalogue record for this book is available from the British Library.

Hardback ISBN: 978-1-78239-925-4
Trade paperback ISBN: 978-1-78239-926-1
E-book ISBN: 978-1-78239-927-8
Paperback ISBN: 978-1-78239-928-5
Printed in Great Britain by Bell & Bain Ltd, Glasgow

Atlantic Books
An Imprint of Atlantic Books Ltd
Ormond House
26–27 Boswell Street
London
WC1N 3JZ

www.atlantic-books.co.uk

For the brothers –

Tam Tam, Bee Boy and Li'l Tigs

CONTENTS

ILLUSTRATIONS & MAPS

Colour Section

Contents of the FedEx package sent by Al-Qaida in 2010 (© PA)

Chapel of St Radegund fresco (*DeAgostini/Getty Images*)

Cressac Chapel fresco (*Corbis*)

Illustration from the manuscript of William of Tyre's *History of Deeds done beyond the Sea*, 12th century (*Ann Ronan Pictures/Print Collector/Getty Images*)

Illustration from the manuscript of William of Tyre's *History* and its *Continuation*, 13th century (*Bibliothèque nationale de France*)

Illustration of Reynald de Chatillon's seal as Prince of Antioch (From *The Crusades: The Story of the Latin Kingdom of Jerusalem*, by T. A. Archer and Charles Lethbridge Kingsford, London & New York, 1894)

View from across the Orontes river by J. Redway (1841) (*Print Collector/Getty Images*)

Reynald's stronghold at Kerak in Oultrejordan (*Marco Tomasini/Shutterstock*)

The Muslim stronghold of Shayzar (© *Maxime Goepp, www.orient-latin.com*)

The citadel of Aleppo (*Valery Shanin/Shutterstock*)

The castle on the Ile de Graye (*Mildax/Shutterstock*)

Contemporary portrait of Saladin, *c*. 1180 (*Ann Ronan Pictures/Print Collector/Getty Images*)

Illustration of Reynald's seal as Lord of Oultrejordan (From *La Palestine* by Baron Ludovic de Vaux, Paris, 1883)

Portrait of Manuel I Comnemos and Maria of Antioch (*DeAgostini/Getty Images*)

Church of the Holy Sepulchre in Jerusalem (*Nickolay Vinokurov/Shutterstock*)

The Horns of Hattin in Galilee, Israel (*Zeromancer44/Wikimedia Commons*)

Illustration from the *Chronica Maiora* by Matthew Paris, 13th century (*Fine Art Images/Heritage Images/Getty Images*)

Maps

Prologue

Sana'a, Yemen, 29 October 2010

The Sana'a office of the global courier company FedEx is on Hadda Street, a busy, dusty drag of upscale shops and restaurants in the Yemeni capital. Among the customers dropping off packages that Friday was a veiled woman who said she was Hanan al-Samawi, an engineering student. She left a box for shipping to the city of Chicago, Illinois.

Inside the box was a Hewlett-Packard LaserJet printer, some traditional Yemeni clothing, a souvenir model of Yemen's famous mud skyscrapers and a few English books, including a torn copy of *The Mill on the Floss* by George Eliot.

Inside the printer were 300 grams of the industrial explosive PETN, more than enough to bring down a jetliner in flight. It was primed to detonate over Chicago.

The plot was the work of the Islamist terror group, Al-Qaida in the Arabian Peninsula. The device's living targets were the people of Chicago, but the bomb was not addressed to them. It was addressed to an old enemy, the most hated and feared of the crusaders who battled the forces of Islam in the Middle Ages.

The bomb was addressed to a man who had been dead for more than 800 years. It was addressed to Reynald de Chatillon.

Introduction

A MONSTROUS UNBELIEVER

> *Reynald was the most perfidious and wicked of the Franks. He was the greediest, the most determined to destroy and do evil, to violate agreements and solemn oaths, to break his promise and to lie.*
>
> Imad al-Din[1]

Twenty-first-century terrorists address their printer-bomb to a long-dead Frankish knight.

The crusades live.

This might surprise most Westerners, for whom the crusades are little more than a dim and dusty story of knights fighting Saracens in the deserts of the Middle East. In fact the legacy of the crusades is very much alive, for they were the crucible in which the forging of the modern world began.

The series of religio-military expeditions, which marched from Western Europe to seize Jerusalem from the Muslims, were the first counter-attacks by Western Christendom against the expanding civilization of Islam – a civilization then superior in medicine, science, mathematics, commerce and much else. The states created in the Levant, settled by the crusaders and then fought over for two centuries were the Christian West's first colonial experiment. The movement began with the staggeringly successful First Crusade, which captured the Holy City of Jerusalem in 1099. Half a century later came the Second Crusade (1145–9), when Reynald de Chatillon went to the East. The Third Crusade of 1189–92 is perhaps the one best lodged in the Western psyche, given its leading men: King Richard the Lionheart, for Christendom, and his chivalrous adversary, the sultan Saladin, for Islam.

Crusades were not directed just against Saracens in the Orient. Religious fervour and the spirit of conquest drove the frontiers of Christendom in all directions. Crusades were launched against Muslims in Iberia, Eastern European Slavs, heretical Christians and even the Greek Christian Byzantine Empire.

Usually, in the twenty-first century, Western awareness of the crusades remains vague, carrying with it (if anything) some inchoate guilt for 'Christian aggression'. In the year 2000, Pope John Paul II's apology for the Church's errors was widely taken to include the crusades. But long before crusading fervour dwindled, Islam's knowledge had been transferred to the West, opening the way to the modern scientific method and the long path to the Enlightenment during the seventeenth and eighteenth centuries. Islamic civilization, set into a defensive posture, stagnated and its power waned. This impotence lies behind much of today's desperate Islamist extremism. In 1492, the Catholic *Reconquista* finally triumphed, with the defeat of the last Muslim kingdom in Spain. In the same year, and sponsored by the same Catholic monarchs, Columbus discovered the New World, assuring the supremacy of the Christian West. The dangerous idea that set these tectonic shifts in motion was spearheaded by men such as Reynald de Chatillon.

Among Muslims there is no guilt for the violence of the crusading wars, nor are they seen as distant historical events. Rather, there is a widespread belief that the Islamic world is still engaged in a virtuous battle against the crusader onslaught. Any loss of Islamic land – whether it was to medieval Frankish crusaders like Reynald, the Catholic *Reconquista* in Spain, the Zionist armies in Palestine in 1948 or the American-led occupation of Iraq in 2003 – forms part of this historical perspective. The crusades are seen by some as an ongoing scourge, one that has inflicted an open, festering wound on Islam. The militant Islamists of the Islamic State of Iraq and Syria (ISIS) describe all their Western enemies as 'crusaders', whether they are tourists on a Tunisian beach, the President of the United States or concert-goers in Paris. Bitterness over the crusades was certainly a motivating factor for the terrorists of Al-Qaida in the Arabian Peninsula (AQAP) when they addressed their cargo bomb to Reynald. After the attempt, which luckily failed,[2] AQAP wrote in their English-language propaganda journal, *Inspire*:

> *Today, we are fighting a war against American tyranny. This is a new crusade waged by the West against Islam. Therefore we wanted to put things into proper perspective. This current battle fought by the West is not an isolated battle but is a continuation of a long history of aggression by the West against the Muslim world.*[3]

Addressing the package to a crusader, AQAP pronounced, would 'revive and bring back this history'. But why choose Reynald de Chatillon in particular as the embodiment of this crusader enemy? Why not Godfrey de Bouillon or Raymond of Toulouse, leaders of the First Crusade? When they seized Jerusalem from the Muslims in 1099, their troops perpetrated a massacre so vile that on the Temple Mount their horses waded in blood up to their knees. Or why not the much more famous Richard the Lionheart, whose mere presence terrorized armies, and who festooned his bridle with the heads of Saracens that he had killed?

Reynald is reviled even more than those crusaders of malign memory. He epitomizes the crusades' enduring legacy of enmity between Christian and Muslim. The Muslims called him 'Arnat', or simply 'al-Brins' (the Prince), and he was a figure of hatred and terror from the first. For twelfth-century Muslims chronicling the war against the crusaders, Arnat was 'The most treacherous and wicked of the Franks'.* Likened to Abu Lahab, the loathsome enemy of the Prophet Muhammad, Arnat was blamed for spreading 'disorder, devastation and ruin'. He was 'one of the most devilish and recalcitrant Franks', 'the most hostile to the Muslims and the most dangerous to them', 'a monstrous infidel and a terrible oppressor'.

In the present day this reputation as a Muslim bogeyman remains as potent as ever. The typical modern Muslim view of Reynald is of someone 'fanatical, greedy and bloodthirsty'.[4] He 'aroused more hatred between Arabs and the Franks than had been caused by decades of wars and massacres'.[5] As *Inspire* explains, AQAP's FedEx bomb was addressed to Reynald in particular because he was 'one of the worst and most treacherous of the crusade's leaders'.

When you get to know what Reynald did – the blasphemy and trauma he inflicted on Islam – it is not surprising that many Muslims still detest the man and his legacy. He was the most effective and ruthless military opponent of the Muslims, particularly of Saladin, who has been elevated in posterity to almost saintly status. And Reynald's shocking exploits (or mad escapades, depending on your

* The crusaders were usually known as 'Franks' or 'Latins': 'Franks' because the largest contingents came from what is now France, and Old French was the lingua franca of the crusader states; 'Latins' to distinguish them from Greek Christians.

point of view) sent tremors through the religious sensibilities of the Islamic world. He struck at the very heart of the faith itself. Reynald's strategy could even be said to be the spark that lit that never-ending jihad, the Holy War, which Islamist groups, including AQAP and ISIS, still prosecute today.

While Reynald's name lives in infamy in the bestiary of Islamism, in the West he has been relegated to almost complete obscurity. Modern historians have usually dismissed him as a peripheral maverick, a 'knight-brigand' or a 'parvenu'. This is a surprising mistake, given his substantial influence in the crusader states. Equally surprising, when his impact is admitted, traditional Western historical narrative usually echoes the negative Islamic view of Reynald. In contrast to his Muslim foes and crusader rivals, who are seen as tolerant and compromising, Reynald is portrayed by Western historians as a greedy, selfish bigot and as an inveterate warmonger. He is 'crude, thick-headed and stubborn', 'aggressive, unadapted and incomprehending'.[6] In the traditional historical narrative, Reynald is cast as the arch-villain of the crusading epic. He is even made responsible for the crusaders' greatest military disaster. Some recent scholars have sought to redress the balance, pointing out Reynald's contribution and his embodiment of 'traditional crusading values', but their influence has been largely limited to academic circles.[7]

For instance, I mentioned Reynald to a Swedish friend who lives in the Middle East and has an interest in the region's history. 'Oh, yes,' she said, 'he was that horrible man who threw prisoners off the walls of his castle.' Now while Reynald was responsible for many acts of violence and cruelty, and the walls of his mighty fortress at Kerak are easily high enough to throw a man to his death, there is no evidence of this actually occurring. A quick trawl of the Internet, though, finds this story to be common currency, sometimes with gruesome embellishments. As a Kerak travel guide claims:

> *One of his [Reynald's] more notorious pleasures involved encasing*
> *the heads of his prisoners in wooden boxes so that, when he flung*
> *them off the castle walls, he could be sure that they hadn't lost*
> *consciousness by the time they hit the rocks below.*[8]

Across all sorts of websites – whether entertainment, travel or 'historical' – the same picture of Reynald is drawn: he is 'notorious', 'barbarous' and 'despicable', and his 'reputation for treachery, betrayal and brutality is unsurpassed'.[9] This goes for other media, too. In a BBC documentary series on the crusades, Reynald was called a 'manic aggressive'.[10] And the Reynald character in historical novels is usually wicked, while in films he has been portrayed almost as a caricature of the bad guy. In Ridley Scott's crusading Hollywood blockbuster, *Kingdom of Heaven*,[11] the excellent Brendan Gleeson plays Reynald as a sort of violent buffoon and a member of the Order of the Knights Templar – shorthand, in this view of the crusades, for the embodiment of unreconstructed Christian militancy. The real Reynald was certainly violent – consistently and extremely – but in a violent time. He was never a Templar. Nor was he a buffoon.

Reynald's bad press began in his own lifetime. The Muslim chroniclers wax vitriolic about him, and key crusader sources are also hostile; the greatest historian of the Latin East, Archbishop William of Tyre, who knew Reynald personally, was a political opponent and had other reasons to dislike him, as we shall see. The second main Frankish record is the chronicle of Ernoul, squire of the prominent crusader noble Balian of Ibelin, another bitter rival of Reynald. Still, there are sources that provide different glimpses of the man and, despite the bias against him, we can piece together a picture of Reynald that is surprisingly positive.

The truth reveals the epic life of Reynald de Chatillon as one of the most important of the crusading period. Famous all over Christendom, Reynald was an embodiment of the chivalric ideal. His knightly virtues were notable enough to promote him from obscurity to woo princesses and win royal power in one of the great romantic stories of the age. Via humiliation and harsh imprisonment, he rose to confront emperors and sultans. A ruthless, brutal grudge-holder, he inflicted revenges so savage and spectacular that they still echo down the ages. A renowned warrior, he led crusader armies to one of their most comprehensive military victories and inflicted on Saladin his most decisive reverse, adding years to the survival of the Latin Kingdom of Jerusalem. A daring tactician, he waged an unprecedented, unrepeated campaign against his Islamic enemies in their own back yard. Reynald became the pre-eminent figure in the crusader Kingdom of Jerusalem, a colossus in the struggle for Palestine that obsessed the Christian world through the twelfth century. Reynald's personality, his external enmities and internal rivalries dominated the last crucial years of the kingdom. And amidst cataclysmic defeat, his death would be decisive in its fall.

Uncovering the true story of Reynald de Chatillon means revising some other accepted truths about the crusades. This book emphasizes how appeasement and treachery – rather than Reynald's aggressive policies – undermined the Kingdom of Jerusalem. It will put Reynald's undoubted aggression and other attributes into context, while telling the extraordinary story of what was, for good or ill, one of the more remarkable medieval lives. It is a life that has been ignored, obscured and misrepresented for too long.

Vézelay, Burgundy, 31 March 1146

Dressed in his rough white monk's habit, the frail figure of Abbot Bernard looked out from a makeshift wooden platform across a crowd of many thousands of souls.

Jutting up from a rolling plain, the steep hill of Vézelay loomed behind him, crowned by a massive Romanesque basilica, the abbey-church of St Mary Magdalene. So many had come to hear Bernard speak that the multitude had overflowed the great church and the town itself. They had moved down to this new site in the spring meadows, where this sea of humanity – townspeople, peasants, priests, the flower of the nobility, King Louis VII himself – waited for the speaker to begin. They had gathered to witness Bernard, abbot of the pioneering monastery of Clairvaux, spiritual spearhead of the Cistercian order and the greatest orator of the age, preach the crusade.

The actual words of Bernard's speech are lost, but we can be sure of much of the content. Expressed through Bernard's inimitable, potent, mellifluous rhetoric, it would have echoed the proclamation recently issued by Pope Eugenius III, the papal bull *Quantum Praedecessores*. So Bernard would have described the recent catastrophic loss of the city of Edessa, one of the key crusader cities in the East, to the fierce Turkish warlord, Zengi. He would have described the suffering of the Christians of Edessa and the danger its fall posed to the Holy City of Jerusalem. He would have urged the men present, and especially the nobility – the warriors – to enlist alongside the king in his armed pilgrimage to the East, to fight for Christ and the Holy Land. He probably dangled the carrot of glory, honour and other earthly rewards for the successful crusader. Without doubt he promised heavenly rewards to anyone who 'took the cross'. These rewards included a complete remission of their sins.

Bernard's pale body looked 'almost lifeless', but his words carried immense power. Whatever he said, it had an almost miraculous effect. That day, wrote an onlooker, Bernard was 'heaven's instrument', bestowing on the multitude 'the dew of the divine word'.[12] The crowd was gripped and inspired. Then and there, thousands committed to the crusade. When Bernard finally called all those who wished to make the 'noble journey' to step forward and take the cross, the response was overwhelming. 'Crosses!' the crowd roared. 'Give us crosses!'

At sunset they were still sewing crossed strips of material to the shoulders of the new crusaders. A supply of cloth had been brought, in anticipation, but this soon ran out and, in their frenzy, people tore off their own clothes to be used. Bernard himself joined them, ripping up his habit for the cause. In the fading light the beautiful Queen Eleanor and her entourage of young damsels dressed up as Amazons and galloped around the fields, further whipping up the ecstatic crowds.

'I opened my mouth,' Bernard later wrote to the Pope. 'I spoke; and at once the *crusaders* have multiplied to infinity. Villages and towns are now deserted. You will scarcely find one man for every seven women. Everywhere you see widows whose husbands are still alive.'[13]

One of those dead men walking – and almost certainly among the passionate crowd at Vézelay that day – was a youthful knight full of zeal and ambition, but with meagre prospects, a certain Reynald de Chatillon.

Chapter 1

DEAD MAN WALKING

*Edessa is taken as you know, and the Christians are sorely
afflicted because of it; the churches are burnt and abandoned,
God is no longer sacrificed there. Knights, make your decisions,
you who are esteemed for your skill in arms; make a gift of your
bodies to Him who was placed on the cross for you.*
Troubadour song of the Second Crusade

Renown is easiest won among perils.
Tacitus

Reynald de Chatillon was born sometime around 1125. He was a
younger son of Hervé II de Donzy, Count of Gien and Lord of Donzy,
a Burgundian town less than thirty miles from Vézelay. Lying about a
day's ride from Donzy was another of the family dominions, the town
for which Reynald was named, Chatillon-sur-Loing.[1] The River Loing,
memorably painted by the Impressionist Alfred Sisley, is a tributary of
the Seine. It rises in Burgundy and winds down past attractive medieval
villages such as Villiers, Moret and Grez-sur-Loing with its graceful

twelfth-century bridge. Chatillon (the present-day Chatillon-Coligny) is not one of the most picturesque of the towns along the Loing and reveals few traces from Reynald's time. The only vestige of the little castle is the ruined tower of the donjon, and this was built in 1180, long after Reynald had left for the Holy Land.

We don't know exactly what Reynald's connection with Chatillon was. He may have been born there or lived there for a while in his youth. He may have been assigned the town as a fief. Peter of Blois calls him 'Lord of Chatillon'. Whatever his connection, it was not strong enough to keep Reynald in France. As for so many other young men in the Middle Ages, especially around the twelfth century, the call of the Holy Land – that almost legendary Outremer ('beyond the sea') – proved too strong.

In Western Europe at the time daily existence was harsh and living conditions rudimentary, even for the noble classes. Life expectancy was short, but then a long life might not have been much to gloat over. The climate was unforgiving and the winters chilled both peasant hovel and noble castle alike. Food was bland, monotonous and unhygienic, and water was often contaminated. Medicine was no more than base superstition, with treatment usually exacerbating any malady, often fatally. The economy was based on the hard labour of subsistence agriculture – a precarious existence on the edge of permanent poverty, catastrophic in years of famine and blight. The population eked out its days almost exclusively in villages that were isolated, even over short distances, by difficult, dangerous roads, local warfare and linguistic differences. Most towns were small, cramped and filthy behind their old walls, with embryonic levels of trade. The feudal system of serfdom left many peasants in complete thrall to their lords and masters.

In this rigidly hierarchical world, social mobility was virtually non-existent, and improvement by education was possible only via the Church. Literacy – indeed learning in general – was monopolized by the clergy, which ruled the souls of all Western Christendom, with power centred on the Papacy in Rome. In this time of profound, ubiquitous religious faith, the Church wielded wide temporal powers and the Pope claimed supreme spiritual authority, even over the greatest rulers, such as the German emperor and the kings of England and France. Bishops were mighty lords in their own right and even lowly priests held their parishioners' uneducated minds in thrall. They dangled the carrot of everlasting bliss to those who followed their bidding, while terrifying their flock with graphic images of the tortures of hell.

By the twelfth century, however, the world was beginning to change. A spirit of adventure was abroad, and it was clearly strong in young men like Reynald de Chatillon. He lived in a time of questioning and searching, of pushing boundaries and breaking new ground. Sometimes this period is called the 'Twelfth-Century Renaissance', though the term goes in and out of fashion. Populations were on the move as new towns, outside the feudal system, were being founded and granted trading privileges. Cities like Paris and London were expanding fast and, encouraged by the crusades, international trade routes were opening apace, enriching maritime cities like Venice and Amalfi, bringing in new foodstuffs, materials, technologies, luxuries and ideas from the Orient. There was an explosion of artistic creativity; freed by new inspirations and technologies, architecture abandoned classical strictures and flowered into the spectacular, soaring 'Gothic' style. Music and literature threw up seminal works such as *The Romance of the Rose*, the songs of the wandering goliards and the poetry of the troubadours, leading to the remarkable discovery (or invention) of 'romantic love'. It was also a time of enquiry; in the famous phrase of the twelfth-century churchman Peter of Blois, a new generation of scholars – like the radical Peter Abelard – was 'clambering onto the shoulders of giants'. The 'giants' were the classical thinkers such as Aristotle and Galen, whose works were becoming known in the West. They fuelled the growth of the first universities in Paris and Oxford, the legal school in

Bologna and the great medical schools of Salerno and Montpellier. This expansion in learning was facilitated by the crusades, which brought Christian intellectuals into contact with classical authors preserved by Islamic scholarship, and opened Western eyes to the relatively advanced Islamic sciences, philosophy and mathematics. These learnings were as fundamental as Arabic numerals (including the vital zero), which displaced the cumbersome Roman system. The enquiring minds of the day devoured the new knowledge with exhilaration.

The popularity of pilgrimages was another expression of this restless zeitgeist. Whether wending their way to the shrine of Thomas Becket in Canterbury, following the route to Santiago de Compostela in Spain, visiting St Peter's in Rome or taking the long journey to the Holy Places in the Promised Land, twelfth-century roads were increasingly thronged with pilgrims on the move. And of course a crusade was, at its simplest, no more than an armed pilgrimage. The clearest manifestation of this outward-looking urge to spread Christendom was actual geographical expansion. The Second Crusade was far more than just another expedition aimed at Palestine; it was an early and emphatic expression of European colonialism. While King Louis VII of France and Emperor Conrad III of Germany led their armies eastwards, there were also crusading offensives in Iberia, one of which led to the capture of Lisbon from the Moors. Militant, expansionist Christianity pressed northwards as well, with the launch of the Wendish Crusade in the Baltic. In all directions, the frontiers of Christendom were being extended.[2]

Within Christendom, too, boundaries were being pushed back as the wilderness was tamed. Bernard's own Cistercian order was at the vanguard of this muscular spirituality. The white monks reformed lax practices in the Church and represented a new purity in Western monasticism. They also embodied their ideals by building monasteries in remote locations, turning forests into tilled fields. Bernard's personal quest for truth led him to find the Lord in nature; his monastery of Clairvaux was built in a 'desert', a wild, remote valley, which the labour and ardour of the monks transformed into fertile gardens and a prosperous abbey.

This was the energetic world of increasing opportunity into which Reynald was born. Nothing specific is known about his youth, but this is not unusual, even for the most famous medieval figures. The same goes for the man who would become his greatest adversary, Saladin. While we have little information, we also have no reason to assume that Reynald's upbringing differed from the typical upbringing of a male born into the knightly class. As such, almost everything he knew would have predisposed him to respond positively to the call for a crusade. The Pope's bull, the king's desire to make the journey, Reynald's background, situation and education – all these would have made his decision quite straightforward.

Traditionally young noblemen were sent by their family to be brought up in another lordly household. There they would serve as a squire and be prepared for knighthood. Whether Reynald was raised in his family seat at Donzy, or elsewhere, he would have been instilled with the same martial values and the ideals of chivalry. The ruling class was first and foremost a warrior class, and its most prized values were those of the soldier, capable of winning glory for himself and his lineage and of defending his lands, his womenfolk and his vassals with the sword. The draughty baronial halls of Reynald's youth would have echoed to the sound of the *chansons de gestes*, songs of the great deeds of real-life heroes from the First Crusade, of semi-legendary heroes like Oliver and Roland, the soldiers of Charlemagne, and of Lancelot and the wholly legendary heroes from the Arthurian myths. Reynald would have known these stories for sure.

These were the early days of heraldry, before formal, inherited coats of arms, when nobles were choosing their own emblems for their shields, banners and personal seals. In a time of helmets, which obscured the face, these signs were vital for identification in battle. They were also powerful symbolic statements about the wearer. The symbol Reynald chose for himself was the swan, the chivalric bird par excellence, enshrined in the earliest known cycle of *chansons*, known as the *Chevalier au Cygne* (the Swan Knight). The first part of the cycle is the *Chanson d'Antioche* (the Song of Antioch), which sings of the First Crusade down to the capture of the great city of Antioch in 1098. It continues with the *Chanson de Jherusalem*, taking the story on to the capture of Jerusalem in 1099. Both these songs were in wide circulation in northern France during Reynald's youth. In choosing the swan as his emblem, Reynald was perhaps revealing a romantic streak and was consciously associating himself with this tradition, and with a real-life hero of these *chansons*, the greatest knight of the First Crusade, Godfrey de Bouillon. After the capture of Jerusalem, Godfrey was chosen as the leader of the Franks in the East. In a saintly rejection of worldly glory, he refused the title of king, agreeing only to be 'Guardian of the Holy Sepulchre'. Legend had it that Godfrey was descended from a swan – the Swan Knight of the *chansons*.

The books of chivalry and the stories of the *chansons* reveal the pattern for the knightly ideal. Central to them were the fame and glory that a knight would win on the battlefield in the service of his lord. And if the battle was against heathens, on crusade, on behalf of Holy Mother Church, then even better. At the time the crusaders were seen as:

> *heroes who from the cold of uttermost Europe plunged into the intolerable heat of the East, careless of their own lives, if only they could bring help to Christendom its hour or trial... nothing to be compared to their glory has ever been begotten by any age.*[3]

A knight would also win glory in the service of his lady, following the principles of 'courtly love', a twelfth-century fashion in romantic manners and verse that was closely intertwined with the Second Crusade, through Eleanor of Aquitaine. Wife of Louis VII, the queen controlled most of southern France in her own right. She was also a great patron of the arts, especially of the troubadours, the southern French singers of the *chansons* and lays of courtly love. The adventurous Eleanor accompanied her husband on crusade and, from the very start, her presence added a sheen of glamour, especially for a youthful knight. She made sure everyone noticed her, and while churchmen disapproved of her extravagant displays, no virile young bachelor, especially one – like Reynald – with a taste for the flamboyant and dramatic, could fail to have been enamoured by the Amazonian queen on that remarkable day at Vézelay, and further seduced by the attractions of the crusade.

And of course if a knight did not go on crusade, far from winning the regard of a beautiful lady, there was the risk of the reverse. Just as women in the First World War handed shaming white feathers to non-combatants, so it is said that Eleanor and her ladies distributed spindles and distaffs to those reluctant to take the cross. It was clearly a knight's honourable duty to defend the faithful in the East. This obligation was accentuated because the recently captured city of Edessa had been the first city to turn Christian, a fact stressed by the crusade's promoters, such as Bernard of Clairvaux. Further spurring a good knight into action were the lurid reports of the sufferings of Edessa that filtered back to the West. The *Lament on Edessa*, for instance, was a contemporary poem on the catastrophe that Zengi's armies inflicted on Edessa's people:

> *Like wolves among a flock of lambs [they] fell upon them in*
> *their midst.*

> They slaughtered indiscriminately, the martyrs let out streams
>   of blood,
> They massacred without compassion the young and the
>   children.
> They had no mercy on the grey hairs of the elderly or with the
>   tender age of a child.[4]

Not to avenge the venerable city's destruction would be dishonourable. As Pope Eugenius put it, in his crusading proclamation:

> It will be seen as a great token of nobility and uprightness if
> those things acquired by the efforts of your fathers are vigorously
> defended by you, their good sons. But if, God forbid, it comes to
> pass differently, then the bravery of the fathers will have proved
> diminished in the sons.[5]

Certainly those who took the cross, but then returned without completing the pilgrimage, suffered shame. Count Stephen of Blois was one of the chief knights of the First Crusade, but he deserted during the excruciating siege of Antioch and fled in disgrace to France. His wife Adela, the steely daughter of William the Conqueror, was humiliated by her husband's cowardice. She made her feelings clear to Stephen, even in the most intimate of moments:

> Being frequently reproved by a variety of persons for this conduct,
> Stephen was compelled both by fear and shame to undertake a
> fresh crusade. Among others, his wife, Adela, often urged him to
> it, reminding him of it even amidst the endearments of conjugal
> caresses.[6]

Goaded by Adela's cruelly timed taunts, Stephen returned to the Holy Land to make amends. This time he fought through appalling hardships on the journey and completed his vow of pilgrimage to Jerusalem. Hopefully both he and Adela were satisfied that he achieved final redemption when, hopelessly outnumbered, he died bravely in battle against the Egyptians at Ramleh in 1102.

In any case, the quest for glory and the avoidance of shame are two sides of the same coin. As one Muslim adversary of the crusaders put it, bravery results from 'contemptuous disdain of being considered a coward and acquiring ill repute'.[7] Reynald would have seen it no differently.

And if the promise of glory on its own was not enough, then the example of the astonishingly successful First Crusade would have provided further motivation, which both Bernard and the Pope actively exploited. The participants had won glory in their lifetime, and immortality in the *chansons*. They also won earthly wealth and power: new counties, principalities and kingdoms were being created in the East, and new men were being raised in rank, becoming counts, princes and kings. There was property to be had too, especially in cities like Jerusalem, where the Muslim population was killed or expelled. A poor crusader – even the lowliest commoner – could suddenly find himself the owner of a palatial mansion. And there was booty: sacks of it. Along with the knowledge of the ages, stories – together with hard golden and silver evidence – of the fabled wealth of the East spread quickly back to Western Europe and acted as sparkling lures for those eking out a subsistence living. Writers such as Fulcher of Chartres, working in the newly formed crusader states, painted a glowing picture of life in the Holy Land, to tempt new crusaders to leave their hand-to-mouth existence and stake their claim to the cornucopia of riches:

Those who were poor [in the West], here God makes rich. Those who had few coins, here possess countless bezants;* and those who had not a villa, here, by the gift of God, already possess a city.[8]

Fulcher was exaggerating, but from a general truth. Life in Outremer was dangerous and uncertain, but it was also wealthy. People lived in cities famous since antiquity, splendidly built in stone by the ancients and enriched by centuries of international commerce. Floors were covered in carpets, not strewn with reeds. Levantine towns had pure, running water, sewers and public baths. Food was varied: savoury, spiced and sweet. To the conquerors, however lowly, luxuries unimaginable in the West, such as silk clothing, sugar and oranges, were easily affordable. For those bridling in Europe under the feudal yoke, there were also clear social benefits. In Outremer the lowest Frankish peasant was immediately superior to the vast majority of the conquered (Muslim and native Christian) population. Still, most crusaders preferred to return to their homes after visiting the holy sites or campaigning for a season against the heathen. This made for a relatively small number of permanent expatriates and plenty of opportunities for ambitious immigrants of whatever class. Indeed, the crusaders suffered from an endemic manpower shortage in the East. This was something the Church well understood, which was why propaganda like Fulcher's was so important. The Church needed to emphasize the rewards of crusading. The general message of Christian preaching may have been non-violence and the holiness of poverty, but when it came to the crusade, there was no contradiction between worldly and spiritual enrichment. As Fulcher put it, 'God wishes to enrich us all.'[9]

For the rulers and great lords there were obvious risks to going on

---

* The ancient Byzantine *hyperpyron* or 'bezant' was the standard gold currency of the Levant. Muslim dinars adhered to this standard as well.

crusade, and the Pope recognized these by expressly guaranteeing protection to the lands and goods of anyone who took the cross. These great leaders were among those who would typically sail to the Holy Land in the spring, campaign for a season and then return home. Their wealth was back in Europe, and the Holy Land offered few additional prospects and much greater risk. Exceptions – such as the powerful Count Fulk of Anjou, who gave up his fief for life in the Holy Land – were few, and Fulk was compensated with the kingship of Jerusalem itself.

For those with little to lose, however, the potential rewards of a crusade were compelling and well worth the gamble. As Flora wryly observes to Phillis in the twelfth-century poem *The Debate of the Knight and the Clerk*, 'It is not love that makes young knights brave. It is poverty.'[10] The ambitious Reynald fell into this category, for although the Old French version of William of Tyre, the *Estoire d'Eracles*, tells us that Reynald was 'well-born', he was also 'not a very rich man'. The lords of Donzy were affluent, middle-ranking barons and the family's fortunes were on the up, but Reynald was a younger son. He had no fortune of his own and, critically, no certainty of inheriting land. His most valuable possessions were probably the tools of his trade: chainmail, longsword and, if he was lucky, a good warhorse. Indeed, as a landless younger son in the twelfth century, Reynald would have had little hope of a prosperous future. The tyranny of primogeniture meant that his oldest brother would inherit the family titles and property. For a man like Reynald, the crusade was literally a God-given opportunity to win a fief of his own in the East, settle down there and achieve a social standing and lifestyle far beyond his expectations in France.

The First Crusade provided brilliant, tempting examples of what could be achieved by an energetic, ambitious younger son who was prepared to take the cross – and a few risks. Bohemond of Taranto, the great Norman hero of the First Crusade and first Frankish Prince of Antioch, had been without a patrimony in his native Italy. Godfrey de Bouillon himself – Reynald's model – was also a younger son. Peter of Blois, who penned an idealized portrait of Reynald in which he is depicted as a kind of warrior saint, tried to suggest that Reynald was not moved by earthly gain; he claimed that Reynald chose the crusade over worldly wealth by abandoning an advantageous marriage to go to Outremer.[11] From what we know of Reynald's later life in the East, this story seems very unlikely, and we can be sure that the desire for worldly advancement – in social rank and wealth – figured highly in his decision to take the cross.

An alternative course for younger sons was to enter the Church; this was the career path of Baldwin of Boulogne, younger brother of Godfrey de Bouillon. By the time of the First Crusade, Baldwin was already a wealthy and powerful bishop, but he cast the cloister aside for the crusade. He became the first crusader Count of Edessa and, in 1100, succeeded his brother to become King Baldwin I of Jerusalem. Like the ambitious Baldwin, Reynald was clearly not suited to the peaceful, contemplative life.

Indeed, completely the opposite.

If not destined for the priesthood, a young nobleman had one profession open to him – warrior. Young aristocrats were bred and raised to fight. These days it is hard to imagine what this entailed. It was not a matter of rough-and-tumble horseplay to toughen the youngster up, interspersed with some fencing and sparring. No, horseplay meant the serious horsemanship of the joust, with sharpened spears, and rough-and-tumble the lethal business of the tournament mêlée. A squire's upbringing was more than just a school of hard knocks. It was the creation of a killing machine, where the paramount virtues were bravery, honour, skill at arms and the ability to deliver the telling blow with the greatest effectiveness, with ruthless intent and without scruple or hesitation. No double maths, followed by biology, for Reynald. His lessons were: charging with the couched lance, hunting with spear and crossbow, wrestling in full armour, killing with the longsword, killing with the dagger.

Picture the terrifying child soldiers of Africa, with a veneer of courtly manners, and you may get an idea of what was being bred in the castle courtyards of the twelfth century, or in the knights' schools that produced masters of violence like Reynald or the unparalleled William Marshall, another 'new man' who hauled himself up from obscurity through force of arms. The big difference between the twelfth-century squire and the traumatized African kids is that medieval children were not doing something seen as evil. Unlike the vacant-eyed seven-year-old killers in Liberia, kidnapped and forced into senseless murder outside any existing social norms, the knight, however vicious, was a pillar of society. His development formed a vital part of the social order, and both religious and secular authorities validated the rectitude of his actions.

What a boy is bred to do, the man will do. In twelfth-century Europe there were trained killers running wild in lands where war was unfortunately often in short supply. Tournaments were one way in which knights vented these martial passions, and these mock-battles were critical to a knight's training. Reynald took part in tournaments and enthusiastically embraced the pageantry that went along with them. He was certainly among the target audience of crusading propaganda, such as the song *Chevalier, Mult Estes Guariz*. This song's lyrics are a stirring secular call to holy war, and would have been sung in the halls of nobles such as the lords of Donzy. It was designed to appeal directly to Reynald and his ilk, by likening the coming crusade to a tournament:

> *God has organized a tourney between Heaven and Hell…*
> *the Son of God the Creator has fixed a day for being at Edessa;*
> *there shall the sinners be saved… who will fight fiercely*
> *to wreak the vengeance of God.*[12]

Of course, tournaments were never enough to sate the desires and energies of medieval warriors. The oversupply of fighting men resulted in chronic banditry and feuding, frequently led by frustrated younger sons. The crusade harnessed this pent-up violence for praiseworthy ends. As the monk Guibert of Nogent wrote:

> In our own time, God has instituted a Holy War, so that the order of knights and the unstable multitude who used to engage in mutual slaughter in the manner of ancient paganism may find a new way of gaining salvation.[13]

This had also been an important feature of the First Crusade, which tried to impose the 'Peace of God' in Europe, while channelling the ferocity of the knightly class against the infidel. According to the chronicler Fulcher of Chartres, Pope Urban II had proclaimed:

> Let those who have been robbers now be soldiers of Christ. Let those who have been hirelings for a few pieces of silver now attain an eternal reward.[14]

Abbot Bernard himself, in his relentless letter-writing and preaching tours in support of the Second Crusade, repeatedly berated warring nobles and urged them to take vengeance on the heathen rather than kill each other. 'Put a stop to it now,' he said of their feuding:

> It is not fighting but foolery. Thus to risk both soul and body is not brave but shocking, is not strength but folly. But now O mighty soldiers, O men of war, you have a cause for which you fight without danger to your souls: a cause in which to conquer is glorious and for which to die is to gain.[15]

This was great news for Reynald. Raised as a warrior, he probably knew little beyond the rules of knighthood. Peace was no good for him. He had few skills and no penchant for peace. Twelfth-century warriors, like the troubadour Bertran de Born, revelled in their calling:

> *Whoever may plough and cultivate his land, I have always*
> *taken trouble about how I may get bolts and darts,*
> *helmets and hauberks, horses and swords, for thus do I*
> *please myself; and I take joy in assaults and tournaments,*
> *in making gifts and making love.*[16]

This was what Reynald excelled at. It was what his upbringing and all his instincts drove him to do. The genius of the crusade was that it provided him with a way to get his kicks and exercise his skills in a legitimate, praiseworthy manner. For Reynald, it was an obvious choice. It is no good retrospectively, and anachronistically, criticizing him or his contemporaries for this. It was the way things were. The code of chivalry put strictures on knighthood, yes; but at its core it promoted ferocity. This applied to any knight worth his salt. The knights who went on crusade were born, bred and brainwashed for the task. So too were the Saracens they fought, who saw themselves as fighting their own version of holy war, the jihad. The entire culture around Reynald was one of barely varnished brutality.

An example of the dehumanizing upbringing experienced by young warriors is provided by one of Reynald's enemies in the East, Usama Ibn Munqidh. While crusader knights are often depicted as rude, crude barbarian soldiers without any refinement, their Islamic opponents are usually shown as culturally and intellectually superior. This is inaccurate. Oriental civilization was overall undoubtedly superior in many ways; however, the Islamic Middle East at the time of the crusades – for all its relative sophistication – was riven by wars between rival princes and was ruled, like the Franks, by a bellicose warrior class, whether Turkish, Kurdish or Arabic. Usama was the archetype for these opponents of the crusaders – an Arabic 'warrior and gentleman' who is seen as the epitome of 'Arab civilization as it flourished at the time of the crusades'.[17] Usama, like Reynald, was brought up first and foremost as a warrior. In one of his poems he wrote:

> My whole ambition was to engage in combat with my rivals,
>   whom
> I always took
> For prey.[18]

His life was spent endlessly training for warfare. When he was not practising in arms and chainmail (Frankish mail was best), he was practising through the proxy of hunting. Instead of chasing boar and partridge along the Loing and roe deer in the rolling hills of Burgundy, Usama hunted francolin on the banks of the Orontes, leopard and lion in the dense thickets along the River Jordan. His father, who (typically for these warrior lords) was 'greatly addicted to warfare', taught him to kill from an early age. In his memoirs Usama describes how, using his little knife, he carefully sawed the head off a sleeping snake, while his father watched proudly.

Another of Usama's anecdotes is even more revealing of the moral make-up of those men who fought each other during the crusades. When he was ten years old, Usama tells us, he hit one of his family retainers with a stick. When the servant pushed back at him, Usama simply:

> pulled a knife from my belt and stabbed him with it. A big
> attendant of my father named Asad the Leader came, examined
> him and saw the wound, out of which flowed blood like bubbles of
> water every time the wounded man breathed. Asad turned pale,
> shivered and fell unconscious.[19]

The man Usama had stabbed died later that day.

Remarkably, Usama does not tell us this story to shock us with his actions, or to examine the rights and wrongs of a ten-year-old boy casually killing a man on a whim. Rather, he uses it to illustrate 'some men's weakness of soul and faintness of heart, which I did not think possible among women'. To him, the sudden, callous murder is something that passes without comment. The ability to kill with such nonchalance had been instilled from his earliest years and would have been regarded as normal – even desirable – in a young medieval nobleman, whether Christian or Muslim. The only thing that shocks Usama about this event is the fact that his father's big, strong attendant could faint at the sight of blood; something Usama was obviously well used to, even by the age of ten.

Dealing with blood was also one of the things Reynald would have had to master early in his development. As the monk Roger of Hoveden wrote, first-hand experience of violence was a vital part of a knightly education in the twelfth century:

> He is not fit for battle who has never seen blood flow, who has not heard his teeth crunch under the blow of an opponent, or felt the full weight of his adversary upon him.[20]

Once in the East, Reynald would soon reveal his propensity for decisive action and extreme violence. It was a trait that appalled and shocked his enemies and sometimes his fellow Christians, but it was far from unique.

This is of course not to say that fighting men never thought beyond the violence of their trade. Usama was a poet and author, and so were troubadour knights like Bertran de Born and William IX of Poitiers. We do not know if Reynald was able to read – most knights could not – but even if he was not literary, a knight's military activities had other dimensions, most importantly religious ones.

For modern readers it is sometimes difficult to understand how Christianity – the religion of 'turn the other cheek' – could have condoned, let alone blessed and encouraged, such violence in its name. It is a problem that the Church wrestled with as well, and the crusade was one of their solutions. Ever since St Augustine's theory of a 'just war' in the fifth century AD, a Christian justification of aggression had been available.[21] Many theorists had developed these ideas after Augustine, and by the twelfth century 'the duty of the duly ordained soldiery' was well accepted as a vital part of society. In his pioneering work of political science, *Policraticus*, the brilliant cleric John of Salisbury, Reynald's contemporary, wrote that a knight's duties were:

> To defend the Church, to assail infidelity, to venerate the
> priesthood, to protect the poor from injuries, to pacify the
> province, to pour out their blood for their brothers (as the formula
> of their oath instructs them).[22]

Clearly twelfth-century Christendom saw no contradiction in mixing religion and violence.

Along with clerical theorists like John of Salisbury, the temporal legends of King Arthur and the Holy Grail – with their conjunction of religious and military images and storylines – confirm that knights saw themselves as spiritual warriors, fulfilling a holy duty. The most perfect expressions of this were of course the Military Orders, 'the new knighthood' championed by Abbot Bernard. The warrior monks of orders like the Knights Hospitaller and the Knights Templar were a:

> new kind of knighthood and one unknown to the ages gone by. It
> ceaselessly wages a twofold war both against flesh and blood and
> against a spiritual army of evil in the heavens.[23]

The righteous fervour that drove Reynald and his comrades to kill and die for the Lord is reflected in the conviction that inspires the Islamic militant of today. The ISIS suicide bomber or Al-Qaida operative sees no dichotomy between the violence he embraces and Islam, the 'religion of peace' (the very word 'Islam' has the same root as 'salaam', the word for peace). Similarly, for Christian knights, religion and warfare mixed without problem. This combination was most perfectly enshrined in the person of a crusader. As Abbot Bernard said, 'If he dies, it is to his benefit. If he kills, it is for Christ.'[24]

The evidence of his later actions suggests that Reynald was hardly the typical pious type, but he need not have been spiritual in any way to be inspired by the crusading ideal. Seeing the Holy City was a romantic vision, which inspired monk and warrior alike. Crusading would have fulfilled the duty of knighthood, as he saw it, and Reynald would also have been motivated by the promise of the remission of sins. Any medieval Christian would have responded to these stimuli. This was a time of fervent religious belief, when paradise was an almost tangible garden of delight, and the tormenting fires of hell burned fiercely just beyond the grave. And the grave was not far away. The papal indulgence of full remission of sins, promised by Eugenius III to all who took part in the Second Crusade, would have been an extraordinary opportunity for a young knight of Reynald's time. Many of them already had blood on their hands and plenty of sins to expiate, by an early age. The pilgrimage to Jerusalem had long been a way for warriors to wipe the slate clean, without having to leave the world of sin and join the Church. The terrifying Fulk Nerra ('The Black'), Count of Anjou, twice went on pilgrimage to Jerusalem as penance for murder. The great thing about the crusade, which made it even better than a pilgrimage, was the opportunity it gave for knights to earn the religious benefits of pilgrimage, but as warriors intending to fight, not as pilgrims peacefully visiting the holy places. Abbot Guibert of Nogent, a chronicler of the First Crusade, observed that:

Now they may seek God's grace in their wonted habit and
discharge their own office, and no longer be drawn to seek
salvation by utterly renouncing the world in the profession of
the monk.[25]

Or as the troubadour Aymer de Pegulhan wrote:

Behold, without renouncing our rich garments, our station in life,
we can obtain honour down here and joy in paradise.[26]

The crusade was tailor-made for King Louis VII of France as well. As a second son, the pious Louis was not originally destined for the throne and had been brought up in the cloister. When he was thrust into the kingship after the death of his brother, the crusade suited his ardent Christian zeal, but more practically it enabled Louis to fulfil his inherited obligations and save his soul as a king and soldier, without having to retire to the contemplative life. For Louis, the crusade was also a way to expiate the terrible guilt he felt for burning the church at Vitry in 1142. During a dispute with his powerful vassal Count Theobald of Champagne, King Louis had stormed the town of Vitry and burned the church, where many citizens had taken refuge. More than 1,000 perished in the flames.

Like kings, even crusaders (Reynald among them) sometimes went too far in their militancy, shocking priest and knight alike. But just because a man's crusade might stray from the righteous path into one of evil did not mean there was not a godly motivation for it in the first place. Abbot Bernard himself observed that 'Hell is full of good wishes and desires.' Over the centuries this saying has mutated a little – 'The road to hell is paved with good intentions.'

Bernard of Clairvaux was canonized in 1174, just twenty-one years after his death. The holy St Bernard – abbot, oracle and spiritual warrior – was one of the embodiments of the questing twelfth-century spirit that engendered, embraced and exploited the crusade. That very earthly warrior – adventurer, social climber, pilgrim and cold-blooded killer – Reynald de Chatillon was another.

Chapter 2

THE WILD EAST

Why should one who has found the East so favorable return to the West? God does not wish those to suffer want who, carrying their crosses, have vowed to follow Him, nay even unto the end. You see, therefore, that this is a great miracle, and one which must greatly astonish the whole world.[1]

When Abbot Bernard spectacularly launched the Second Crusade at Vézelay in 1146, he was consciously echoing an epoch-making speech of fifty years before; on a platform at Clermont in 1095, Pope Urban II had unleashed the crusading idea onto an unsuspecting world.

Ostensibly Urban was responding to a plea for help from the Greek Orthodox Christians of the East. For more than four centuries the Byzantine Empire, the Greek successor to the Roman Empire, had barred the expansionist forces of Islam from flooding into Europe. But in 1071 at Manzikert they had suffered a calamitous defeat at the hands of the Seljuk Turks. Anatolia and almost all their Asian territories had been overrun. In 1081 Alexius Comnenos became emperor, and in 1095 he asked for reinforcements from the West. Alexius was interested in a crack force of mercenaries, but Urban did not simply pass on a straightforward call for recruits; instead, sensing the opportunity to put the Church in the forefront of something big, he created a potent hybrid of pilgrimage and holy war – a crusade.

Medieval Christianity was superstitious and obsessed with pilgrimages. An arduous journey to a holy place associated with a saint brought great rewards for the pilgrim. At the pilgrimage site the saint's deeds and often his or her relics – usually a body part or an object associated with their life – could be venerated. Prayers would be answered and, in recognition of the pilgrim's devotion, sins would be forgiven. Of course the most respected of all pilgrimage sites were the holy places in Palestine, associated with the life and death of Christ himself. Urging the belligerent feudal knights of Western Europe to take Christ's resting place from the infidel, while also promising remission of sins, was a stroke of genius. Fifty years later Bernard was building on Urban's example to inspire a new generation to buy into the crusading brand.

Urban's idea had quickly spiralled out of his control. The earliest incarnation of crusading fervour was the disastrous popular expedition led by Peter the Hermit. In 1096 his horde of fanatical peasants trekked across Europe towards the Holy Land, chanting prayers and perpetrating massacres, usually on hapless Jewish communities in their path. As soon as they moved from Byzantine to Muslim territory, the Turks quickly slaughtered them. Peter the Hermit was among the few who escaped. Not far behind tramped the great armies of the First Crusade proper. While the war-weary Byzantines were appalled by Peter's hopeless rabble – hardly the contingent of fighting men they had hoped for, when they asked the West for help – the Emperor Alexius was even more disturbed by the endless columns of fearsome, heavily mailed knights advancing towards his capital of Constantinople.

Luckily for Byzantium, the crusaders saved their aggression for the Muslims and, against all the odds, went on to capture the ancient cities of Edessa and Antioch and, in July 1099, the Holy City of Jerusalem itself. After fulfilling their vows, most crusaders returned to their homes in Western Europe, but many remained in the East, to become the ruling class in the lands they had conquered. They set up four independent crusader or 'Latin' states, imposing their feudal form of government on the conquered populations of Muslims and native Christians. These colonies occupied a country rich in trade and fertility – and richer still in the medieval imagination. For centuries men would leave their homes to fight for these lands, many of them expecting no reward except in heaven. It was a landscape covered in classical and biblical sites. It was also vulnerable – in most places just a narrow band of territory between the Mediterranean Sea and the desert, running from Anatolia in the north to the borders of Egypt in the south.

The northernmost of these domains was the county of Edessa. It was centred on the ancient city of Edessa (present-day Sanliurfa in Turkey), which had become the first officially Christian polity in the world during the second century AD. The county was sparsely populated, spreading across the vast savannahs between the Euphrates and Tigris Rivers. With most of the population made up of Armenian and other native Christian groups, the county had formed a barrier against the surrounding Muslim enemies. This barrier had been smashed when the Turkish warlord Zengi stormed the city of Edessa in 1144.

South of the county of Edessa lay the principality of Antioch, which stretched along the Mediterranean shore from Cilicia to the port of Jabala and the border with the county of Tripoli. Its capital was Antioch, the largest urban centre between Constantinople and Cairo. Antioch had been in Byzantine hands until as recently as 1078, and the emperors of Byzantium maintained a passionate (and legally compelling) claim to suzerainty over the city. This was a constant challenge for its Latin rulers.

The next state down the coast was the county of Tripoli. It occupied the littoral between the massive castle of Margat in the north and the

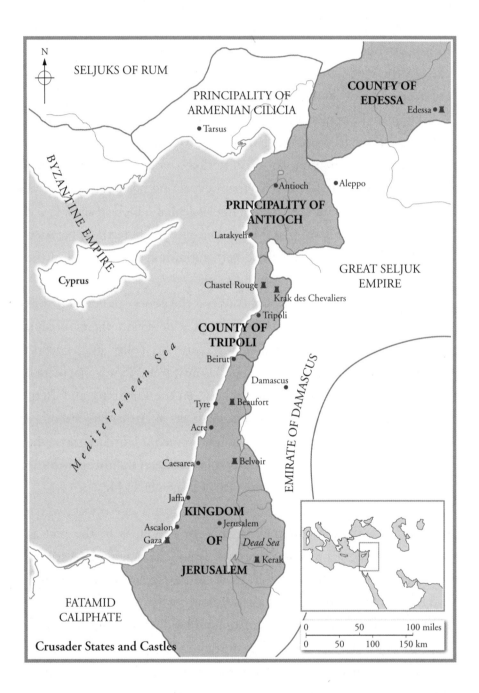

N

SELJUKS OF RUM

PRINCIPALITY OF
ARMENIAN CILICIA

• Tarsus

**COUNTY OF
EDESSA**

Edessa • ⚔

B
Y
Z
A
N
T
I
N
E

E
M
P
I
R
E

• Antioch   • Aleppo

**PRINCIPALITY OF
ANTIOCH**

Latakyeh •

Cyprus

GREAT SELJUK
EMPIRE

Chastel Rouge ⚔   ⚔
                  Krak des Chevaliers

• Tripoli

**COUNTY OF
TRIPOLI**

Beirut •

M
e
d
i
t
e
r
r
a
n
e
a
n

S
e
a

• Damascus

Tyre • ⚔ Beaufort

Acre •

E
M
I
R
A
T
E

O
F

D
A
M
A
S
C
U
S

Caesarea •   ⚔ Belvoir

Jaffa •

KINGDOM

Ascalon •   • Jerusalem

Gaza ⚔

OF

Dead Sea

⚔ Kerak

JERUSALEM

FATAMID
CALIPHATE

Crusader States and Castles

0		50		100 miles
0	50	100	150 km	

environs of Beirut in the south. To the east it took in the mountains of Lebanon, site of mighty crusader strongholds like *Krak des Chevaliers*, which looked down on the Muslim territories beyond. These crags were also the home of the Assassins. An extreme heterodox Islamic sect, the Assassins used their trademark brand of political murder to maintain independence from Christian and orthodox Muslim powers alike.

The southernmost Latin colony was the largest and most powerful – the Kingdom of Jerusalem. It boasted the most magnetic pilgrimage sites, including Nazareth and all the religious sites related to Jesus' life as described in the New Testament. The kingdom also included crusader Palestine's most important ports, Acre, Tyre and Jaffa, and fielded the strongest army of all the Latin states. Its eastern boundary was long and porous, however, with the Jordan River fordable at numerous points. Reaching right down to the Red Sea, the great fief of Oultrejordan ('beyond the Jordan') was created to defend the long southern stretch of this border fronting onto the desert. All of the kingdom's southern side was bounded by desert and was open to incursions from the Egyptians, who were especially irksome due to their stubborn hold on the coastal city of Ascalon, the only city in Palestine still in Muslim hands.

Unable to expand further against Islam, the crusaders built a web of castles across the Levant to defend their borders and dominate the conquered territory. Behind their castle walls, the Franks settled into a precarious stalemate of perpetual cross-border raiding, punctuated by major battles. Sometimes there would be temporary truces, usually with feuding Muslim emirs buying off the ever-aggressive crusader knights. Instability was chronic. Nomadic Turcoman hordes might sweep through at any time, ravaging Muslim and Christian territory alike. And every pilgrimage season brought welcome contingents of new crusaders, eager to combat the surrounding foes.

Among these enemies, most crusaders would have included the venerable, magnificent, but ramshackle Byzantine Empire. From time immemorial the empire had been the world's Christian superpower, and it still dominated extensive territories across Eastern Europe, the Balkans and Greece. In Asia, however, it faced relentless waves of migrating Turkish tribes from the east. The brilliant emperor Alexius I Comnenos (1081–1118) had retaken the offensive, and under his energetic son John (1118–43) and his grandson Manuel, the Byzantines had pushed back enemies on a number of fronts. But apart from some coastal territory, most of Anatolia remained in Muslim hands. The crusaders distrusted the Greeks, whom they saw as shifty, effeminate Orientals, obsessed with fashion and obsequious etiquette. The sophisticated Byzantines in their turn looked down upon the Franks as dangerous, uncouth barbarians. Even the common Christian heritage could be more divisive than unifying – the Latin and Greek Churches, run from Rome and Constantinople respectively, having split in the 'Great Schism' of 1054.

Imperial preoccupations with their European provinces meant that the Byzantines rarely entered directly into crusader affairs, but when they did, tensions between Greek and Latin Christians often led to violence. Successive emperors in Constantinople provoked the crusaders by claiming sovereignty over previously Byzantine-held territories like Antioch. Constantinople also wanted Greek patriarchs to preside over the Eastern Church, especially in great bishoprics like Antioch and Jerusalem. As Reynald de Chatillon would learn, these claims were sometimes pressed by force.

There was another rival Christian state in the region, too – the small Armenian kingdom on Antioch's northern border. The Armenians were a warlike, fiercely independent people who had carved out a realm from the Byzantine province of Cilicia and were constantly probing Antiochene territory. Both Armenians and Greeks could be unhelpful, unreliable and sometimes downright hostile to the Franks – Reynald would fight them both in time – but, unlike the Muslims, the Christian powers of the Near East were not set on extermination of their co-religionists. The Franks may have regarded Byzantium with suspicion, but it was also a powerful ally of last resort, a strategic Christian counterweight to Muslim power. Now and again Greeks, Armenians and Franks overcame their differences and managed to mobilize together against the reviving expansionist pressure of Islam.

At the beginning of the crusading period, after the death of the powerful Seljuk sultan Malik Shah, the Islamic Near East was politically and militarily fragmented, wholly unprepared for the irruption of heavily armed Frankish knights. This was greatly to the benefit of the early crusaders, who established their enclaves between the Muslim powers in Syria to the east and Egypt to the west. To hold onto their hard-won conquests, the Franks' overriding strategic imperative was to prevent the various Muslim powers of the region coalescing. Most worrying was the doomsday scenario of Egypt and Syria working in concert. Luckily Syrian and Egyptian Muslims did not get along.

In Cairo the ruling dynasty was the Arabic Fatimid caliphate. The Fatimids were Muslims of the minority Shi'ite sect, implacably opposed to the orthodox Sunni Islam that was prevalent in Syria. The Egyptians were ruling much of Palestine, including Jerusalem, when the First Crusade conquered it, and in the early years of the Kingdom of Jerusalem they made several major counter-offensives. They also launched frequent raids from their garrison behind Frankish lines at Ascalon. The Egyptian fleet, the largest in the region, was a persistent threat to Christian shipping and to the crusader coastal cities. Egypt, with its ancient trade routes, fertile delta and intensive agriculture watered by the annual inundation of the Nile, was immensely rich and had virtually unlimited supplies of manpower, but it was often weakened by power struggles at court, not least between the caliphal figureheads and their chief ministers, the viziers, who ruled in all but name. In the middle of the twelfth century Egypt was not an immediate threat to the survival of the crusader states.

More acutely dangerous were the Muslim emirs of Syria on the crusaders' eastern borders. These were mostly orthodox Sunni Turks, warlords who owed a nominal allegiance to the Sunni caliph and the sultan in far-away Baghdad. This allegiance was reflected in the local rulers' acceptance of symbolic robes of investiture sent by the caliph, and in the use of titles like *atabeg* (roughly, 'governor'). By the middle of the twelfth century, the most dangerous of these chieftains were the Zengids, descendants of the Turkish *atabeg* Zengi, conqueror of Edessa. Early in 1146, one of Zengi's eunuchs, feeling slighted by his master, waited until the *atabeg* was in a drunken stupor and then murdered him. But Zengi's death brought no respite for the Franks. In the fortress city of Aleppo, only fifty miles from Antioch, ruled Zengi's son, the new *atabeg* Nur al-Din Mahmud.

Nur al-Din was a terrifying adversary. A brilliant general, he was brave, too, and a formidable warrior, personally wielding bow and sword in battle, to the great concern of his retainers. He was an ardent orthodox Muslim, and the chronicler Michael the Syrian complained that he treated non-Muslim subjects badly, forcing Christians to cut their hair, and ordering Jews to wear a red symbol on their turbans and their right shoulder, to mark them out. To Muslims, he commanded respect and devotion. He was honest, approachable and shunned personal wealth. He was also pious and dedicated to jihad. The city of Jerusalem was holy to Islam, as well as to Judaism and Christianity, and Nur al-Din was committed to its recapture and the utter extirpation of the Frankish presence in the East. He had even built a great pulpit destined for the holy mosque of Al-Aqsa, on Jerusalem's Temple Mount.

After having Zengi's murderers cruelly executed, Nur al-Din had imposed his authority on northern Syria, unifying many of the competing Muslim emirates under his rule. In November 1146, he snuffed out a crusader attempt to reoccupy Edessa, and in savage retaliation obliterated the Christian presence there for ever. By March 1148, when Reynald arrived in Outremer with the Second Crusade, Nur al-Din was already chipping away at the remaining crusader fortresses in the county of Edessa and threatening the principality of Antioch.

The other powerful Syrian entity confronting the Latin states was Damascus. This ancient city was hostile to the crusaders, but had also worked with them when any other Islamic ruler became too powerful. Both Nur al-Din and his father Zengi had been thwarted by alliances of convenience between Damascus and Jerusalem. In the mid-twelfth century, Damascus was ruled by Mu'in al-Din Unur, a pragmatic politician who was quite prepared to deal with the crusaders and, vitally, an opponent of rising Zengid power.

In the long run, though, if Aleppo, Damascus and Cairo could work together, uniting Syrian and Egyptian Islam in jihad, the Latin states would be caught between the hammer and the anvil. Fundamentally, whatever local understandings with the crusaders could be reached, Muslims could not tolerate a Christian power ruling in Dar al-Islam – the lands of Islam – especially in the Holy City of Jerusalem. As the poet al-Qaysarani wrote:

> *This matter has been decreed and Jerusalem is as good as purified.*
> *There is no purification for it except when it runs with blood.*[2]

From the Muslim point of view, underlying even the most civil of inter-faith relations was an undertone of anger, disdain and revulsion. Muslim writers of the time reveal their attitude in the inevitable curses, whenever the Franks are mentioned: 'may God defeat them', 'God curse them', 'may God clear the land of their pollution'. Ibn Jubayr, who travelled through Frankish territory in the 1180s, has some decent things to say about their society (the Franks' fair taxation, for instance), but loathes them viscerally. The city of Acre 'stinks and is filthy, being full of refuse and excrement'. The Christian queen is 'a sow', the king 'a pig'[3] and all the unclean polytheists should suffer extermination. Muslims regarded the crusaders as 'polytheists', seeing the curious Christian belief in the Trinity of Father, Son and Holy Spirit as worship of three separate gods. It is decreed in Islam that polytheists who do not convert deserve one fate – death. When Muslims developed superficially cordial relationships with Franks, as did the aristocratic Arab chieftain Usama Ibn Munqidh, at heart they still despised their Christian friends and strove to bring about their annihilation. Among other things, Usama derided Frankish medicine, justice, education, sexual morals and honour. The one quality he did allow those 'devils of Franks' was courage.

Courage was a quality Reynald de Chatillon would show in abundance, but any traveller to Outremer required plenty of it. Even a peaceful pilgrimage to Jerusalem was a perilous undertaking. Storms and pirates beset the spring and autumn sailings to Palestine. The land route was even riskier, plagued by robbers in Europe and, beyond the borders of Christendom, by hordes of warlike infidels, bent on killing or enslaving any Christian who fell into their grasp. Once in the Holy Land, the pilgrim was prey to an unhealthy new climate and fatal diseases. And then there was the return journey.

Whether the crusader intended to stay in Outremer or campaign just for a season, he would have to face a well-armed and implacable foe, whose forces far outnumbered his. During the half-century before Abbot Bernard launched the Second Crusade, entire expeditions from Lombardy, Bavaria and Aquitaine were destroyed crossing Turkish territory in Asia Minor. Before even reaching the crusader states, the men were dead, the female camp followers and children sold as harem-girls and slaves. The crusader settlers defending their hard-won gains had also suffered crippling defeats. At Ramleh in 1102, for instance, in the heart of the Kingdom of Jerusalem, the Egyptian army trapped and destroyed a Frankish force. King Baldwin I barely escaped with his life, while a host of noble lords lost theirs. At the *Ager Sanguinis*, the Field of Blood, in 1119, Turcoman cavalry annihilated the army of Antioch. Prince Roger of Antioch himself was among the dead.

Everyone knew the risks, and many crusaders made wills before they left. Indeed, in his preaching Bernard made it clear that crusaders should assume they would not come back, that they were giving their lives for the cause. To die in God's work would bring life everlasting and a remission of sins. 'I call this a blessed generation,' he wrote:

> that can seize an opportunity of such rich indulgence as this,
> blessed to be alive in the year of jubilee, this year of God's choice.
> The blessing is spread throughout the whole world and all the
> world is flocking to receive this badge of immortality.[4]

Despite, or partly because of, the great peril of the task, Reynald and his blessed generation flocked to take the cross. Bernard said that he was 'sowing the Crusade'; and this was the greatest harvest yet. The expedition that was to be called the Second Crusade would number in its ranks Emperor Conrad of Germany, King Louis VII of France, Count Theobald of Champagne and many more of the greatest nobles of Christendom. Beyond the vague aims of avenging the fall of Edessa, shoring up the Christian forces in the East and somehow taking the Holy War to the heathen, the crusade had no specific plan of campaign. Nor did the organizers offer any specific lure of new territory to conquer, or great treasure to share. None was needed. For a restless crop of warlike young men like Reynald, the seed of the crusade fell on fertile ground.

St Simeon, Syria, 19 March 1148

On a calm day after long weeks of unseasonable storms, a tattered flotilla of ships limped out of the west towards the coast of Syria.

To the south loomed the Bald Mountain. To the north were heaped the monumental ruins of a long-forgotten ancient city and its port.* Dead ahead rose St Simeon's Mount, where the younger of the stylite hermit saints lived on his pillar for almost seventy years. And in its shadow, by the mysterious white rock of St George, lay the harbour of St Simeon, port of Antioch, the greatest city of the crusader states.

The leaking ships carried King Louis and his nobles on the final leg of a gruelling nine-month odyssey. The voyage from Atalya, a Byzantine town in southern Anatolia, should have taken just three days, but the weather had tormented the crusaders with mountainous seas and contrary gales. The journey had stretched to a frustrating three weeks.

When the ships hove into view, the Latin Patriarch of Antioch, Aimery of Limoges, hastily assembled a reception committee on the shore. As King Louis' vessel drew up to the quay, a choir began to sing the *Te Deum*. With Aimery reciting blessings for their safe arrival, Louis VII and his men disembarked.

An arduous journey of horrors was over. Two years after Bernard of Clairvaux had inspired it, the Second Crusade had finally arrived in Outremer.

---

* These were the remains of Seleucia Pieria, founded by Seleucis I in 305 BC.

Chapter 3

KNIGHT-ERRANT

A handsome bachelor and excellent knight.
Ernoul

The French contingents of the Second Crusade, under King Louis VII, set out for the Promised Land from the German-French border town of Metz in June 1147. They followed the German army, which had left the month before. Under the command of Emperor Conrad, the Germans led the way across Europe. Their journey east took them through the European provinces of the Byzantine Empire. The Germans created such havoc as they crossed imperial territory that the locals took to killing any stragglers. Inevitably the following French army encountered constant hostility, towns barred shut, sky-high prices and unburied German bodies spreading disease. It was said that 'the Franks suffered less from the armed Greeks than from the dead Germans'.[1]

The *basileus* Manuel Comnenos, Emperor of Byzantium since 1143, was a determined leader who fought tirelessly to enhance the power and prestige of his realm. Although he pursued a generally pro-Frankish policy, he was very concerned about the threat that such large foreign forces posed to his empire. He treated his unwanted visitors warily. To Byzantine Greeks, like the chronicler John Kinnamos, the crusade was a 'handy excuse' for the Franks' real motive: to gain possession of Byzantine land 'by assault and trample down everything in front of them'.[2] As a result they were very inhospitable, and thoroughly alienated the crusaders. But the astute Manuel was right about the danger. Amongst the crusaders there were many who loathed the schismatic eastern Christians and coveted their immense wealth. Manuel shunted Conrad and his army across the Bosphorus to Asia as quickly as possible to avoid any attack on Constantinople.

Manuel managed relations a little better with King Louis and the French, whose army arrived at Constantinople on 4 October 1147. Reynald would surely have been as impressed as any by the greatest city in the world, 'Rich in renown and richer still in possessions'.[3] The foundation of the capital of the Eastern Roman Empire dated back to the mists of antiquity. The city boasted stupendous walls, rebuilt by Justinian, marble palaces decorated with gold, and countless churches and shrines containing treasures and holy relics. These included the largest church in the world, Santa Sophia, under its cavernous dome. Many of the French, led by the outspoken Bishop of Langres, openly advocated an attack on the metropolis, but Manuel again managed to coax his unwelcome guests into Asia. He was helped by Byzantine agents spreading stories of great German victories, to spur the French knights on.

The French hurried after the Germans, keen to claim their share of the spoils, but instead of piles of booty, they found themselves passing cairns of human bones. They soon encountered the beaten remnants of Conrad's army, including the badly wounded emperor himself. The Seljuk Turks had been waiting for them. If the crusaders are to be believed, the Turks had been kept well briefed by the 'treacherous' Byzantines. As soon as the ponderous German force moved out of Greek

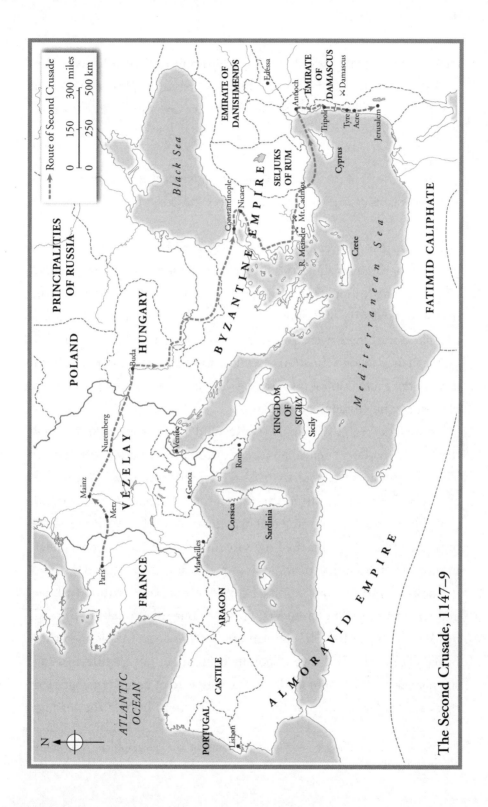

The Second Crusade, 1147–9

territory, the mobile Turkish cavalry had simply obliterated them. The Germans' treasure was plundered, the men massacred, the women and children sold as slaves. The Syrian chronicler Gregory the Priest wrote that:

> *the countries of the Turks were filled with the spoil of the Franks,*
> *and talents of silver were sold as if they were lead.*[4]

The direct route was now barred. Instead of trying to fight his way past the victorious Seljuks, Louis decided to take the long way round and skirt Asia Minor. This would at least keep the crusaders inside the narrow coastal strip of Byzantine territory. That offered scant comfort, though, as the Greeks were now seen as 'common enemy' with the Turks, rather than as fellow Christians. Reynald was probably no different from most of the French in taking a strong dislike to the Greeks, whom they blamed for the crusade's misfortunes.

As for the real (Muslim) foes Reynald had come to fight, they remained a shadowy enemy haunting the fringes of the crusaders' march. The French knew the potency of Turkish warriors – they had seen the effects of their handiwork in the traumatized Germans – but Reynald probably did not have his first real experience of warfare with the Turks until the French army reached the sinuous valley of the River Meander in south-west Anatolia (near modern-day Aydin) in December 1147.[*]

Ranks of Turkish warriors lined the southern bank of the Meander and tried to block the crusaders' crossing. But the crusaders attacked head-on across fords in the river and forced a passage. In this and other initial clashes the Turks were soundly beaten, but later, while crossing the narrow pass of Mount Cadmos, the vanguard of Louis' army ignored the king's order to camp at the top of the climb. Instead the leading

---

[*] The Meander's coiling course gave its name to the geographical term for a winding river bend.

troops carried on, leaving the centre unprotected. The Turks attacked in earnest and inflicted severe casualties. In the chaos, packhorses and men plummeted to their deaths in the deep ravines, and the king himself barely escaped. Luckily he was not recognized. When his horse was killed, Louis managed to clamber up a steep outcrop of rocks and fend off his attackers with a sword. Even more damaging than the casualties, who included many prominent knights, was the fact that the defeat at Mount Cadmos abruptly removed any sense of military superiority the French force may still have enjoyed. It also further diminished Louis' already-poor reputation as a military leader, and sowed discord in the army. Additionally, there was obvious tension between Queen Eleanor and those around Louis who disapproved of her. Reynald, and everyone else present, could not have failed to notice the contrast between the gaudy Eleanor and her hedonistic followers on the one hand, and the pious Louis and his dour ecclesiastical advisers like Odo of Deuil on the other.

The blame for the fiasco at Mount Cadmos was laid partly at Eleanor's door. The vanguard that day had been led by a great lord from Poitou – and thus a vassal of the queen – called Geoffrey de Rancon. Queen Eleanor was travelling with Geoffrey as they crossed the mountain. It was said Geoffrey had disobeyed the king's orders and continued to a more comfortable camping ground at Eleanor's request. Additional evidence of the queen's influence was seen in the fact that Geoffrey might well have been put to death for his catastrophic breach of discipline, but his life was spared – possibly due to Eleanor's protection.

Mauled and demoralized, the crusaders soon added cold and hunger to their misery. As they trudged towards Atalya on Anatolia's south coast, they were driven to the extremity of eating their horses. At Atalya they were barred from the city and further aggravated by the high prices of the few goods on offer. They suffered continual Turkish attacks and, eventually, a plague. All of this they blamed on the Greeks, who then inflicted one last trial on the crusaders, charging an exorbitant 5,000 marks to ship the king and his nobles on the short journey to Antioch. Thanks to appalling weather, that normally short journey turned into three tortuous weeks, which ended at St Simeon on 19 March 1148. Meanwhile the foot soldiers and camp followers were obliged to take the harsh 500-mile land route to Antioch in the dead of winter across the passes of the Anti-Taurus Mountains. Ravaged by disease and hunger, harassed at every step by the agile Turkish horse archers, thousands of infantrymen even defected, to fight as mercenaries for the Muslims. It is likely that Reynald travelled with the king and his barons and so was spared the horrors of this land journey, but – noble or not – everyone on the crusade had endured months of frightful hardship.

The Prince of Antioch, Raymond of Poitiers, had been awaiting King Louis' arrival with increasing anxiety, and as soon as he heard of the crusaders' landfall, he hurried the fifteen miles from Antioch to the coast. Raymond greeted King Louis reverently. He then conducted the royal party up through the hills to the city, with all the pomp he could muster. Everything had been prepared for a grand entry, and the clergy and people of Antioch greeted the crusaders with the 'greatest magnificence'. It was not only the king who benefited from Raymond's hospitality. The French knights, probably including Reynald, were showered with generosity. According to William of Tyre:

> Raymond showed the king every attention on his arrival. He
> likewise displayed a similar care for the nobles and chief men
> in the royal retinue and gave them many proofs of his great
> liberality. In short, he outdid all in showing honour to each one
> according to his rank. [5]

Certainly Queen Eleanor of France would have been very happy to see Prince Raymond again. Raymond was Eleanor's uncle, brother of her father, Duke William X of Aquitaine. Like Reynald, Raymond of Poitiers was a younger son born in the West. Also like Reynald, Raymond had been without lands of his own. However, unlike Reynald, his father was one of the most powerful magnates in Christendom, Duke William IX of Aquitaine.

In 1136 Raymond, then at the court of King Stephen of England, received a job offer from Outremer. Prince Bohemond II of Antioch had been killed in battle with the Turks – his head had been embalmed and sent to the caliph in Baghdad. Antioch was without a prince, and the rights of the principality passed to Bohemond's only child, the young princess Constance. Constance's mother Alice acted temporarily as regent, and King Fulk of Jerusalem marched north to protect Antioch, but his forces could only stay temporarily. In the long run, Constance needed a husband to run the principality and lead its troops in the constant warfare against Antioch's Muslim and Christian neighbours. A delegation was sent to the West, and the role of Constance's husband and Prince of Antioch was offered to Raymond of Poitiers. He quickly accepted the deal. He then had to journey to the East in secret, disguised as a poor pilgrim to avoid the clutches of King Roger of Sicily, who also had designs on Antioch. On his arrival, Raymond married Constance, even though she was only ten years old.

On many levels Raymond was a perfect choice for the role. He was one of the great knights of the age, handsome, brave and monstrously strong. William of Tyre admired his many virtues:

> Lord Raymond was of noble blood and ancient lineage. He was very tall and in personal appearance extremely pleasing. He was young and his cheeks were still covered with the light down of youth. He was handsome far beyond all the kings and princes of the world, and he was affable and agreeable in conversation. In fact, his entire bearing was in every respect that of a charming

*and elegant prince. Experienced in military matters and expert in
the use of arms, he easily surpassed all his predecessors.*[6]

Even the Byzantines, with whom he had very tense relations, admired
Raymond personally. 'He was a man like the legendary Heracles,'[7] the
chroniclers wrote, 'surpassing Priam with his goodly spear of ash'.[8]
Perhaps the best indication of Raymond's effectiveness, though, is what
his enemies thought of him. 'Among all the kings of the Franks, there
was none more feared by the Turks,'[9] wrote Gregory the Priest, and the
Muslim historians agreed:

> *This accursed one was among the Frankish knights who were
> famed for their gallantry, valour, power of cunning and great
> stature, and he had acquired special repute by the dread which he
> inspired, his great severity and excessive ferocity.*[10]

Raymond could not read, but he was a great patron of the arts,
especially poetry, which flourished during his reign. He had an indolent,
sybaritic streak and his court, with its blend of Western, Byzantine and
Arab influences, was luxurious and sensual. True to the tastes of his
father, William IX of Aquitaine, he fostered the fad for courtly love. All
this suited Eleanor perfectly and she revelled in her stay in Antioch.

The fashion for courtly love had been born in William IX's court
in Poitou. The duke was one of the earliest troubadours and, like
her uncle Raymond, Eleanor had enthusiastically embraced her
grandfather's tradition, sponsoring troubadours, encouraging poetry
and the conventions of courtly love in her circle. Princess Constance,
Raymond's now twenty-one-year-old wife, would also have been familiar
with the conventions, which would be formally laid down by Andreas
Capellanus for Eleanor of Aquitaine's daughter, Marie of Champagne.
His work *De Amore* (*About Love*) included such guidelines as: 'The easy

attainment of love makes it of little value' (number 14) and 'He whom the thought of love vexes, eats and drinks very little' (number 23). It must have been thrilling – and daunting – for Constance suddenly to be surrounded by the most fashionable and romantic court in Christendom, as Eleanor and her entourage basked in the heady, licentious atmosphere of Antioch. Nobody was immune to the spellbinding attractions of Outremer, as the Muslim traveller Ibn Jubayr discovered when he saw a Frankish woman:

> most elegantly garbed in a beautiful dress from which trailed, according to their traditional style, a long train of golden silk. On her head she wore a golden diadem covered by a net of woven gold and on her breast was a like arrangement. Proud she was in her ornaments and dress, walking with little steps of half a span, like a dove, or in the manner of a wisp of cloud. God protect us from the seduction of the sight.[11]

Antioch had been founded back in 300 BC by one of Alexander the Great's generals and it had thrived for centuries. In Roman times it was third-biggest city of the empire, after Rome and Alexandria. The city had a great Christian heritage as well, which was very much alive for Reynald and his fellow crusaders. Antioch was where Christ's followers were first called Christians. It was where St Peter set up his first bishopric, long before he became Bishop of Rome. The Patriarch of Antioch therefore rivalled in prestige the Patriarchs of Jerusalem and Constantinople, and the Pope. The Apostle Paul had worked in Antioch too, writing his epistles in a cave on the slopes of Mount Silpius. In Reynald's time the cave was venerated, and the crusaders built a Romanesque church there – the only relic of Frankish Antioch still standing today. Although it had declined from its heyday, Antioch was still a great metropolis in the twelfth century and it was by far the wealthiest and most populous city controlled by the crusaders. It was 'beyond all description and impregnable', according to Stephen of Blois; its ramparts were said to be topped with 24,000 crenellations, for anyone who bothered to count.

The city sat at the end of profitable trade routes from the Orient. Antioch's port of St Simeon bustled with vessels from the Italian merchant cities of Pisa, Genoa and Venice, shipping soap, glass, carpets and the luxuries of Asia to eager consumers in the West. The famous 'silks of Antioch' were dyed, and precious stones from all over Asia were worked. Ironically, as the peril of Muslim unity increased, Antioch's wealth had grown, too. The strong rule of Zengi and his son Nur al-Din made their lands safer for travellers, and caravan traffic swelled as a result.

Around the city the territory was untamed. The home of lion, boar and leopard, it made glorious hunting for a young knight. It could be perilous, too; one notorious leopard, living in a ruined church near the outpost of Apamea, claimed many human victims, including a formidable Frankish knight. The Muslims called it 'the leopard which fought the jihad'.[12] Closer to the city itself, the land was rich and its deep brown soil was fertile. The plains and hills around were lush with crops, grape vines and fruit trees heavy with figs and citrus that ripened all year long. On the mountain slopes the prevailing wind from the sea was strong enough to bend the trees towards the east, but it also provided a cooling breeze for the great city and its famous gardens, blooming with red and saffron-yellow roses.

Antioch was full of exquisite villas, gardens and rippling fountains in which the citizens were happy to frolic, to the astonishment of newcomers. Fed by five aqueducts dating from Roman times, even the common houses boasted running water and were luxurious beyond the dreams of Westerners, used to the chilly, echoing castles of Europe. According to Willebrand of Oldenburg, who passed through Antioch at the beginning of the next century, the houses looked like mud huts on the outside, but on the inside they were palaces of mosaic, marble and porphyry. They were hung with silk from China and ornamented in rich carpets from Persia. New incenses of the East stimulated the nose; and oranges, pomegranate and sugar – unknown in the West – pleased the palate. Sultry slave girls and courtesans satisfied other senses, and public baths were a revelation. To the newly arrived crusaders, used to the relative austerity of Western Europe, the *Poulains* (as the Syrian-born Franks were called) were rightly notorious for their ostentation and decadence. They lived a precarious and lavish lifestyle punctuated by violence, their profligate excesses stimulated by the ever-present threat of disaster.

The twenty-something Reynald slotted neatly into this environment. Along with the harsh realities of his military calling, he had a taste for luxury and for show. And despite his relative poverty and lowly status, he clearly had the talents to back up his ambition and move in the most gilded of circles. The glimpses that we catch of Reynald from the contemporary sources build a picture of a very able young man, one who made his name with his courage and fighting skills, but who also made an impact in other ways. The only way a poor young bachelor could break into the upper echelons of a hierarchy dictated by birth was by proving himself as a knight. And Reynald seems to have conformed quite closely to the contemporary ideal of a courtly, chivalrous knight-errant.

The key virtues of chivalry, which any true knight required, were *franchise, prouesse, largesse, cortoisie* and *loyauté*: nobility or rank (of birth), military prowess, generosity, courtesy and loyalty. These all went together to make a man *preux* ('valiant') – a *preudhomme* – the truly valiant or chivalrous man.[13] We find Reynald described in almost exactly such terms. Even the Old French version of William of Tyre, usually very critical of Reynald, describes him as '*loyau*' and '*sage, cortois et de bon afere'* ('wise, courteous and of noble rank'). Ernoul says he was *'haus hom et bon chevalier'* ('high-born and a fine knight'). In battle, Reynald fought with the greatest *'prouesse'*. The one knightly quality not explicitly accorded to him is *largesse* (generosity), but while he was still a poor knight in Antioch, Reynald did not have anything to be generous with. However, there is reason to think he might later have met this criterion as well.

We don't know what Reynald looked like, but most crusaders were clean-shaven – something that was unusual for the local cultures, and especially shocking to the Armenians, for whom a beard was an essential sign of manhood. The ideal knight was also slender; 'If the knight is thin and tall,' wrote Usama Ibn Munqidh, 'the Franks admire him more.' Reynald was certainly good-looking – a 'handsome bachelor', according to his contemporary, the chronicler Ernoul. He also might have had the courteous gift of the gab – he had 'milk and honey in his voice', according to Peter of Blois.[14] Most importantly, Reynald had the crucial quality of any knight, bravery, in spades. All in all, the attractive and well-mannered Reynald might indeed have been amongst those knights who found favour with Eleanor and her suite. His knightly qualities and adventurous spirit would also have fitted well with the courtly-love convention in which a knight idealizes a high-born lady as his love, performing deeds of valour to win her favour. The beautiful Princess Constance herself would have made a perfect object to put on a pedestal as his 'lady'.

Eleanor and her damsels dallied in Antioch without distress, but the frivolity could only last so long. Prince Raymond needed men like Reynald for their military skills, not for their manners. Although he was a formidable warrior, Raymond had his faults. He could be lazy, rash and had an uncontrollable temper. He also loved to gamble – surely a poor choice of vice for a man who, the chronicles say, was 'greatly dreaded by the enemy, but unlucky'.[15] Raymond also lacked skills as a statesman and strategist. On his erratic watch, the Armenians in Cilicia had taken territory from Antioch; they had also seized some strategically sited mountain castles belonging to the Knights Templar. The Templars, along with the other powerful Military Order of the East, the Knights Hospitaller, were vital elements in the defence of the Latin states. They garrisoned key frontier fortresses and provided substantial contingents of elite mounted knights to crusader armies.

The Seljuk Turks in Anatolia were also menacing, though they were mainly absorbed in conflict with the Byzantines. Most temptingly for Raymond, the arrival of such a large contingent of warriors with the Second Crusade was a chance finally to take the offensive against Nur al-Din. Perhaps they could seize one of the key Muslim strongholds east of the Orontes River, such as the fortress town of Shayzar, or even Nur al-Din's mighty capital of Aleppo itself.

Eleanor supported Raymond's strategy, which made sense – Nur al-Din was undoubtedly the greatest threat to the Franks at the time – but the queen's stance widened the gulf between her and her husband. The pious Louis was not keen to help Raymond. He preferred to continue southwards first and complete his pilgrimage to Jerusalem. Eleanor was angry enough to suggest a separation, pointing out that under the rules of consanguinity they were too closely related to be legally married. If Louis went south to the Kingdom of Jerusalem, she threatened to remain in Antioch with her vassals. Relations between King Louis and Prince Raymond quickly soured. Meanwhile the liaison between handsome Uncle Raymond and his beautiful niece became ever closer. William of Tyre is explicit about what happened:

> *Frustrated in his ambitious designs, [Raymond] began to hate*
> *the king's ways; he openly plotted against him and took means to*
> *do him injury. He resolved also to deprive him of his wife, either*
> *by force or by secret intrigue. The queen readily assented to this*

*design, for she was a foolish woman. Her conduct before and
after this time showed her to be… far from circumspect. Contrary
to her royal dignity, she disregarded her marriage vows and was
unfaithful to her husband.*[16]

When the rumours reached Louis, who was still besotted with the
lovely Eleanor, he was devastated. In the dead of night he left Antioch
to continue his journey to Jerusalem. He did not take his leave of
Raymond. The king's men seized Eleanor and dragged her from the
town by force.[*]

When Louis left Antioch for Jerusalem, it is not known whether
Reynald went with him, or whether he stayed to serve under Raymond
in Antioch. The latter is more likely. Certainly a few years later the
Old French version of William of Tyre, known as the *Estoire d'Eracles*,
confirms that Reynald was working in Antioch as a mercenary soldier.
What is certain is that, having experienced the lifestyle of Outremer at
first hand and seen the opportunities on offer, Reynald decided to stay
in the East.

After leaving Antioch, Louis fulfilled his vow of pilgrimage and toured
the holy sites. The German emperor Conrad was also in Jerusalem,
having recovered from his wounds. They began a long series of debates
with the King of Jerusalem, Baldwin III, about how best to use the
substantial forces they had gathered. Eventually, in July 1148, Conrad
and Louis, along with the army of the Kingdom of Jerusalem, led their
remaining crusaders against the great Muslim metropolis of Damascus.
The capture of Damascus would have been a strategic triumph for the
crusaders and could have shifted the balance of power in their favour.

---

* After the crusade, Eleanor's marriage to Louis was annulled and she married a
man more to her tastes, the energetic, warlike, impious and hot-blooded Henry
Curtmantle, who went on to become the great King of England, Henry II.

It would have rid the Latin states of a powerful Muslim enemy, while winning rich new lands and untold treasure. But there were strong objections to the plan, among them the obvious problem that the populous, well-armed and high-walled city would be a very hard nut to crack. Also, Damascus was a friendly power. Unur's regime had been a useful counter-balance to Nur al-Din's growing strength, and Damascus actually paid an annual tribute to the crusaders. In hindsight, a direct attack on Nur al-Din in Aleppo might have been more sensible and, if successful, would have left Damascus isolated and easier to capture. But this was of course the strategy proposed by Raymond of Poitiers, which Louis had rejected.

The outraged Damascenes put up a robust defence, and as crusader casualties increased, so did frustration and disunity in the Christian camp. The local Frankish nobility, with all their interests committed in the East, had a love-hate relationship with the new crusaders. While they welcomed reinforcements from the West with open arms, they emphatically did not want outsiders grabbing all the spoils. Rather than risk a conquered Damascus going to newly arrived crusaders like the ambitious and acquisitive Count Thierry of Flanders – who wanted Damascus for himself – the jealous local barons preferred to undermine the campaign. Rumours brewed of large bribes paid by the Muslims to local Frankish leaders to betray the crusade. After just four days, the siege was lifted and the magnificent Frankish army retired in disorder. Preoccupied with Nur al-Din in the north and estranged from the King of France, Raymond and the troops of Antioch were not even present at the debacle.

King Louis and the Emperor Conrad returned, chastened, to Europe. The great crusade launched with such ardour by Bernard of Clairvaux had been a total failure. Bernard never really lived it down. Following the disaster of the Second Crusade, the balance of power in the Levant began to shift decisively and ominously towards Islam. Chroniclers reported a rain as red as blood in Jerusalem, and red snow in June.[17] William of Tyre wrote pessimistically:

> From this time, the condition of the Latins in the East became
> visibly worse. Our enemies saw that the labours of our most
> powerful kings and leaders had been fruitless and all their efforts
> vain; they mocked at the shattered strength and broken glory
> of those who represented the substantial foundations of the
> Christians. With impunity they had scorned the actual presence of
> those whose very names had formerly terrified them. Hence their
> presumption and boldness rose to such heights that they no longer
> feared the Christian forces and did not hesitate to attack them
> with unwonted vigour.[18]

The aggressive activity of the Muslim armies after their victory at Damascus meant that even if Reynald, as we suspect, stayed in the north and missed the rest of the crusade, he would have had his fill of fighting around Antioch. Nur al-Din's policy was one of constant jihad and eventual annihilation of the Christian invaders. He was on the warpath, and everything in the north of the Latin states was about to change. This change would throw up all sorts of possibilities for an up-and-coming soldier of fortune.

The Walled Fountain, near Inab, 29 June 1149

It had been a long, hard night for the men of Antioch. The Turks had harassed them relentlessly through the hours of darkness, pushing back the outposts of Prince Raymond's army, overrunning his outer lines of defence and seizing the high ground. The Franks were camped on a low-lying plain, near a spring known as Fons Muratus, hemmed in by marshes and hills. On the surrounding ridgelines, the morning sun revealed dust rising from ranks of Turkish cavalry, 6,000 strong. Raymond's force was outnumbered by four to one.

As a rising wind blew the dust in his eyes, Raymond could reflect on how his own actions had led to this potentially disastrous position.

Word had come to him in Antioch that Nur al-Din was besieging the powerful citadel of Inab in the north-west of the principality. Raymond had responded with his habitual bravery and impetuosity. Some of his captains advised caution, but the rash Raymond would not be overruled when it came to warfare. Without waiting for the bulk of his cavalry to arrive, he pressed on.

On 28 June, Raymond caught Nur al-Din's forces by surprise, inflicting a sharp defeat. He could then have taken refuge in one of his nearby fortresses to wait for reinforcements, but his pride kept him in the field. He did not want to show any fear of Nur al-Din.

Nur al-Din was at first reluctant to engage, suspecting that Raymond's force was just the vanguard of a larger army. When scouts reported that Raymond had camped in the open, without reinforcements, the atabeg saw his chance.

The next morning Raymond realized the enormity of his mistake, but it was too late to withdraw. He resolutely 'drew up his lines in battle formation, stationed his knights in order, and prepared to fight at close quarters'. The two armies came together and engaged hand-to-hand in the choking gloom of dust clouds that blotted out the sun. The Frankish knights fought desperately, launching their most potent tactic – 'their famous charge' – at the Muslims, but they were too heavily outnumbered. In the chaotic mêlée the field-army of Antioch was virtually annihilated. Raymond 'fought valiantly, like the high-spirited and courageous warrior he was, but finally, wearied by killing and exhausted in spirit, he was slain by a stroke of the sword in the midst of the slaughter which he had wrought'.[19]

After the battle, the people of Antioch, picking through the piles of dead, only identified his naked, mutilated corpse by some recognizable marks and scars on his remaining body parts. Raymond's head and right arm had been hacked off and taken to Nur al-Din, who paid their bearer a handsome reward. The prince's skull was set in a silver case and sent as a gift to the caliph in Baghdad.

Chapter 4

ARRIVISTE

Many there were, however, who marvelled that a woman
so eminent, so distinguished and powerful, who had been
the wife of a very illustrious man, should stoop to marry
an ordinary knight.

William of Tyre

The defeat at the Walled Fountain in June 1149 was as calamitous as Roger of Antioch's downfall on the Field of Blood thirty years before. 'The flower of the army and the prince' was destroyed, leaving Antioch at the mercy of the Muslim invaders. Nur al-Din swiftly captured the strategic castles of Harim, near Antioch, and Apamea on the Orontes. He then ravaged the principality, right up to the walls of Antioch itself. To underline the extent of his conquest, Nur al-Din rode to St Simeon and bathed ceremonially in the Mediterranean. Antioch, though, held out. The city's intimidating defences and its determined populace deterred Nur al-Din, as did the threat of Byzantine retribution if he attacked. After all Antioch was officially – if not effectively – subject to Byzantine sovereignty. When King Baldwin of Jerusalem hurried north to take charge of the leaderless principality, Nur al-Din made a truce and withdrew beyond the Orontes River.

If Reynald was soldiering in Antioch at this time, he may have been one of the few lucky survivors from the battle at *Fons Muratus*. More likely he was serving in the garrison at Antioch, perhaps even in the palace guard. His subsequent closeness to Princess Constance would fit with this possibility. Either way, from this time on it is overwhelmingly likely that Reynald was plying his trade in Antioch, as a mercenary in the pay of King Baldwin III.

Baldwin needed someone to fill the vacuum left by Raymond's death, but the heir to the principality of Antioch was Bohemond, the son of Raymond and Princess Constance. Bohemond was only five years old. According to William of Tyre:

> *Great was the anxiety of King Baldwin of Jerusalem at this time on behalf of Antioch and the lands adjacent to it. He feared lest, deprived as it was of the protection of its prince, it might fall into the hand of the enemy and suffer the pitiable fate of Edessa.*[1]

Again Antioch needed a military leader 'to undertake the duties of the prince and to rouse the people from their state of dejection'.[2] Again the princess needed a husband – at least until her infant son Bohemond came of age. The most powerful man in the principality was now Antioch's spiritual leader, the wealthy, worldly and controversial patriarch, Aimery. In the wake of the slaughter at *Fons Muratus*, as Nur al-Din's army approached Antioch, Aimery – contrary to his usual tight-fisted habits – paid for mercenaries to defend the city and showed effective leadership. As a stopgap, Baldwin left him in charge of administering the principality until a spouse was found for Constance. At this stage Baldwin would also have made arrangements to strengthen Antioch's standing army and provide for their pay. This is where Reynald fitted in – 'as a mercenary in the pay of the king'.[3] It was a respectable job in which he could showcase his knightly skills (hunting, killing, and so forth), but certainly not the glorious achievement that an ambitious knight would have dreamed of when leaving Burgundy. Yes, he was fighting the Holy War, but there was little fame to be won in the endless round of petty raids and skirmishes. Reynald, we can be certain, was after something more. In Antioch, after the death of Raymond, that 'something more' may suddenly have appeared more attainable.

Widowed heiresses in the Latin states were a very valuable commodity and a tried and tested means to social mobility. In Outremer, baby Frankish boys proved less resilient than girls. And if he survived the multiple ailments of infancy, a young man's life expectancy was still very short, thanks to the ever-present swords and darts of the enemy. This meant there was an endemic shortage of fighting men. And because even the greatest lords frequently fell in battle, this led to a regular supply of rich widows for aspiring and able knights. Even the highest ranks were achieved through marriage: Raymond of Poitiers had become a prince by marrying Constance, and in 1131 Count Fulk of Anjou had become King Fulk of Jerusalem through his marriage to Queen Melisende. The view of the time was that while a woman could be the rightful holder and transmitter of authority in a fief, effective rule required a man, especially in the unremitting warfare of Outremer. Most powerful heiresses were quickly married off, husbands being carefully selected for their prowess, wealth, connections and the additional fighting men they could bring to the party.* Reynald would prove a master at using this critical tool of political marriage.

Princess of the great city of Antioch and now back on the marriage market, Constance was one of the most eligible women in the world.

---

* For instance, starting in 1183, Princess Isabella of Jerusalem would be married off four times for her royal birthright. Her husbands were: Humphrey IV of Toron, Conrad of Montferrat, Henry of Champagne and Amalric II, King of Cyprus.

Still only around twenty-two years old, she was not just rich and powerful, but beautiful as well. Raymond was not cold in his grave before the suitors began to queue up; and they included a candidate from Byzantium. The Emperor Manuel saw an opportunity to bring Antioch firmly under his control by marrying Constance into the imperial family. Manuel himself had been considered as a husband for Constance in his youth, but now he was married – though not very happily – to a homely German. He sent his brother-in-law, Caesar John Roger of Sorrento, to Antioch to ask for Constance's hand. Unfortunately, the age gap between Constance and the widower John Roger was even greater than that between Constance and her first husband, Raymond. As a young girl she had had no choice but to acquiesce, but as a grown woman Constance was not keen to rush into a new match, especially not to another much older man. Poor old John Roger was summarily rejected. According to Manuel's imperial secretary, John Kinnamos, the disappointed suitor took the rebuff to heart:

> In these circumstances the Caesar John went to Antioch, but achieved nothing of what he had come for (because he was aged); Constance regarded him with displeasure and he returned to Byzantion; when sickness beset him, he tonsured his locks and donned the black garb [of a monk].[4]

But whatever their age and attractiveness, Constance would probably have rejected any Byzantine suitor. She was unwilling to subject herself and her city to closer rule from Constantinople. Most of her subjects – and the Franks of Outremer in general – agreed with this policy and would have preferred her to choose a Frankish consort. In opposition to the Byzantine option, King Baldwin provided his own succession of prospects. William of Tyre describes how the king repeatedly:

advised the princess to choose one of the nobles as a husband, by
whose counsel and efforts the principality might be governed. There
were in the land at that time a number of noble and distinguished
men attached to the camp of the king. Among them were Ives de
Nesle, count of Soissons, a distinguished man, wise and discreet, of
great influence in the kingdom of the Franks; Walter de Falkenberg,
castellan of St Omer, who was later lord of Tiberias, a discreet
man and very courteous, wise in counsel and valiant in arms; and
also Ralph de Merle, a noble of the highest rank, experienced in
the practice of arms and noted for his good sense. Any one of these
seemed with justice quite capable of protecting the region.[5]

Many of the virtues that qualified these knights to lead Antioch were precisely the same as those applied elsewhere to Reynald. The suitors were *sage*, *cortois*, noble and valiant. They also had advantages that Reynald did not – great influence, in the case of Ives de Nesle, Count of Soissons. But it did not matter how well suited they were. One after the other, Constance sent them all packing.

Meanwhile the strategic situation in Antioch was becoming critical. Nur al-Din remained on the offensive, pressurizing the Frankish possessions to the east, in what remained of the county of Edessa. Then, in May 1150, another disaster befell the Franks. Count Joscelin II of Edessa had succeeded in holding off Nur al-Din from what remained of his county, and had recently even dealt the Zengid forces a severe defeat. Nur al-Din's armour was amongst the booty and, in a show of bravado, Joscelin sent the captured chainmail to Nur al-Din's father-in-law, the powerful Seljuk chieftain Mas'ud, with an arrogant message: 'Here is your son-in-law's armour. Next you will be receiving something more serious.' Soon afterwards Joscelin was riding from his lands to a conference in Antioch when he fell into the clutches of a band of Turcoman marauders. Some said he was captured while lying unconscious after a fall from his horse; others that he had left his escort to answer a call of nature. The freebooters sold him to a Jew in Aleppo as a slave. To Joscelin's misfortune, the Jew recognized him and sold him for a quick profit to Nur al-Din. The *atabeg* had Joscelin blinded, bound in chains and flung into a pit. The historian Ibn al-Athir wrote that Joscelin's capture was:

> *one of the greatest successes for the Muslims because the count*
> *was an intransigent devil, fierce against the Muslims and cruel.*
> *His capture was a blow to all Christendom.*[6]

Still lacking a prince, Antioch was too weak to come to the aid of the now-leaderless Edessa. With Joscelin a prisoner of war, the remaining fortresses of the county fell in steady succession. When the end was clearly in sight, Joscelin's wife Beatrice sold the remnants of her county to Emperor Manuel. However, the *basileus* had not done his due diligence on the purchase: the county of Edessa was extinguished in July 1151 with the fall of Joscelin's great castle at Turbessel. The first state created by the Franks in the East was gone. Antioch had lost its eastern bulwarks and was more exposed than ever.

The extinction of Edessa drummed home to every Frank in the East just how fragile their establishment was. After Edessa, Antioch could be next. The pressure mounted on Constance to take a husband, but still she was not ready. William of Tyre disapproved:

> *The princess… dreaded the yoke of marriage and preferred a free*
> *and independent life. She paid little heed to the needs of her people*
> *and was far more interested in enjoying the pleasures of life.*[7]

Independence here, of course, had significance beyond Constance's personal liberty. The freedom of Antioch from vassalage to either the king of Jerusalem or the Byzantine emperor was also at stake. King Baldwin decided to mount a full-frontal assault on Constance and invited her down the coast to Tripoli, where the leaders of the Latin states were gathered for a summit.

> The king, well aware of her predilection, called a general
> council at Tripoli, consisting of the nobles of the kingdom and
> the principality… After subjects of general interest had received
> careful attention, the matter of the marriage of the princess was
> given consideration.[8]

The arguments of the council could not sway Constance, so King Baldwin brought out his secret weapons; Constance's intimidating aunts, the dowager Queen Melisende of Jerusalem and the Countess of Tripoli, Hodierna, ambushed their niece and berated her for putting Antioch in jeopardy. Along with the efforts of King Baldwin and Count Raymond II of Tripoli, they used every feminine wile to convince her to accept one of the very eligible barons on offer. Nothing worked. Queen Melisende was a dominant personality, who had ruled for a time in her own right. In full termagant mode, she had ridden roughshod over kings and princes, but Constance was made of even sterner stuff. She adamantly refused all-comers. William of Tyre ascribed her fussiness to the typical folly of women. A modern guess might be that Constance was simply enjoying her independence. We are bound to wonder, however, whether she stubbornly rejected all her official suitors because her eye and her heart were already drawn elsewhere. According to William of Tyre, 'the pleasures of life' that Constance preferred involved a certain young nobleman from Burgundy:

> The Lady Constance, widow of Prince Raymond of Antioch,
> who, after the fashion of women, had refused many distinguished

*nobles, secretly chose as her husband Renaud de Chatillon, a
knight in the pay of the king.*[9]

We cannot be sure how long the affair had been going on before it
became public. By 1153 Constance had set her heart on Reynald, but
the engagement was still secret. Perhaps the princess believed in what
Andreas Capellanus would make his thirteenth precept of courtly love,
'When made public, love rarely endures.'

In 1153, King Baldwin III launched a major offensive against the
fortress city of Ascalon, on the southern borders of his kingdom. The
lone town on the Levantine coast still in Muslim hands, Ascalon had
been a persistent strategic problem for the Latin states since the First
Crusade. The city was powerfully fortified, well stocked with arms
and provisions and contained a numerous and determined garrison.
Ascalon barred the route to Egypt and was a base for constant raids
into Frankish territory. Over more than fifty years 'the Bride of Syria'
had resisted everything the Franks could throw at her. This time they
were determined to capture the city, and Baldwin summoned all the
forces at his disposal for the campaign. This included Reynald de
Chatillon. It is here, at Ascalon, that we find the earliest mention of
Reynald in the contemporary sources and, for the first time, have his
whereabouts specifically attested. According to a terse William of Tyre,
'two high-born men of France' were marching as mercenaries in the
army of the king: 'Reynald de Chatillon and Walter of St Omer; these
last two served the king for pay.'[10]

Intriguingly, Reynald is mentioned here in the same breath as Walter
of St Omer, another brave young knight from France who arrived on
crusade with Louis VII and had been stationed in Antioch. Walter had
been a popular candidate for Constance's hand, and would later make
a great catch of his own in Eschiva of Bures, Lady of Tiberias. That
marriage would make Walter Prince of Galilee, the most important fief

in the Kingdom of Jerusalem. The close link to Walter is another reason to think that, during his time in Antioch, Reynald was in the circle of Princess Constance. Clearly Reynald and Walter were two of a kind – men on the make, young bucks who stood out equally for their skill in war and their vaulting levels of ambition. But if Walter was the early favourite in the marriage stakes, he turned out to have been only a wingman for his friend. Reynald struck it lucky first, because during the siege of Ascalon, as the *Estoire d'Eracles* recounts, Constance finally revealed her choice for husband and new ruler of Antioch:

> *Constance the Princess of Antioch, who had refused many great*
> *barons, gave her heart to a bachelor of France who was not a*
> *very rich man, but wise, courteous and of high rank. A handsome*
> *bachelor and a fine knight, his name was Reynald de Chatillon.*[11]

What made Constance choose Reynald over the many other, more obviously advantageous suitors? The sources strongly support the contention that love was a factor. Constance 'gave her heart' to the 'handsome bachelor' and 'greatly desired' him. In Raymond, she had been used to a husband who was renowned for his good looks. The handsome Reynald ticked this box. Also, unlike the much older Raymond and the rejected John Roger, Reynald was for once a lover in Constance's own age group. And along with the physical attraction, Reynald fulfilled many of the qualities of the romanticized ideal of the knight; and while he was not wealthy, his lineage was theoretically very impressive. In a move typical of the upwardly mobile families of the day, the Lords of Donzy had conveniently found noble blood dating back to Roman times. They traced their descent to the aristocratic Roman clan of the Palladii.[12]

In the conventions of courtly love, the passion between an aspiring knight and his lady was a celibate one, but sometimes the literary expressions of love and service could cross the line and become physical. This is apparently what happened in this case. The brave young knight-errant had truly won his princess. William of Tyre even hints at what was essentially an elopement. Constance 'secretly' became engaged to Reynald, and the assent of the king was merely a rubber stamp.

The match was clearly not all about blind passion, though. The princess would not have bestowed her principality, and the inheritance of her son, on a poor man – however handsome and well mannered – without good reason. Yes, Reynald's courtly qualities would have helped. More importantly, Reynald was serving as a knight in Antioch, so Constance had ample opportunity to observe what really mattered: his skills as a leader and as a warrior. To outweigh his lowly status, these qualities must have been truly exceptional. Still, William of Tyre wrote wickedly:

> Many there were, however, who marvelled that a woman so eminent, so distinguished and powerful, who had been the wife of a very illustrious man, should stoop to marry an ordinary knight.[13]

The snobbery reflected in William's dismissive phrase 'ordinary knight' could not halt Reynald's inexorable rise. According to many observers, the young man had outstanding abilities, some of them grudgingly admitted even by William himself. The marriage was certainly acceptable to King Baldwin, who, if he had any choice in the matter, must have thought Reynald capable of ruling well and, at the very least, of performing the critical princely role to 'guard the land'. Reynald had already proved himself trusted by the king as one of his leading warriors. One version of the marriage story – that of Ernoul – portrays it as Baldwin's idea, and pre-approved by his barons. Indeed, if he needed any more proof of Reynald's mettle, Baldwin saw it at first hand during the siege of Ascalon. While William of Tyre cannot bring himself to praise Reynald's actions there, his mention of Reynald's presence is a hint that something special occurred.* The chronicler Michael the Syrian, who spent time in Antioch and knew Reynald personally, is explicit: the 'Lord called Reynald' played a significant role at Ascalon, 'running the gauntlet of death, in peril of his life'. The Syriac historian Gregory the Priest also writes of Reynald's 'heroic deeds' during the siege. It is possible Reynald put on an especially good show on this very public stage, in the knowledge that he was going to ask the king a big favour.

Reynald asked for Baldwin's consent while in the field at Ascalon, in front of the leading nobles and bishops of the Latin states. In doing so, Reynald gave a glimpse of one of his most striking personality traits – a flair for the theatrical, a penchant for the dramatic and emotional gesture. Instead of straightforwardly and discreetly asking for Constance's hand, when he came before King Baldwin, the *Estoire d'Eracles* recounts that:

> *Reynald fell at his feet and begged him very humbly to not refuse*
> *him such a great honour, because with the help of God and the*
> *support of the king, he would strive to defend the land of Antioch*
> *and would always be at his command.*[14]

Ascalon finally fell to the Franks in August 1153. From Cilicia in the north to the borders of Egypt in the south, the entire littoral was now in Frankish hands. By the time of this great victory, Reynald was openly engaged to Constance. They went public only after King Baldwin gave his approval: 'She did not wish this to be made public, however, until she had secured the authority and consent of the king, her cousin, under whose protection her principality lay.'[15] As well as marrying for love,

---

* Another, even more striking example of William of Tyre glossing over Reynald's military prowess would occur some twenty-four years later.

Constance showed in her choice that the interests of Antioch were currently better served by owing allegiance to the King of Jerusalem than to the Emperor of Constantinople.

The royal stamp of approval did nothing to diminish the scandal, however. The marriage was the talk of Outremer:

> *Reynald returned to Antioch and immediately married the lady who greatly desired him. Many marvelled, and gossip spread throughout the land, but no matter what people said, Reynald de Chatillon became Prince of Antioch.* [16]

To the consternation of many and the delicious gossip of all, the landless soldier of fortune had won the heart of a princess and become ruler of one of the greatest cities in the world. He had succeeded beyond his wildest dreams. The question now was whether he would prove worthy of his good fortune.

The Citadel, Antioch, summer 1154

The impregnable citadel of Antioch sat high above the city on the crest of Mount Silpius. Far below, Antioch spread out between the slopes of the mountain and the Orontes River, with the great Cathedral of St Peter at its heart. It was a beautiful city, decked with gardens and fountains, 'the chief city of all of Syria, watered by the Orontes and refreshed by the west wind'.

Colossal walls built by the Roman Emperor Justinian encircled the town, studded by 360 massive towers clad in great blocks of stone. To the east, the fertile plains of the principality stretched into the distance. To the west, through the haze, rose St Simon's Mount. On that hot summer day, looking out from the tower of the citadel, it would have made a magnificent sight for the Patriarch Aimery.

But the elderly patriarch was not enjoying the view. Chained to the top of the tower, he was naked, his bald head and his entire body burning in the scorching summer sun. Before casting him onto the turret, the soldiers had beaten him savagely. Blood seeped from his cuts and dripped onto the dusty stonework. Attracted by the blood, flies and blood-sucking creatures buzzed around him, settling on his wounds.

As a final flourish, Reynald had made his men smear Aimery's body with honey, so that the stings of wasps and bees added to his torment.

The message was clear.

You did not cross the new Prince of Antioch.

Chapter 5

DIABOLIC DARING

The prince, who was an arriviste, was… driven out of his mind with rage. He took the Patriarch and led him shamefully to the donjon of Antioch. Then he did even greater devilry: He tied the Patriarch, who was priest and sacred bishop in the see of the holy St Peter, to the top of the tower, even though he was a sick old man. There he had him smeared with honey and left in the burning sun all day, to suffer the heat and the flies in great torment.

Estoire d'Eracles

After Prince Raymond's death in 1149, the Patriarch Aimery of Limoges had promptly taken charge of Antioch and organized an effective opposition to repel Nur al-Din. Since then the patriarch, 'who was a rich and powerful man, widely obeyed throughout the land', had been in day-to-day control of the affairs of state. As such, he had opposed any marriage for Princess Constance, knowing that a new prince would leave him sidelined. At King Baldwin's council in Tripoli, for instance, Aimery's influence had been critical in helping Constance hold firm against the pressure of her aunts. William of Tyre recorded that, in rejecting the plans for her marriage, the princess:

> *was guided by the advice of the patriarch. He, being a very artful and subtle man, is said to have supported her in this mistake, in order that he might have a freer hand in the government of the land – a thing which he greatly desired.*[1]

When Reynald married Constance in 1153 and took over the reins of power, Aimery made his displeasure obvious. Reynald was not in a position to ignore such a dangerous rival, and kept him under observation. Aimery continued to bad-mouth Reynald all over town, but in undermining his prince's position, he was taking a great risk. The bishop 'spoke about him [Reynald] in private and even in council as though he did not fear or respect him in the least'.

However, Aimery had misjudged his opponent. As a 'new man', without wealth or allies to bolster his position, Reynald could not tolerate dissent. He had to stamp out this challenge to his authority. Here we see one of Reynald's traits clearly displayed – his capacity for decisive and memorably gruesome action. 'Moved to violent and inexorable wrath', the prince, wrote William of Tyre:

> *Laid violent hands upon the patriarch and with diabolic daring caused the venerable man to be seized and ignominiously conducted to the citadel which towers above Antioch.*[2]

Reynald was not just acting out of anger. He had another motive for mistreating the patriarch – his wealth. Reynald needed money. As we know, he was not a rich man, and a prince had many expenses. He had to maintain a standing army and keep a court with the requisite *largesse*. The Greek historian John Kinnamos tells us that Reynald 'felt extreme poverty' and so laid a trap for the patriarch, whom he 'knew to be very wealthy'. Reynald invited Aimery to the palace and, 'entertaining the bishop privately, he asked him for money'. The patriarch refused to help Reynald and, 'because he was unable to persuade him', the prince seized Aimery, thrashed him brutally and set him naked on the tower. According to Kinnamos, the treatment had the desired effect because, sometime during his agonizing, insect-plagued day in the burning Syrian sun, the patriarch caved in. He 'gave way, offering to yield all his wealth' to Reynald.

William of Tyre also disapproved of Aimery, whom he thought corrupt and unfit for office, but Aimery was still Patriarch of Antioch and an assault on him was an assault on Holy Mother Church. Suddenly the priest, whom William criticized as an 'unlettered man from the Limousin, whose life was far from noble', became 'the aged priest, a successor of Peter, the chief of the apostles'. Aimery's arrest and torture were 'a most abominable act', the 'mad conduct of the foolish prince'.[3] William lamented the fact that nobody stood up for the poor old man: 'No one, for piety's sake, offered him any relief from the relentless rays of the sun or tried to drive away the flies.' Given that twelfth-century historians were almost exclusively clergymen, attacking the Church or its ministers was a surefire way to generate negative coverage. Reynald's bad reputation starts here. So extreme was this event, however, that secular society was scandalized as well. King Baldwin of Jerusalem sent emissaries to Antioch reproving Reynald for his outrageous act and warning him to turn from his wicked ways. Reynald eventually relented and 'released the patriarch, but not without heaping much abuse upon him' – and not without seizing Aimery's vast wealth.

The outrage is not surprising. One of the cardinal duties of the feudal leader was to defend the Church, to 'venerate the priesthood and protect the clergy'. Violence towards men of the cloth was reprehensible, and Reynald was roundly condemned both by his contemporaries and by posterity. However, he was not the only lay lord in the Latin states to quarrel with the Church. Raymond, his predecessor as Prince of Antioch, had quarrelled with his patriarch, the rich and arrogant Ralph de Domfront. Raymond had the patriarch deposed and replaced by Aimery. At one stage Ralph was 'shamefully bound and treated ignominiously like a man of blood'[4] (in other words, like a murderer). He died in exile in Rome, still striving for papal support to reclaim his bishopric. King Baldwin I of Jerusalem had also fought bitterly with his patriarch, Daimbert, while King Baldwin II was suspected of poisoning the patriarch Stephen of La Ferté in 1130. Money and land lay behind all these clashes. Raymond coveted Ralph's famous wealth, while the kings of Jerusalem needed the Church's gold reserves to pay their troops, and Church lands to enlarge their demesne. But none of these leaders attracted the censure subsequently aimed at Reynald for his treatment of Aimery. The difference lies in the overt, unique style of savagery utilized by Reynald. When he had to act decisively – and be seen to act decisively – in crushing Aimery, Reynald was able to conceive and execute his response in a way so dramatic that everyone would pay attention, and no one would forget.

Interestingly, in contrasting Reynald with the other knights who could have married Constance, William of Tyre uses the word 'discreet' for the rejected suitors. The implication is perhaps that the successful suitor, Reynald, was indiscreet. This is born out by his flamboyant, extravagant actions. Reynald could certainly put on a show – whether of anger or, if needed, of contrition. After torturing the patriarch and stealing his treasure, he made a demonstration of remorse, dressing Aimery in his regalia and leading him through the streets of Antioch. The charade did not placate Aimery, who 'was no less enraged against him'. The patriarch eventually fled to exile in Jerusalem, where he remained for years, plotting incessantly, even with Antioch's traditional political foe (and theoretical overlord), the Byzantine emperor. He was always on the lookout for an opportunity to take vengeance on Reynald and wrote repeatedly to the emperor, offering to betray Reynald to him.

With his chief adversary gone, other dissent cowed by the virulent crushing of the patriarch and, no doubt, his treasury enriched, Reynald got down to the business of running Antioch. Later historians have belittled his contributions as prince – Jonathan Phillips, for instance, dismisses him as 'far inferior' to Raymond of Poitiers[5] – but, in the eyes of his contemporaries, Reynald demonstrated excellent qualities as leader in a very challenging role.

The prince had the task of protecting the magnificent patrimony of Antioch for his stepson Bohemond, and maintaining its independence in the face of a range of threats. First, Reynald had to keep internal order. The patriarch was not the only potential source of a challenge to his rule. There was a complex web of communities in Antioch, where the Frankish conquerors and their Italian merchant allies formed only a small minority. There were many Greek and Syrian Christians in Antioch, too, members of the Orthodox, Nestorian, Jacobite and other churches. The loyalty of these people was dubious. Also questionable was the loyalty of the substantial Christian Armenian population, and that of the Muslims living in the principality. While these communities might usually be loyal, if central authority weakened, they could not be relied upon.

This underlying mistrust was seen after Prince Raymond's death in 1149. When the Patriarch Aimery took control of Antioch, a curfew was imposed on all non-Frankish inhabitants. As well as fending off the forces of Nur al-Din outside the walls, the Franks kept watch on their fellow citizens inside the city. All non-Frankish inhabitants were disarmed and forbidden from going around after dark without a torch.

Normally all communities lived in peace with each other in their own neighbourhoods, and were judged by their own peers according to their own traditional laws. Reynald wisely did nothing to disturb

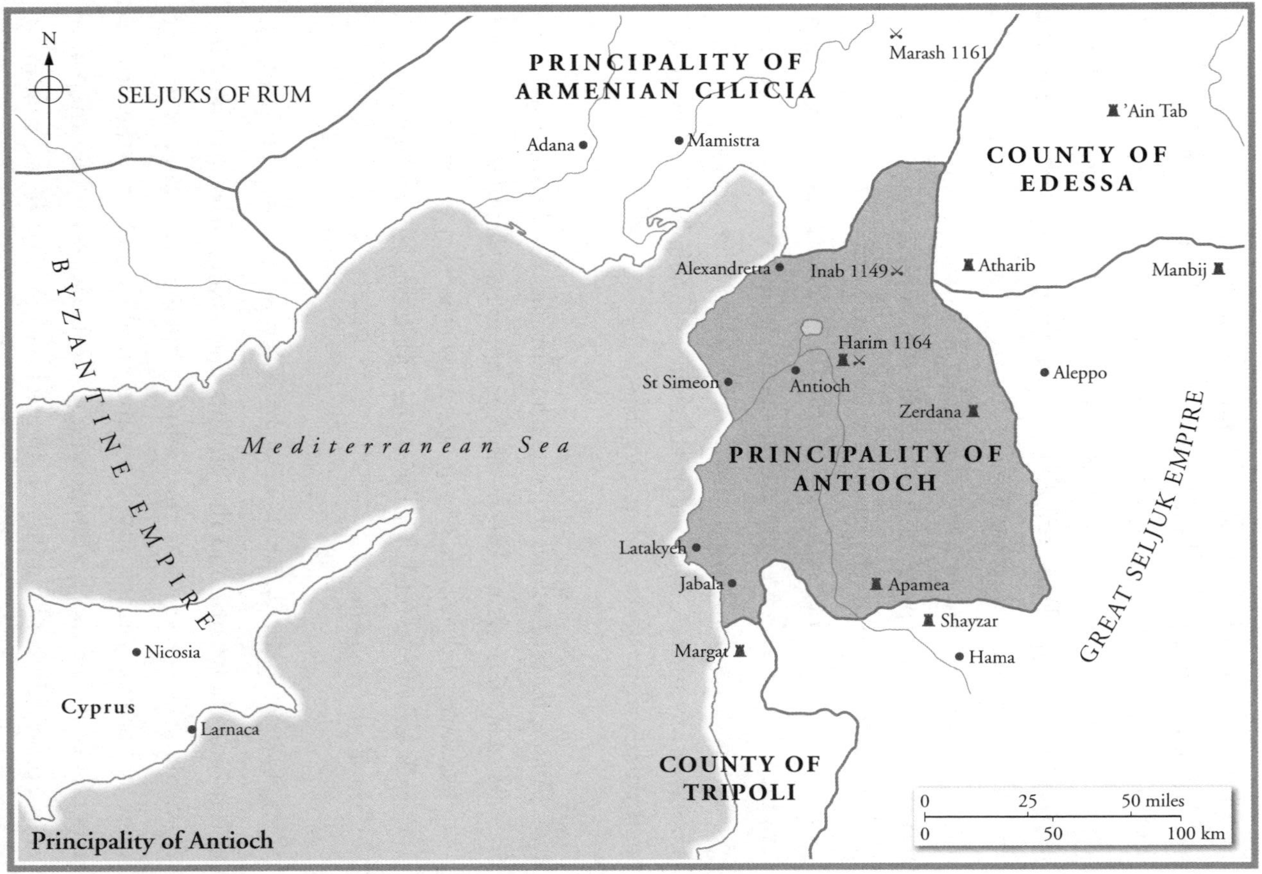
N
SELJUKS OF RUM
PRINCIPALITY OF
ARMENIAN CILICIA
Marash 1161
'Ain Tab
COUNTY OF
EDESSA
Adana
Mamistra
Alexandretta
Inab 1149
Atharib
Manbij
Harim 1164
St Simeon
Antioch
Aleppo
Zerdana
BYZANTINE EMPIRE
Mediterranean Sea
PRINCIPALITY OF
ANTIOCH
GREAT SELJUK EMPIRE
Latakyeh
Jabala
Apamea
Shayzar
Nicosia
Margat
Hama
Cyprus
Larnaca
COUNTY OF
TRIPOLI
0
25
50 miles
0
50
100 km
Principality of Antioch

this modus vivendi, showing the trademark crusader tolerance of the different local Christian sects, most of which preferred any overlord to the Byzantines and their Greek Church. He was careful to maintain cordial relationships with all the communities under his aegis. In December 1156, for instance, he attended the consecration of a new chapel built by Latins for the Monophysite Syrian Church and dedicated to the Syriac saint, Barsaumo. The ecumenical congregation included Franks, Armenians and prominent Syrian Christians, including the future Syrian archbishop, the chronicler Michael the Great. There is no evidence of Reynald mistreating Muslim subjects in his territories. Indeed, in his later career he would collaborate with them on more than one occasion, and there is evidence that he even made an effort to learn Arabic.[6] Along with Muslim citizens and visiting merchants, however, reminders of the underlying enmity with Islam were always present in Frankish territory. A Muslim traveller from Granada, Ibn Jubayr, was particularly distressed by what he witnessed:

> *Among the misfortunes that one who visits their land will see are*
> *Muslim prisoners walking in shackles and put to painful labour*
> *like slaves. In like condition are the Muslim women prisoners,*
> *their legs in iron rings. Hearts are rent for them, but compassion*
> *avails them nothing.*[7]

The chief administrative body of Antioch was the High Court, comprising the prince and the knights and churchmen who held fiefs from him. This court was the political cabinet and also dealt with civil and criminal issues involving the Frankish nobility: the prince's feudal vassals. Frankish commoners – the burgesses – had their own court, presided over by a jury of their fellow citizens. To aid him in his administration, the Prince of Antioch had a deputy, his seneschal, to control the treasury and a constable to run the army. Revenues were mainly raised from the prince's extensive demesne and from tolls and duties on imports and exports.

Very soon after his marriage, Reynald began the everyday work of a feudal lord, signing charters and grants in his capacity as prince. He is seen signing jointly with his wife: *Ego Raynaldus, Dei gratia Antiochorum princeps, unaque Constantia, Bohemondis Junioris filia* – 'I Reynald, by grace of God Prince of Antioch, with Constance, daughter of Bohemond the Younger…' His first recorded act as prince, in tandem with his wife, was to confirm the privileges of the Venetians resident in the principality, and to reduce their duties on silk from 5 per cent to 4 per cent and on other merchandise from 7 per cent to 5 per cent. A year later Reynald and Constance granted the Pisan merchant community and its church a reduction of tolls and ceded them some property near Latakyeh and a house in Antioch. In 1155 Reynald officially confirmed the gift of some mills, given by a burgess of Antioch to the Hospitallers.

Even Muslim subjects benefited in many ways under Frankish rule. Typically, Muslim villages paid a portion (around one-third) of their crops to their Christian overlords, a token tax on fruit and olive oil and a small poll tax, but otherwise were not interfered with. So light and fair was Frankish rule, complained Ibn Jubayr, that many Muslims were 'seduced' into preferring Frankish rule to Muslim:

> This is one of the misfortunes afflicting the Muslims. The Muslim community bewails the injustice of a landlord of its own faith, and applauds the conduct of its opponent and enemy, the Frankish landlord, and is accustomed to justice from him.[8]

It appears that Reynald adhered to these norms, but his relations with the different interest groups in Antioch were not always plain sailing. He seems to have quarrelled with the merchants of Genoa, and in 1155 a letter from Pope Adrian IV to Patriarch Aimery ordered that the patriarch should excommunicate Reynald, unless he followed the Pope's instructions and reimbursed the Genoese for damages done to them. Generally, however, once the uppity patriarch had been dealt with, Reynald's domestic affairs seem to have been relatively stable.

Reynald also worked diligently at international diplomatic relations and at protecting the future of the ruling dynasty. Early in his reign he looked very much to his homeland of France to provide international backing. For instance, in 1155 he wrote to King Louis VII requesting his aid in the form of another crusade. Unfortunately the letter's language reveals little of Reynald's character. It is written in a standard, rhetorical style, rehearsing the perennial complaints of the Franks in Outremer: 'The mouth cannot express, nor the hand write of the misfortunes and anguish which we have to endure...' But the main thrust of the message was more interesting: Reynald was asking the king to find suitable husbands for his stepdaughters. Maria and Philippa were 'of an age to be married' and were 'more than beautiful in both face and form'. There is a certain irony, of course, in the parvenu Reynald insisting that none of the vagabond local knights were good enough for Maria and Philippa. The letter demonstrates his genuine concern for the family into which he had married, and also underlines his interest in, and understanding of, the use of political marriages – a recurrent theme in his life. This time he was unsuccessful in his matchmaking, but a few years later he would organize Maria's engagement to the most eligible fiancé in the world.

Reynald's own marriage, with its blend of love and pragmatism, proved a success. Princess Constance quickly bore Reynald three children – two sons, Baldwin and Reynald, and a daughter, Agnes. Very different fates awaited the children and the three stepchildren of the minor knight from Burgundy: one would marry a spy of Saladin; one would die heroically in battle; another would be cruelly murdered in Byzantium. Reynald's blood-descendants would be kings and emperors.

Unfortunately the younger Reynald did not father any of them. Though medical care in the East was much more advanced than in Europe, the frailty of baby boys in Outremer was notorious. The little Reynald died in infancy.

His father had little time to grieve. The external threats to Antioch were Prince Reynald's main concern. The only secure border was to the south – with the Frankish county of Tripoli. There the promising young Count Raymond III had ruled since his father's murder by the Assassins in 1152. Born and bred in the East, Raymond was a brilliant and ambitious politician, who is generally cast by Western historians as a hero of crusader history. Dark-complexioned, with a piercing gaze, Raymond was closely related to the royal family of Jerusalem and nursed a long-held and destabilizing desire to become king. Slight in build, discreet and gifted with patience and foresight, Raymond had a character that was the opposite of Reynald's bluff warrior. They differed in their strategic approach, too; Reynald would never trust Count Raymond's predilection for appeasing the Muslims. Over time, the cunning Raymond would prove Reynald's greatest political rival among the Franks and their clashes would undermine the Latin states at a critical period. For now, the relationship between the arriviste in Antioch and the youthful count in Tripoli was harmonious.

To the north of the principality of Antioch, the lush Cilician plain was disputed with the warlike Armenians. In the years before Reynald's accession, this fiercely independent Christian people, led by the aggressive and fearsome Thoros II, had taken control of most of Cilicia. Soon they would be confronted by the new Prince of Antioch. To the east, Nur al-Din of Aleppo remained the greatest threat. Antioch's inland border had previously lain far beyond the Orontes River, but Nur al-Din's conquests meant that the effective eastern frontier now ran from the Anti-Taurus Mountains in the north down to the Orontes and along the river to the region of Shayzar.

At the beginning of Reynald's reign, Nur al-Din was still focused on dominating Muslim Syria and he did not exert much pressure on Antioch. In 1154, however, he finally took control of Damascus, uniting that Muslim power centre with Aleppo. This was an ominous strategic setback for the Franks, who had benefited from Muslim political fragmentation in Syria since the time of the First Crusade. At this stage Nur al-Din's control of Damascus was still uncertain enough for him to pay a tribute to the Kingdom of Jerusalem in return for a truce, but there were clear signs of danger for the Franks. The forces of Aleppo and Damascus, united under a strong leader, would be hard to resist. While Reynald did not have the strength to decisively defeat Nur al-Din, or even to capture any of his main strongholds, he could not afford to sit back passively and allow the *atabeg* to act with impunity.

To take the fight to his enemies, Prince Reynald had a variety of military forces at his disposal. First he had the knights, the medieval fighting machine par excellence. Most of these were raised via the feudal services owed to him by his noble vassals. Some knights were drawn from the prince's own personal 'demesne' lands, but most knights were provided by magnates such as the Mazoirs, lords of the great castle at Margat, and by many other smaller vassals who owed the service of just one knight – often themselves. The total number of knights available in Antioch had been around 700 at the time of the Field of Blood in 1119, but since then much of Antioch's territory had been lost. Reynald might not have been able to count on more than 400. There were also the sergeants, mostly foot soldiers, who were provided by ecclesiastical lords and the burgess citizens of the towns. Then there were the Turcopoles, light cavalry after the Turkish fashion, a mixture of native Christians, sons of mixed Frankish and Syrian parents and Muslim converts. Alongside these was a standing mercenary force, composed of soldiers of fortune like Reynald himself.

Once he had established his authority and stamped out internal dissent from the patriarch and any other doubters, Reynald harnessed all his forces and set about patrolling his borders with unremitting vigour. According to Ernoul:

> From the moment he became prince, he wore no silk, no proud colours or rich furs, whether squirrel, blue or grey. Instead he always wore his mail hauberk and his leather jerkin.[9]

So, now aged about thirty, the new Prince of Antioch put aside ostentation, eschewed his previous frivolities and the luxuries that came with the throne, and committed himself to his main task – warfare. Ernoul's comment suggests that, as we suspected, the young Reynald had indulged in the good things in life – at least in couture – even before he became prince. Later he would prove, very publicly, that although he campaigned incessantly, he had not abandoned his taste for luxury, or his fashion sense.

The new prince plunged with gusto into the constant raids and counter-raids of the frontier, inflicting 'plundering and devastation' on the districts around Aleppo.[10] Rustling livestock, looting villages, taking captives for ransom or for sale as slaves – all these provided much-needed revenue and weakened the enemy's economy. As the modern crusades historian R. C. Smail put it, such warfare 'was both a profitable pastime for feudal magnates and an instrument of policy'.[11] Ambushes and skirmishes wore down an opponent's military strength. Pitched battles were rare and, with able-bodied fighting men always at a premium, the Franks tended to husband their resources and avoid risky confrontations. Usama Ibn Munqidh noted this Frankish reticence to engage. To him, the Franks were above all nations 'the most cautious in warfare'.[12] In keeping with this tradition, Reynald was not a general who charged recklessly to destruction, but neither could he afford passivity.

He went toe-to-toe with Nur al-Din and met with both successes and setbacks. In 1156, troops from Aleppo defeated a Frankish force, presumably Reynald's, that had been ravaging Turkish territory around Harim. The heads of the slain Frankish warriors were paraded through the streets of Damascus. It was a sign of the far greater violence to come.

Reynald's earliest substantial campaigns, however, were not against the Muslim enemy that had brought him to the East.

There were plenty of Christian rivals to deal with first.

Chapter 6

A VIOLENT SINNER

They took and pillaged cities and towns. They seized gold and
silver and silks in great quantities. They raped virgins and married
women alike.

Estoire d'Eracles

In crusader Antioch, the strategic situation was never a simple one of
Christian versus Muslim. Some modern writers have dismissed Reynald
as an anti-Muslim bigot, ascribing to him the ignorant prejudices
of newly arrived crusaders, as opposed to the realism of those born
in the East, who were more accustomed to, and more accepting of,
their Muslim neighbours. In fact Reynald seems to have grasped the
strategic realities rather well. Like all the leaders of Outremer, instead
of focusing all his energies against the heathen, he was quite prepared
to fight against his co-religionists if necessary. Reynald's main task
was to maintain the integrity of Antioch, repelling Armenians to the
north and Muslims to the east, while steering a narrow path between
the might of Byzantium on the one hand and the ambitions of the
kings of Jerusalem on the other.

The elephant in the Antiochene room was the Byzantine Empire. Antioch was legally a vassal state of Byzantium. Bohemond I of Taranto, first crusader Prince of Antioch, had paid homage to the emperor for his principality, and imperial suzerainty had been repeatedly reaffirmed ever since. Most recently, Raymond of Poitiers had bowed to the emperor John Comnenos in 1138 and to his son Manuel in 1145. Raymond had to kneel in abject submission beside John's tomb before Manuel would grant him an audience. The emperor had then insisted on the even more humiliating imposition of a Greek Orthodox patriarch in Antioch although, showing wise regard for Frankish sensibilities, Manuel had not exercised this clause. When Raymond was killed in 1149, Manuel hoped to gain closer control over Antioch, but his efforts to dominate the province via a marriage to Constance had failed. He was not pleased to see the ancient metropolis pass to the adventurer Reynald.

Reynald ostensibly owed more to Baldwin and Jerusalem than to Manuel and Constantinople, but while he had been King Baldwin's sword for hire and the king had blessed his marriage, in keeping with established Antiochene policy, Reynald attempted to steer an independent course. He was quite happy to work with the emperor if it suited him.

In 1155, Manuel asked Reynald for help. The Byzantines had a problem with the Armenians in Cilicia. The rebellious Armenian prince, Thoros II, who had been imprisoned in Constantinople, had escaped some years before and returned to his homeland. Since then he had carved out an Armenian realm from the Byzantine province and had conquered the major cities, including the capital, Tarsus, and had killed the governor of Mamistra. William of Tyre, who always had a soft spot for the emperor Manuel, had no such feelings for the savage Armenian:

> *This man [Thoros] by his capricious and unloyal acts had often fallen under the displeasure of the emperor and incurred his*

*rebuke. Since his lands were far distant from the empire and
his residence in the high mountains was difficult of access, he
often descended into the plain of Cilicia and carried off booty
and spoils. He preyed without scruple upon the land of his lord
in every way and brought heavy and unmerited trouble upon
the faithful subjects of the empire, without regard to rank or
condition.*[1]

Manuel had sent his kinsman, the handsome, mercurial Andronicos
Comnenos, to tame Thoros, but Andronicos had been well beaten.
It was clear that for Byzantium to dislodge Thoros, the emperor
himself would have to lead a massive expedition across Asia Minor.
But Manuel's attention and resources were tied up in the west; in Italy
and on the seas he was at war with the Normans of Sicily, while in his
Balkan provinces he was occupied with restive Serbian subjects and
belligerent Hungarian neighbours. The cynical reality of Near Eastern
politics is seen in Manuel's next attempt at a solution for the Cilician
problem – an alliance with the Greeks' traditional enemies, the Seljuk
Turks; Manuel arranged for the Seljuk Sultan of Iconium, Mas'ud, to
invade Cilicia. Already bitter enemies of the Greeks, the Armenians
were especially outraged that the emperor would stoop so low as to
incite the Muslims against them. Unfortunately for Manuel, Thoros
managed to defeat the Turkish incursion too, and continued to expand
his domains at the empire's expense. In 1155, Manuel tried a different
proxy and turned to his 'vassal' in Antioch to do his dirty work for him.
The emperor, wrote William of Tyre, asked Reynald:

*To send forth his knights and keep Thoros away from the lands of
the empire, that the possessions of his Cilician subjects might be
safe from such raids. If money were needed for the purpose, he
himself would send a sufficient sum.*[2]

Money most certainly was needed. Byzantine gold alone might have won Reynald over, but in addition he had his own *casus belli* with the Armenians. During the reign of Prince Raymond, Thoros had taken control of some castles previously held by the Knights Templar in the mountain ranges between Antioch and Cilicia, notably the great fortress of Baghras. This chain of fortresses was pivotal to Antioch's defensive system and had to be retaken. Reynald demanded the return of the castles, on the basis that 'the brethren [the Templars] fought for all Christendom, so they should get back what belonged to them'. Thoros said no. Typically Reynald wasted no time in his response: 'The prince, who was valiant and chivalrous, greatly desired to serve the emperor.' He 'at once summoned a large force of cavalry and proceeded to Cilicia, where he repulsed Thoros and completely destroyed his army'.[3] Even William of Tyre describes Reynald's part in this as a 'valiant deed'. In a battle near the coastal city of Alexandretta, Thoros was soundly beaten: 'Reynald chased Thoros from the land, fell upon the houses of those who had helped him and destroyed them utterly.' Thoros fled to safety, then made peace with Reynald and returned the disputed castles to the Templars.[4]

Despite Reynald's victory over the Armenians, things turned out badly for the emperor. The Franks regained their fortresses, but Cilicia remained outside imperial control. Worse (from the emperor's viewpoint), Reynald and Thoros got over their differences and became the best of allies. The problem was that Manuel did not keep his part of the bargain. The campaign had been very costly to Reynald, who expected 'great gifts' in return, but the emperor's 'sufficient sum' of gold did not materialize. Or, as William of Tyre put it, 'the honourable recompense which he hoped to receive for his valiant deed seemed slow in arriving'. Reynald was enraged. Money – or the lack of it – was a sore point for him. The expenses of the Prince of Antioch were crippling. He had to redeem his debts, pay his mercenary troops and show the *largesse* required of any feudal overlord worth his salt. The Armenian campaign stretched his finances to breaking point. As he showed with his swift vengeance on the patriarch, Reynald was not one to tolerate a slight. He could not afford, politically or economically, to let the emperor off the hook. The prince was determined to make Manuel pay – in gold and in suffering. This time Reynald found a truly extreme way to make his point. The result was another 'shameful act'.[5] In the spring of 1156, Reynald invaded the island of Cyprus.

The island was Christian. It was peaceful, fertile, wealthy and, though Byzantine territory, it enjoyed friendly political relations and mutually profitable trade links with the Latin states just sixty miles away on the mainland. Assaulting the island ran the risk of full-scale retribution from the empire, but Reynald did not mind. As he prepared his attack 'in a piratical fashion',[6] some of the Franks in Jerusalem – perhaps the party sympathetic to Byzantium – sent warning to the Cypriots. It did not help. There was not enough time to reinforce the garrison, which was only sufficient to deter the infrequent raids of Egyptian corsairs. The Greek general Michael Branas tried to defeat the invasion at Nicosia, but against Reynald's effective generalship and battle-hardened troops, the island's militia had no chance. As William of Tyre commented:

> All the forces of the island, such as they were, had been assembled; but Prince Renaud, marching upon them, at once defeated their army and shattered their forces completely so that thereafter no one might dare to raise a hand against him.[7]

Reynald captured Branas and the governor, Manuel's nephew, the *Protosebastos* John Comnenos. He then proceeded to sack the island with appalling savagery. The inhabitants were 'Subjected to the monstrous tyranny of the prince of Antioch, who treated them as if they had been enemies of the faith and detestable parricides'.[8]

The army of Antioch ran amok. They looted and burned, raped and plundered. They mutilated the Orthodox priests and murdered with abandon. According to William of Tyre:

> [Reynald] completely overran the island without meeting any
> opposition, destroyed cities, and wrecked fortresses. He broke
> into monasteries of men and women alike and shamefully abused
> nuns and tender maidens. Although the precious vestments and
> the amount of gold and silver which he carried off were great,
> yet the loss of these was regarded as nothing in comparison with
> the violence done to chastity. For several days Renaud's forces
> continued to ravage the whole country; and, since there was none
> to offer resistance, they showed no mercy to age or sex, neither
> did they recognize difference of condition. Finally, laden with a
> vast amount of riches and spoils of every kind, they returned to
> the seashore.[9]

On the shore, Reynald realized they did not have space to transport the vast herds of livestock they had seized. He wrung the last few bezants out of the traumatized islanders by selling their animals back to them. He did find space amongst the booty, however, for the most valuable captives – bishops, priests and nobles – who were shipped back to Antioch as hostages until their ransoms were paid. The island was left destitute and in ruins.

After many centuries, the cruelty of the Cyprus invasion still baffles and shocks. The Cypriots were innocent victims caught in the middle of short-term quarrels and long-term geopolitics in which they played no part. Late payment of a debt does not seem to justify such violent revenge, but Reynald had to collect somehow and, unfortunately for Cyprus, the island was Byzantine territory within reach – and a soft target. Michael the Syrian says that Reynald attacked because the

Cypriots were mistreating Franks on the island. Even if true, this would have been no more than a secondary motive. The atrocity sent a clear message to the *basileus* that his betrayal would not be tolerated. Thoros and his Armenians, who hated the Byzantines even more than the Franks did, tagged along with the invasion and added some excesses of their own. Amongst other things, the Armenians excused the attack as recompense for the hurt suffered when Manuel allied against them with the Muslim Seljuks. The Byzantines had also killed Thoros' brother, Stephane, by throwing him into a cauldron of boiling water.

Reynald's attack on Cyprus now appears shocking and abominable – and it was – but it was not exceptional for the time. If the islanders had been Muslims, it would have passed without much comment. What shocks one Christian chronicler is not the atrocities themselves, but the fact that they were inflicted on Christians. Clerical chroniclers such as William of Tyre and Gregory the Priest were also particularly disgusted at the violence inflicted on fellow churchmen.

Reynald was not the only crusader to bring devastation to Cyprus. In 1162, Count Raymond III of Tripoli would raid the island with great savagery. Richard the Lionheart would actually conquer the island from the Byzantines in 1191 and would later sell it to the Knights Templar. But while these acts are glossed over by historians, Reynald's operation attracts universal censure. Perhaps his raid really was much more savage, though Greek and Latin historians also record Raymond's later attack as one of great slaughter and devastation. Perhaps the difference lay in that extra touch of memorable sadism that Reynald brought to his atrocities: he did not just kill Cypriot priests, but cut off their ears and noses and then sent the horrifically mutilated clergymen to Byzantium, as an unforgettable mark of his wrath.

Reynald's raid won him great riches, but his ill-gotten gains did not go far. William of Tyre remarked with some satisfaction:

Within a short time all the wealth which had been so wickedly
acquired was dissipated; for, as says the proverb, 'Booty wickedly
acquired brings no good results.'[10]

From the bloodbath of Cyprus, however, Reynald could count some positive results. Yes, he earned more hatred from the Greeks and their appalled historians. Yes, by attacking fellow Christians (albeit schismatic Greeks) – and especially by the assaults on the Greek Church and its priests – he confirmed his wickedness, in the eyes of clergymen like William of Tyre and sworn enemies like the Patriarch Aimery. But most of the Franks resented the Greeks and regarded them as hardly better than Turks. If anything, Reynald's atrocity might have won him admirers amongst his Frankish fellows. Most of all, he had boosted his fearsome reputation and, by defying the mighty emperor Manuel, had enhanced his prestige. But he had also stored up plenty of trouble for himself, for he had made a bitter enemy of the most powerful man in the world. Manuel's compassion and anger had been roused by the 'pitiful case of the Cyprians'.[11]

For that outrage, Reynald's blood was forfeit. Luckily for Reynald and his Armenian partners in crime, the emperor, still occupied with adversaries in the West, was in no position to take revenge as yet. The vast machinery of the Byzantine state ground along slowly. The empire had been around for many centuries. She could bide her time and wait for her revenge.

Shayzar, Syria, October 1157

Trapped behind the weakened walls of their citadel, the Turkish defenders in the ancient city of Shayzar faced certain defeat.

The castle in which they held out was normally regarded as impregnable. It ran along the crest of a steep ridge, flanked all along one side by the Orontes River. On the other side the lower town, also formidably fortified, usually provided equal protection. But the previous autumn the suburb had been damaged in an earthquake, and just a few weeks earlier another massive quake had shattered the citadel itself. Shayzar's ruler and his family had been gathered for the circumcision of one of the young princes, when part of the castle collapsed on top of them, killing almost everyone in attendance.

The walls had barely been repaired before the Franks suddenly appeared in strength. They had surrounded Shayzar and attacked with vigour, each commander striving for the glory of being the first to break in. After only a few days the siege ladders went up against the walls and the attackers swarmed over the ramparts. The jubilant infidels then sacked the town with gusto. Most of the inhabitants had escaped to the citadel and were trapped there with the garrison. Along with the hail of arrows and missiles, they could now hear sounds of revelry rising from the houses they had just abandoned, occupied by Franks enjoying their spoils.

The crusader army was just too strong. It was a striking example of that all-too-rare phenomenon in the Latin East – a coalition force from all three Latin states, Antioch, Tripoli and Jerusalem. The local units were further strengthened by a powerful visiting contingent under Count Thierry of Flanders, and by an Armenian army led by Thoros. The united front had been welded together in a common aim by the strategy of Reynald de Chatillon, and that strategy was on the verge of delivering a triumph for the crusaders. Without hope of a relief force, it was only a matter of time before the garrison of Shayzar capitulated.

Confident of victory, King Baldwin suggested that Shayzar be given to Count Thierry as a fief. Agreement was unanimous and everything was set fair for a famous victory. Apparently this time Reynald's impulsive, self-seeking character was in abeyance and his cooperative approach was going to yield long-term gains for all the crusader states.

What could possibly go wrong?

Chapter 7

GUARDIAN
OF THE LAND

He frequently adorned the whole province with his strenuous and glorious deeds of war.

Peter of Blois

After ruthlessly using the innocent Cypriots to teach the emperor a lesson, Reynald was able to return his attention to Antioch's eastern frontiers and its Islamic enemies. In 1157, the magnate Thierry, Count of Flanders, 'a great and distinguished man', came on crusade to the Holy Land. It was his third armed pilgrimage, and as ever he brought with him a large retinue of men to fight for the cross. As with Louis VII and his army during the Second Crusade, the inevitable discussion arose as to where this eager fighting force would be best deployed. Everyone was agreed that 'the arrival of such a great prince with so many noble and valiant men in his train ought not to be futile and without result'.[1] The problem was that each leader looked first to improve his own strategic situation.

Baldwin of Jerusalem was concerned about the growing power of Nur al-Din on his kingdom's frontiers. It was three years since the ruler of Aleppo had added Damascus to his dominions, displacing its ruler, Ibn al-Muqaddam, and uniting the two major cities of Syria for the first time since the crusaders arrived in the East. Damascus and its weak ruler had been so dominated by the crusaders that their emissaries would wander through the city at will, freeing any Christian slaves who wished to return home. Soon after Nur al-Din took control, Damascus threw off its subservience. The crusaders had managed to establish themselves in the Levant largely due to the lack of Muslim cooperation, so Nur al-Din's steady unification of Muslim Syria was a dangerous strategic development. This was well appreciated by William of Tyre:

> This change was decidedly disastrous to the interests of the
> kingdom. In place of a man without power, whose weakness
> rendered him harmless to the Christians and who up to this time,
> as if subject, had rendered them an annual tribute, a formidable
> adversary arose.[2]

Nur al-Din had shown what a different prospect he was, earlier in 1157. King Baldwin had invaded the territory of Damascus, breaking a truce. Nur al-Din had retaliated by inflicting a severe defeat on the army of Jerusalem outside the crusader-held town of Banyas. In desperation, Baldwin had summoned the kingdom's remaining knights to his aid and had even appealed for help to the other Latin states. The Prince of Antioch responsibly answered the call, and it was only the timely appearance of reinforcements under Reynald and Count Raymond III of Tripoli that saved Banyas for the Franks.

Count Raymond would have preferred Thierry and his 400 Flemish knights to fight Nur al-Din along the borders of Tripoli, while Reynald of course wanted Thierry to campaign even further north, around Antioch. After an abortive assault from the county of Tripoli on the fort of Chastel Rouge, Reynald brought all his charisma and persuasive skills to bear. Clearly his sack of Cyprus and torture of the patriarch had not diminished his influence amongst the crusader leaders. On the contrary, after four years of guarding the land of Antioch, the man who could seduce a proud princess had earned the standing to win over the entire leadership of Outremer. They listened to him because:

> Prince Reynald, who was an expert in warfare, and had
> considered the matter deeply, spoke to the King and all his barons.
> His cogent arguments persuaded them all to leave [Chastel Rouge]
> and make straight for Antioch.[3]

The crusader army proceeded to Antioch 'under more favourable auspices', which included the 'most agreeable news' that Nur al-Din, the crusaders' most dangerous enemy, had been taken severely ill. He had been struck by a severe, unidentifiable disease and was rumoured to be dead, or close to death. Typically such a situation would result in chaos and disunity amongst the Muslims, as different emirs scrambled to secure their own part of the ruler's treasure and dominions. Nur al-Din's sickness was no different, as William of Tyre noted:

> The report brought by the messenger proved in fact to be true.
> Nureddin had been attacked by a most serious malady; the ranks
> had become disorganized, and, as is the custom among them when
> the master dies, plundering and unrestrained violence was rife in
> his army.[4]

The Franks needed to capitalize on this confusion with a major offensive. Reynald convinced Thierry and the crusader leaders that the best place to focus the additional Flemish strike force was on the Muslim stronghold of Shayzar.

Shayzar, known to the crusaders as Caesarea-on-the-Orontes, was an ancient settlement dating back to the Assyrian Empire. Later it had been Roman and Byzantine for more than a thousand years, until the late eleventh century. It was the home town of the Arab warrior Usama Ibn Munqidh, whose family, the Banu Munqidh, had ruled there since 1081 when they purchased the city from the Byzantines. It was the linchpin of the Muslim strongholds along the east bank of the Orontes River and its capture would drive a wedge between Nur al-Din's heartland of Aleppo and the territory of Damascus to the south. But its defences were daunting. A castle protected Shayzar's bridge across the Orontes. The lower town was well fortified, the citadel impregnable.

The Franks of Antioch had attacked Shayzar many times before, without capturing it; when the indomitable Norman, Tancred de Hauteville,* was ruler of Antioch (1100–10) he had put Shayzar under tribute, but he had never breached its walls. In 1138 Shayzar had even withstood a fearsome siege by the combined forces of Antioch and the Byzantine emperor John Comnenos. The Byzantines' massive siege engines had battered the ramparts, destroyed towers and houses and killed many of the citizens. But while the lower town had been captured and its Muslim inhabitants massacred, the defenders in the citadel had held firm. Eventually, rising dissension in the Christian camp between Greeks and Latins led to the lifting of the siege.

Reynald was aware, however, that the major earthquakes of the previous twelve months, which had damaged Antioch and Tripoli, had also weakened the defences of many of the Muslim fortresses. The first quake in autumn 1156, which had damaged the lower suburb of

---

* Tancred had style. When the First Crusade passed through Constantinople, he had scandalously sat on the emperor's throne. He later described himself to imperial envoys as 'Ninus the Assyrian, a giant whom no man could resist'.

Shayzar, had also destroyed bastions in the nearby castle of Apamea and other towns. A series of tremors continued for months, and then, after a lull, another massive quake struck in August 1157. Known as the 'Hama earthquake', it was horribly lethal. In the town of Hama, Ibn al-Athir recorded how when a school collapsed, every pupil was killed. The teacher reported that not a single parent came to enquire after any of the children. All their relatives were dead, too.[5] This was the quake that collapsed the citadel of Shayzar on top of the emir, Taj al-Dawla Ibn Munqidh, and his family. The story goes that the emir had a favourite horse, which he could not let out of his sight. That day the horse was standing in the doorway of the emir's residence. When the earthquake struck and everyone rushed for the door, 'the horse kicked the first man and killed him. The people were prevented from leaving and the building collapsed on all of them.'[6]

Of all the Banu Munqidh, only two survived: a princess pulled alive from the rubble, and the warrior Usama, who was away from the city at the time. An emir sent by Nur al-Din had quickly occupied the town and rebuilt the walls, but – given the combination of Nur al-Din's sickness and Shayzar's uncertain defences – Reynald understood that the Franks might never have a better chance of subjugating the city. At first his strategy succeeded brilliantly. After the sack of the lower town, the citadel had no hope of a relief force from the ailing Nur al-Din. Nothing, it seemed, could prevent Reynald winning a great victory. On his watch, Shayzar was finally going to be brought under the control of Antioch. But then, as William of Tyre recorded bitterly, political rivalries intervened:

> Just when it seemed certain that, under the continued pressure, the citadel also might be taken easily together with all who had fled thither for refuge, an insignificant but most annoying source of friction arose among our leaders.[7]

The unanimous view amongst the crusader leaders (including Reynald) was that Shayzar should be given to Thierry of Flanders as a fief, 'to be held by him as a hereditary possession forever'. Shayzar was a patrimony prestigious enough to ensure that Thierry – and the wealth, connections and armed retinue he commanded – would settle once and for all in Outremer. So far everyone agreed. The point of contention was precise: who would be Thierry's overlord? The scandalized William of Tyre recorded that it was Reynald himself, the instigator of the Shayzar campaign, who threw a spanner in the works:

> Prince Renaud alone raised difficulties; he declared that Shayzar with its dependencies had, from the beginning, formed a part of the heritage of the prince of Antioch; hence, whoever held it must pledge loyalty to him as lord.[8]

The proud Thierry, however, refused to pay homage to the upstart Reynald. He would only agree to become a vassal of the King of Jerusalem. Baldwin, unsurprisingly, was ready to take this course, as it would have recognized him as overlord of Shayzar. At Ascalon in 1153, Reynald had sworn to be King Baldwin's man. If the king still believed this oath, it was here that he would have realized Reynald's loyalties now lay elsewhere. The Prince of Antioch simply could not accept the King of Jerusalem as overlord of Shayzar. And, unfortunately for Thierry and Baldwin, Reynald was in the right. It was beyond dispute that Shayzar had always 'belonged' to Antioch. The bishops of Shayzar (who had sold the city to the Muslims) had been suffragans of the Patriarchate of Antioch. The city was included in a planned grant of lands to Raymond of Poitiers by the Byzantine emperor John in 1138, and for the previous sixty years it was the princes of Antioch who had maintained an undisputed claim to the town, a claim they had backed up by constant campaigning. At times Shayzar had even paid tribute to Antioch. By insisting on Thierry's homage, Reynald was loyally fulfilling his role as protector of the lands of Antioch and the patrimony of his stepson, Bohemond. To allow the King of Jerusalem to assume suzerainty of Shayzar would have been irresponsible, and would have set a dangerous precedent for the independence of Antioch as a whole. Indeed, in the face of Thierry's intransigence, Reynald was quite conciliatory. He did not insist on homage being paid to him personally, but was quite happy for Thierry to swear fealty to the young heir to the principality, Bohemond, as long as Thierry recognized the supremacy of Antioch over Shayzar. Thierry's pride would not allow him to accept even this. 'Never have I done homage,' he said, 'except to kings.'

The impasse was total. The united Christian force abandoned the siege and returned to Antioch laden with loot, but without the great prize of Shayzar. Blame for this failure has been laid at Reynald's door. William of Tyre, a partisan of the Kingdom of Jerusalem, implicitly criticized Reynald for enforcing Antioch's rights; and modern historians have seen yet another example of his unbending, selfish ambition and short-sightedness. His conduct overall 'had not been satisfactory'.[9] The implication is that Reynald should have seen the bigger picture. The capture of Shayzar would have been better for the future of the Frankish states as a whole, so he should have overlooked the narrow interests of Antioch. This view does not recognize that Reynald's task as prince was primarily to uphold the rights of Antioch and its ruling family, which he represented. Though they may have been in the East to fight for Christendom, all the leaders of the Latin states put their interests and those of their dominions first. Reynald was no different. Plus, Thierry had caused problems before. In 1148, when the Second Crusade's siege of Damascus had broken down in recriminations and mutual suspicion, Thierry was at the heart of it; 'he is said to have approached each of the kings separately, one after another, and urgently demanded that the city when taken be given to him'.[10] Some of the local barons were incensed that Thierry thought he could waltz in from France and take one of the greatest prizes in the East. Such resentment may well have left them open to the rumoured bribes from the Damascenes to sabotage the siege. At Shayzar, Thierry again played his part in a political fiasco.

Reynald was nothing if not persistent. Having failed to win Shayzar for Antioch, he was not going to let Thierry return to Europe without achieving something. Despite the bad blood between him, Baldwin and Thierry, Reynald still managed to persuade the crusader army to turn its attention to Harim. On a steep, conical hill just a few miles from Antioch, this powerful castle had been captured by Nur al-Din in 1149, after he killed Raymond at the battle of *Fons Muratus*. Led by Reynald, the Franks now attacked Harim with the same energy they had applied to Shayzar, setting up great mangonels that soon pounded the town into submission. They were helped when one of the great stone missiles killed the castellan. Once he died, says William of Tyre, the defenders:

> *Dispersed like sheep when the shepherd is struck down, and,*
> *as sand without lime cannot hold together, so the obstinate*
> *resistance, which they had hitherto shown, ceased.*[11]

There was no dispute here about jurisdiction. Harim belonged to Antioch, and when the castle surrendered in February 1158, it was given to one of Thierry's knights, who immediately swore homage to Reynald for his fief. Reynald repaired the fortifications and left a strong garrison.

Reynald had at least managed to win something from the opportunities offered by Thierry's crusade and Nur al-Din's illness, which, unfortunately for the crusaders, had not proved mortal. The recapture of Harim restored the supremacy of Antioch west of the Orontes, while to the east Reynald's forces successfully maintained an aggressive posture. The capture of Harim, we learn from the Arabic chronicler Abu Shama, 'encouraged the boldness of the Franks and they launched raiding parties into all the districts of Syria, pillaging and sacking fortresses and villages'.[12]

Antioch – and Reynald's position in it – was secure. To the south, King Baldwin III then asserted his authority with a substantial victory over Nur al-Din near the cave fortress of Habis Jaldak, east of the Jordan. A truce was subsequently established between Baldwin and Nur al-Din. The balance of power seemed stabilized all along the frontier.

Then suddenly, in the autumn of 1158, the balance shifted.

Alliances crumbled and priorities were redrawn. Reynald's days as Prince of Antioch – indeed, his very days on earth – were suddenly numbered. His crimes against the empire were finally being called to account. The terrifying news came south from Cilicia like a thunderbolt: the emperor had come.

Mamistra, Cilicia, Easter 1159

Raised up on a dais outside the imperial tent, the Emperor Manuel, in all his exalted glory, sat. He relaxed on a throne glinting with gold and resplendent with precious stones. Flanking him, their massive axes gleaming, stood the tall, blond barbarians of his Varangian Guard. Gathered before the monarch in varying attitudes of servility were the high courtiers of the empire, the hierarchy of the Greek Orthodox Church and emissaries from all the potentates of the Orient. Drawn up around them was Manuel's gigantic army in full array, its formations stretching, legion after legion, into the distance.

Through this great throng came a line of Frankish monks and nobles, unshod, weeping, beseeching forgiveness. At their head trudged a pitiful figure. Barefoot and bareheaded, he wore nothing but a short, rough tunic with sleeves pulled humiliatingly above his elbows.[13] A rope was tied about his neck and he held a naked sword in his hand by the blade. Reynald de Chatillon, great Prince of Antioch, was coming to beg for mercy.

The procession wound its way through the jeers and taunts of the massed battalions, and up to the dignitaries around the emperor. Then it halted, a stone's throw from his presence. Flinging himself to the ground in front of Manuel, Reynald proffered his sword, hilt first, towards the emperor. Behind Reynald, the monks and lords of Antioch knelt down, wailing, begging the *basileus* to acknowledge their pleas.

Reynald lay motionless, abased, prostrate in the dust. His life hung in the balance, at the whim of the emperor.

The 'divine' Manuel Comnenos, born in the purple, *basileus*, despot, Emperor of the Romans, successor of Augustus and overlord of Antioch, ignored him.

Chapter 8

IMPERIAL VASSAL

*Shortly before the coming of the emperor, [Reynald] had wreaked
his fury upon the innocent Cyprians and had perpetrated upon
them and upon their wives and children outrages abominable
in the sight of both God and men. Consequently, he feared the
arrival of the emperor.*

William of Tyre

*He was a man of violent impulses, both in sinning and in
repenting.*

William of Tyre

During the year 1158 the emperor Manuel Comnenos felt secure enough
in his western dominions to turn his attention to the old imperial
territories in Asia and re-establish imperial pre-eminence in Cilicia
and northern Syria. He gathered a huge army and marched southwards.
His first target was the rebellious Armenian, Thoros. To take him by
surprise, the emperor secretly rode ahead of his cumbersome army
with just 500 cavalry. Thoros escaped only by chance, after meeting a

talkative pilgrim who had come across the emperor (and been given a gold piece by him) the previous day. According to William of Tyre:

> So unexpected was the coming of the imperial armies that Thoros, who was then staying at Tarsus, had barely time to flee to the neighbouring mountains before the legions and the chiefs of the army were spreading over the open plain.[1]

Manuel's innumerable host covered the earth. It swiftly recaptured all the cities of Cilicia from the Armenians. The emperor then settled in with his army to winter in Mamistra and prepare for the next stage of his campaign in the spring. His destination, he openly proclaimed, was Antioch; his objective, punishment for Reynald's attack on the innocent Cypriots – that outrage 'abominable in the sight of both God and men'.

The emperor's coming did not concern Reynald alone. The Muslim powers were equally daunted by the arrival of this massive Christian army. Nur al-Din, now fully recovered from his illness, raised troops and warned all his governors to be ready for the Holy War against the emperor, though realistically there was no power in the region capable of resisting such a mighty force. The great expedition confirmed King Baldwin of Jerusalem's strategy; he had already thrown in his lot with Byzantium. In 1157, he had sent to the emperor suggesting an alliance by marriage. In requesting the match, he was also implicitly abandoning Reynald to his fate. The chroniclers go further, stating that Baldwin actively conspired against the Prince of Antioch. Baldwin, it appears, hoped to receive Antioch as a fief from the emperor, once Reynald had been dealt with.

Manuel was on board – he sent his niece Theodora to Baldwin with a huge dowry of 100,000 gold bezants, and many thousands more to distribute in gifts. By agreeing to the marriage alliance with Jerusalem, the emperor was ensuring that Reynald was isolated politically. In the autumn of 1158, while Baldwin was cementing the new Jerusalem–Byzantium axis by marrying Theodora, Reynald was scrambling to find a way out of his very serious predicament. Patriarch Aimery, who had plotted against Reynald ever since his humiliating treatment on the castle turret five years before, again offered to betray his enemy to Manuel. The offer was contemptuously rejected. With his irresistible army in attendance, Manuel needed no help to take care of Reynald.

Reynald found himself isolated. Nobody was foolish enough to ally with him against the full might of Byzantium. William of Tyre gives him credit for developing a 'guilty conscience' about his Cyprus expedition, but self-preservation probably trumped guilt in Reynald's hierarchy of concerns. The humiliating performance of penance at Mamistra was simply the public culmination of a long series of diplomatic negotiations with Manuel over Reynald's fate, and that of his principality. As soon as he heard of Manuel's approach, Reynald consulted with his advisers, such as Gerard, Bishop of Latakyeh, on how to react. There was nowhere to run, no way to hide. It was impossible to fight. The only thing he could do was grovel.

Reynald was negotiating for his life and, with so much at stake, he proved extremely resourceful, demonstrating considerable diplomatic skill. First, he won over some Byzantine nobles who could intercede with the emperor on his behalf. Then the negotiations began in earnest, with Reynald making excuses, begging for forgiveness and promising to behave better in future. He had to offer concessions strong enough to outbid the Cypriots, who were calling for his head. He also had to counter the machinations of his Frankish enemies and of pretenders to power in Antioch, such as King Baldwin and the Patriarch Aimery. Reynald and his team outmanoeuvred them all. Once they had won Manuel round, the final negotiation was the form and extent of the public submission. The upshot was the humiliating show of contrition at Mamistra.

Reynald led the procession of Antioch's nobles and churchmen through the laughing ranks of Manuel's troops and knelt before the emperor. This was a pointedly public display, designed to be seen not just by the Greeks, but also by the ambassadors and chiefs of all the realms of the east. As John Kinnamos observed:

> Astonishment took possession of those who were present, who had come as envoys from the nations in Asia, the Khorezmians and Susans and Ekbatanians, and all of Media and Babylon, whose ruler they call the Great Sultan, and from Nur-ad-Din the atabeg of Aleppo and Yaghi-Basan the Turks' chieftain, and from the Abasgai and Iberians [Georgians], even from the Palestinians [Crusading States] and the Armenians beyond Isauria.[2]

For the Franks, the humbling of Reynald de Chatillon, under the gleeful gaze of their enemies, was mortifying. 'He threw himself on the ground at the emperor's feet,' wrote William of Tyre:

> where he lay prostrate till all were disgusted and the glory of the Latins was turned into shame; for he was a man of violent impulses, both in sinning and in repenting.[3]

And, with Reynald grovelling in the dust, the emperor studiously ignored him.

After a suitably pointed interval, Manuel turned disdainfully towards the prince and laid out his terms. Reynald's life would be spared and he would remain as Prince of Antioch, but with onerous conditions: first, he was to reaffirm the allegiance to Byzantium and surrender the mighty citadel of Antioch to Manuel. Second, Reynald and his army would campaign, if requested, in the service of the emperor. Third, a Greek patriarch would be imposed in Antioch. Reynald agreed, binding himself to the agreement with a series of solemn oaths. Manuel then gestured that he could rise and be forgiven his 'drunken offence' on Cyprus.

So why would Manuel forgive Reynald? The explicit agreement to campaign on the emperor's behalf was new, but although the concessions appeared considerable, they mostly reflected the form of previous professions of Antiochene fealty. The actual arrival of an Orthodox patriarch, for instance, was still unlikely – it would prove too unpopular in Frankish Antioch – even though the tension between Reynald and the Latin patriarch (Aimery used Manuel's visit to return to Antioch from exile) meant there was a greater possibility that a Greek prelate really would arrive from Byzantium. Manuel could also have achieved the same concessions from a regime led by the young Bohemond, or by another of the many Franks – such as the Patriarch Aimery or King Baldwin – who would happily have supplanted Reynald. But getting rid of Reynald would have left King Baldwin with a free hand in Antioch, something the emperor would not risk. Depriving Bohemond, the rightful heir of his principality, would not have looked good either, and would have given the inevitable Frankish rebellion a legal justification. The best way for the empire to control Antioch was not through an unpopular Byzantine governor or an empowered King of Jerusalem. It was in the form of a cowed and pliable Reynald de Chatillon.

Along with that political reality and the extent of his concessions, key to Reynald's survival was the extremity of humiliation to which he subjected himself. The Byzantine court was a theatre of protocol, in which the display was often as important as the message itself. Reynald's own fate was in a sense incidental. The central point of this ceremony was to exalt the emperor and demonstrate his power – and his mercy. Reynald clearly outdid himself here. His show left a deep impression on the observers, amused and astonished the neutrals, satisfied the Greeks and dismayed the Franks.

The Byzantines would also have grumbled that Manuel had a soft spot for the Latin Christians. During his reign Franks held important roles at court and in the imperial administration. Meanwhile the great maritime cities like Venice forged strong trading links with Byzantium. Called *megas* ('the great') by Greek commentators, Manuel was a thoughtful and perceptive leader, who had the capacity to look beyond grudges and take the long view.

Once Reynald had been reconciled to the emperor, he continued to work on him for further concessions. In this he found a supporting voice in King Baldwin, who made the journey north from Jerusalem to pay his respects to the emperor. Despite breaking protocol by dismounting too close to the emperor's tent, Baldwin struck up a close relationship with Manuel, who talked with him at length (though seating Baldwin on a distinctly lower seat than his). Now without hope of running Antioch, Baldwin helped Reynald persuade Manuel that occupying the citadel would be a bad move, as would the imposition of a Greek patriarch. Baldwin warned the emperor that implementing these clauses was sure to cause serious unrest amongst the Franks, as well as among the Armenians and the strongly anti-Greek communities of local Christian Churches, such as the Nestorians and Jacobites. Won over by the charming young king, Manuel agreed not to force the issue, though he did insist that no bishop be accepted from anywhere other than Byzantium.

The next carefully staged event in the programme agreed between Manuel and Reynald was the emperor's ceremonial entry into Antioch. Again Reynald laid on a good show. In April 1159, Manuel marched his army from Cilicia and camped before the walls of Antioch, as his father John had done in 1138. Back then John's army had to attack the town before it submitted. Reynald and Manuel avoided violence this time. King Baldwin and Prince Reynald, along with the leading nobles and churchmen and a great crowd of townspeople, 'streamed forth from the gates to meet him [Manuel] with a show of servile submission', wrote the chronicler Nicetas Choniates.[4]

Wearing a purple robe covered in precious jewels, the emperor in all his splendour rode into the city. To the sound of drums and trumpets, he paraded as though it was a triumph in Byzantium. Some of the Latins had tried to prevent the emperor's entry by warning of threats against his life, but Manuel was not deterred. Still, he took no chances, wearing two layers of chainmail hidden beneath his regalia. Alongside him marched the magnificent axe-bearing barbarians of his bodyguard, blond-haired, 'tall as palm trees'. Reynald's part in this theatre was that of loyal vassal. Unarmed, he walked subserviently beside Manuel's stirrup, holding his bridle like a groom. King Baldwin rode a respectful distance behind, without his crown. On 'stately horses of proud bearing', the cavalcade proceeded along boulevards covered in rich rugs and planted with fresh sprays of flowers like 'a garden of delights'.[5] Every citizen of the town turned out to line the streets. It must have been passing brave to be Manuel that day, the triumphant master of celebrating Greeks, sullen Armenians, frightened Syrian Christians, fascinated Turks and Arabs and murmuring Franks, some of them cheering, perhaps in relief. After worshipping in the great Cathedral of St Peter, they paraded to the royal palace, where they settled in for more than a week of lavish festivities.

The charming Manuel won a lot of friends, not least by his extravagant gifts showered on all and sundry. The town was put completely at the disposal of the emperor, and during his sojourn in Antioch, it was effectively in Greek hands. Even the courts were presided over by Greek judges. Reynald entertained the emperor and his entourage royally. They enjoyed feasts, pageants, the luxurious public baths and much more. Manuel was young and passionate and, according to Choniates, despite being married, he was:

*Wholly devoted to a dissolute and voluptuous life and given
over to banqueting and revelry. Whatever the flower of youth
suggested and his vulgar passions prompted, that he did. Indulging
in sexual intercourse without restraint and copulating undetected
with many female partners.*[6]

It is likely Manuel took full advantage of the varied sensual delights
on offer in Antioch. His roving eye would also have taken in the beauty
of Princess Constance and, even more so, that of Maria, her exquisite
young daughter by Raymond of Poitiers. To the consternation of his
advisers, Manuel even risked life and limb in the grand culmination
of the celebrations laid on by Reynald – a magnificent tournament in
the Western style. Manuel, who was personally brave and a warrior of
renown, insisted on fighting. Unusually for a Byzantine, the emperor
was an expert in the Western knight's speciality: charging with the
couched lance. He had practised this a lot and was known for using a
particularly long and heavy spear.

Now fully reconciled to the emperor and firmly ensconced as Prince
of Antioch, Reynald took advantage of the tournament finally to reveal
his true colours. In complete contrast to the bedraggled penitent of
Mamistra and the servile groom of Manuel's triumph, Reynald took
centre stage. Escorted by the mightiest warriors of his princely guard,
he emerged in splendour that echoed the swan knight of the *chansons
de gestes*. Choniates describes him coming forth 'on a horse whiter than
snow, wearing a cloak slit down the middle and reaching to his feet and
a cap like a sloping tiara, embroidered in gold'.[7] While he did spend
most of his time campaigning in chainmail, when called for, Reynald
was clearly not averse to flaunting his fashion sense.

Wisely, it was decided that the grudge match between the gloating
Greeks and the 'high-spirited and insolent' Franks would take place
with blunted lances. It was a hard-fought battle of 'diverse noble deeds',

with beaten knights fleeing the field or hiding behind their shields in fear, riders knocked from their saddles and victors lauding it over their cowering victims. The only holds barred were when Frankish knights faced the emperor. Jousting against the most powerful man on earth was a no-win situation and the knights drawn to fight him must have agonized at the possibility of unhorsing the *basileus* by mistake or, even worse – heaven forfend – injuring him.

While the Byzantine lords generally came off worse against the more practised Franks, luckily Manuel fared better – he even dashed two knights to the ground at once. His prowess, combined no doubt with judicious Frankish tumbles, enabled him to win the grand prize. The victory crowned an extraordinary propaganda success for Manuel, and left His Imperial Majesty in a very agreeable mood for the more serious business at hand.

Manuel was confident enough in his supremacy even to forgive Thoros, who crept down from his mountain hideout to beg, like Reynald, for mercy. The emperor confirmed the Armenian prince in his dominions as a vassal of the empire and demanded his service immediately – in battle against the heathen.

In that spring of 1159, for the second time, Reynald de Chatillon and Thoros joined a grand Christian alliance against Nur al-Din. But this time the visiting contingent was not just Thierry of Flanders and a few Frankish knights. This time Reynald would march with the whole of the eastern empire at his back. Nur al-Din would have no chance but to capitulate. Aleppo itself would fall. From its camping grounds around Antioch, the great Byzantine war machine, with its innumerable legions and creaking siege engines, rumbled slowly into motion and lumbered inexorably towards the east.

The Zengid emirs were in a state of panic. Nur al-Din sent far and wide for volunteers to engage in the jihad, but while he prepared for battle, he realized the military position was hopeless. As the irresistible

Christian army rolled towards the Orontes, he negotiated feverishly with Manuel to head off the inevitable defeat. When the expeditionary force reached the frontier at the ford of the Orontes, just a few hours from Aleppo, an embassy arrived from Nur al-Din. To the consternation of Reynald and the Franks, who immediately smelt treason, Manuel agreed to meet the envoys.

The truth of the matter was that, just as with the siege of Shayzar, political issues had intervened to thwart the great Christian coalition. This time the problem was back in Constantinople. Word had come to Manuel of serious plots against his rule. He had no choice but to break off his offensive and rush back to the capital. To save some face, he wrung concessions out of Nur al-Din, who, despite his commitment to jihad, bowed to the realities of Byzantium's irresistible might. He promised to fight on the Byzantine side against the Seljuk Turks and agreed to release all the Christian captives languishing in his dungeons. The prisoners included some prominent men, such as the Grand Master of the Temple, Bertrand de Blanchefort, and Bertrand of Toulouse, a claimant to the county of Tripoli. There were also 6,000 others taken during the constant battles of the previous decade and more. Many were French and Germans who had been captured during the Second Crusade. The Franks, disappointed and furious, but powerless to influence Manuel's decision, were forced to watch the Byzantine army simply turn around and 'slink off like foxes'. The jubilant Muslims saw the retreat as a great victory. Nur al-Din was able to point to the precious gifts sent to him by Manuel, including fine horses, mules, robes, jewels and a magnificent brocade tent, as proof of the honour and respect that he commanded, and to which, implicitly, the emperor had been obliged to bow. The *atabeg* had greatly enhanced his prestige and, as a Damascene chronicler wrote, his reputation for 'sureness of judgement and design, ability of management and decision, and purity of intention towards God'.[8]

The Franks had nothing to show for the grand imperial coalition other than the captives released to them by Nur al-Din. There must have been some pleasure in seeing old comrades again, and the release of the Grand Master was significant, but the reappearance of Bertrand was an embarrassment to the incumbent Count of Tripoli, Raymond III. Bertrand's captivity had left him a broken man, however, and even the 6,000 were no great addition to the fighting strength of the Franks. Most were in a pitiful condition after years of harsh treatment. While Reynald and King Baldwin, abandoned again by the Greeks, fell back into their territory, Nur al-Din ostentatiously celebrated his triumph with an immense banquet. Then, to add insult to ignominy, his Turcomans harried the Byzantine rearguard as they marched out of Syria, inflicting serious casualties.

Over the century since the catastrophic defeat at Manzikert in 1071, Byzantine power had slowly been re-established by the great trio of Comnenos emperors, Alexius, John and Manuel, but that recovery was now reaching its zenith. Nobody knew it at the time, but Manuel's great expedition was the last time a Byzantine army would impose imperial hegemony in Syria. For now, the emperor's word was still law, and even though Manuel had departed, Reynald remained at his beck and call. In 1160 the emperor 'commanded' his service in a campaign against Byzantium's greatest enemies, the Seljuks. The emperor attacked up the valley of the Meander. Reynald and a mercenary force hired by the Franks marched northwards alongside Thoros of Cilicia and the Byzantine general John Kontostephanos.* Nur al-Din also fulfilled his commitment, attacking the Seljuks from the rear. The campaign was successful and the Seljuk sultan, Kilij Arslan, was humbled. In a grand ceremonial visit to Constantinople he was treated very much as a vassal. Manuel dazzled him with great banquets, circuses and astonishing gifts

---

* The name of this leading Byzantine family translates as 'Short Stephen'.

of gold and silver tableware. The Turks failed dismally with their attempt to impress the Byzantines in their turn, when one of their noblemen promised to fly across the Hippodrome. The parachute-like pockets of his suit failed to provide the required lift and he plummeted to his death. Overwhelmed on all fronts, Kilij Arslan recognized imperial suzerainty and, amongst other things, reopened the land route across Anatolia to Christian pilgrims travelling to the Holy Land.

Reynald was now firmly in the imperial circle of trust. This is reflected in a letter from Manuel to the German emperor, Conrad, referring to Reynald as 'a prince of my empire'.[9] In this spirit of friendship with the empire, Reynald helped put together a deal that would bring Antioch and Byzantium even closer together. The move would prove very unpopular with the rulers of the other Latin states, especially with the Count of Tripoli. At stake lay which of the ruling families of Outremer would win the lottery of the next marriage alliance with the empire, and this time the jackpot was huge – the post of empress itself. Manuel Comnenos was looking for a bride, and he wanted a Frankish girl.

The emperor's first marriage had been to Bertha of Sulzbach, the plain daughter of the Emperor Conrad. 'Not so much concerned with physical beauty', she also unfortunately had the 'natural trait of being unbending and opinionated', according to Choniates.[10] This unpromising combination meant that Manuel was not very attentive towards her, especially in 'matters of the bed'.

Bertha (or Irene, as she was known as empress) died in 1159. According to Michael the Syrian, she was poisoned by the emperor because of her failure to bear him an heir. Manuel decided that a Frankish replacement would make most sense and, after a decent period of mourning, sent an embassy to the Latin states to look for candidates. King Baldwin of Jerusalem suggested the beautiful Melisende, sister of Count Raymond III of Tripoli. When Manuel indicated his agreement, Raymond III was ecstatic. He was always manoeuvring to improve his station, and the imperial engagement enabled him to revel in dreams of the immense prestige and influence he would wield, with a Caesar as brother-in-law. William of Tyre described how Raymond went overboard on the preparations and blew a fortune on his sister's trousseau:

> bracelets, earrings, pins for her headdress, anklets, rings, necklaces, and tiaras of purest gold. Silver utensils of immense weight and size… all these things were prepared at vast expense and with great zeal; the workmanship alone was evidence of their exceeding great cost.[11]

Count Raymond even built an entire fleet of twelve galleys to convey himself and the bridal party to Constantinople in the high style to which he planned to become accustomed. While all this was happening, imperial envoys arrived in Tripoli to complete the preparations. The Greek delegation 'carefully scrutinized each detail and inquired into the life and conduct of the damsel even to the most secret physical characteristics'.

But then… nothing happened.

The whispers were that the imperial team's report confirmed Melisende's beauty and character, but also cast some doubt on her legitimacy. Her mother Hodierna had indeed quarrelled with Melisende's father, but the gossip was almost certainly false, and in this case nothing more than a red herring. The real reason for the hold-up was the emergence of another candidate, Princess Maria of Antioch – the stepdaughter of Reynald de Chatillon, and a daughter of Constance and Raymond of Poitiers – whom Manuel would have met during his stay in Antioch in April 1159. She was now about sixteen years old, and already famous for her beauty:

> The woman was fair in form and exceedingly beautiful… she was like unto the laughter-loving, golden Aphrodite, the white-

armed and ox-eyed Hera, the long-necked and beautiful-ankled Laconian [Helen of Troy].[12]

While Raymond and Baldwin complained to the emperor about the inexplicable delay of his marriage to Melisende, Reynald was skilfully and secretly exercising one of his greatest diplomatic skills – matchmaking. He was negotiating Manuel's marriage to his stepdaughter. Left in ignorance, Raymond felt his impatience mount until, in the summer of 1161, he dispatched an embassy led by Otto of Risberg to Byzantium, to hurry things along. Otto returned with the shocking news that the emperor had called off the engagement. The summary jilting of his sister, 'like the daughter of a common person', enraged Raymond III. It was a gross insult. It also meant Raymond's vision of a glittering future as a member of the imperial family had vanished in an instant. In retaliation for this dishonour, and for the emperor's refusal to repay his substantial costs, the enraged Raymond took a leaf out of Reynald's book. He hired a gang of pirates to crew his twelve galleys, re-equipped them for war and ravaged whatever Reynald and the earthquakes of 1157 had left intact on Byzantine Cyprus.

In autumn 1161, with Melisende – repudiated and humiliated – fading away in a convent, her replacement, the Princess Maria, set sail from St Simeon for Constantinople, life as empress and, two turbulent decades later, a frightful death.

This affair, which today may seem petty, was political dynamite in the twelfth century. Antioch's gain was Tripoli's loss. Count Raymond was left humiliated and embittered, his county sidelined for good. Meanwhile Antioch gained the protection of a close imperial alliance, and Reynald's prestige was greatly enhanced. The most powerful man in the world, before whom Reynald had demeaned himself at Mamistra, was now his son-in-law.

The scandal may also have had a terrible long-term impact on the crusader states, for though it is nowhere explicitly attested, Raymond's anger at Manuel would have been matched by resentment of Reynald's coup in marrying off his stepdaughter. It may not be a coincidence that the future dealings between the Count of Tripoli and Reynald de Chatillon would be almost exclusively hostile. In the end, Raymond would go to unheard-of – and fatal – lengths in opposition to Reynald's policies, and the rivalry of these two ambitious, vengeful characters would come to dominate and destabilize the crusader states.

In Syria, meanwhile, the peace of the emperor could not hold. Frank and Turk might both pay lip service to Byzantine supremacy, but they were enemies at heart. They soon returned to the perennial low-level frontier warfare. In the last months of 1161, that old bugbear, money, dictated Reynald's actions again. His spies reported that excellent grazing conditions had brought innumerable herds of cattle, sheep and camels to the sprawling grasslands of the old county of Edessa. Most of the pastoralists happened to be Christians, but as the Armenians and the Cypriots had already learned, this meant nothing to Reynald. The peasants were now subjects of the Turks, so they and their animals were fair game. To the south, King Baldwin III had also taken advantage of the good pasturage along the desert fringes. He broke his truce with Nur al-Din to raid across the Jordan and returned laden with booty from unprotected nomads (Muslims in this case) and their flocks.

In November, Reynald followed suit. He struck out for the Euphrates with a sizeable force, perhaps 120 cavalry and 500 foot soldiers. They fell upon the unsuspecting pastoralists, taking them completely by surprise. The haul of robes, riches and especially animals was beyond their wildest expectations. When the band of raiders turned for home 'in great joy', they drove ahead of them a vast, bellowing herd of four-legged loot.

Nur al-Din's governor of Aleppo was his 'wet-nurse brother'* and trusted lieutenant, Majd al-Din. He reacted swiftly to news of Reynald's incursion. While the troops of Antioch returned slowly south-westwards, impeded by their countless prizes, Majd al-Din was hot on their tail with a large force of Turkish cavalry. Guided by some of Reynald's men they had captured, the Aleppans caught up with Reynald's marauders near Marash. On 20 November, the Turks tried to lay an ambush, which was detected by Reynald's scouts. Informed of Majd al-Din's substantial force, Reynald halted his column for the night and carefully considered his next move.

Reynald has been portrayed as impulsive and thoughtless, but while he was decisive by nature, he did take advice. He worked with his advisers to survive Manuel's vengeance after Cyprus and, caught between Majd al-Din's cavalry and the vast herds of livestock, he responsibly discussed the tactical options with his lieutenants. However, just because he took advice did not mean he always made the right decision.

Round the campfires that evening, Reynald listened to two opposing plans: some of his men advised that they should abandon their spoils and make a run for it – the Turks, they said, would be satisfied with retrieving the livestock. Others argued that they should fight – it was unthinkable to surrender meekly such a vast booty. The Franks were outnumbered, yes, but they were better, fiercer fighters than the Muslims. With God's help, they would prevail and return to Antioch with their lives and their wealth intact. The discussion was heated, and all parties had their say, but the decision that November night was Reynald's alone.

---

* They had shared a wet-nurse as infants.

Near Marash, Anatolia, 23 November 1161

A chorus of lowing, bleating, grunting beasts greeted the rising winter sun, glimmering through a haze of dust raised by thousands of shuffling hoofs.

The knights and mounted sergeants cantered like drovers around the waking beasts, whipping and coaxing them into as tight a group as they could. Then the Frankish force drew up into battle formation. According to the *Estoire d'Eracles*, Reynald had chosen his strategy because he was 'chivalrous and brave'. Unsurprisingly, he had decided to fight his way out.

Calmly and methodically the Franks arranged their infantry into a defensive line and the horsemen into their well-drilled *conrois*, the fighting units of the Frankish cavalry, forming a screen between the Turks and the animals. Then, in a slow confusion of dust and noise, the unwieldy mass of sheep, cattle and camels shuffled off in the direction of Antioch, chivvied along by the line of mailed warriors.

The Turks immediately made a ferocious attack, but Reynald's men fought them off. Throughout the day, the Turks launched charge after charge, forcing vicious hand-to-hand combat with sword and mace. Each time the crusaders' 'stout resistance' beat them back. Between charges the Turks harassed the Franks with showers of arrows, but Reynald's strategy was vindicated as the animals and their Frankish escort edged inexorably forward.

The Franks' armour proved effective against the Turkish arrows, and the light Turkish cavalry, just as hampered by the crowds of beasts as the Franks were, could not overwhelm their well-disciplined adversaries at close quarters. For a long time the outcome hung in the balance. However, as the afternoon wore on, some of Reynald's troops began to buckle under the relentless Turkish assault and lost their nerve. 'Most hideously', says the *Estoire d'Eracles*, they broke and ran. As soon as the Frankish defence lost its cohesion, the line crumbled. The Turks were able to get amongst the defenders and begin a terrible slaughter. The Franks, severely outnumbered, were doomed.

Reynald tried to rally his men and plunged into the thickest of the fight, performing 'prodigious feats of valour',[13] but too many of his troops had fled. He had the opportunity to cut his way out and escape, but chose instead to stand and fight to the end, refusing to abandon his remaining men. Eventually he too was cast down. Reynald de Chatillon, Prince of Antioch, was now at the mercy of his most bitter enemy.

Chapter 9

IN THE POWER
OF NUR AL-DIN

*In punishment for his sins, the prince was forced to expiate in his
own person all the crimes which he had committed. A captive,
bound with the chains of the foe, he was led to Aleppo in most
ignominious fashion, there to become, with his fellow captives,
the sport of the infidels.*

William of Tyre

*But one day, when he had triumphed more gloriously than usual
over the sons of dissidence, the Heavenly Potter, wishing to test
the vessel that he had created for honour and glory, allowed him
by a trick of false brethren to be captured by enemies and taken
away to exile.*

Peter of Blois

Reynald and the survivors of his band were made prisoners of war. It was
a terrifying predicament for a crusader. The taking and ransoming of

captives was an established commercial activity for the Franks and their enemies, but while Reynald was likely to be kept alive for a substantial ransom, his men were in far greater danger. Sergeants and common infantry were sometimes given a chance to name a price, but it was rare that a lowly soldier could command a ransom valuable enough to save his life. Ordinary captives might be kept alive for sale as slaves, but it was just as common for Muslim leaders, especially the more zealous – like Nur al-Din – simply to put them to death, sometimes with remarkable cruelty. Turcopoles, the crusaders' native light cavalry, were seen as traitors and apostates by the Muslims and, if captured, were routinely massacred without a second thought. Even after death, the ordeal of a crusader was not over. The Turks liked to decapitate and collect the heads of the corpses, whether killed in battle or butchered afterwards. They would then be tied to their bridles or stuck on their spears. After one battle so many Franks were beheaded that it was said their heads arrived in Damascus 'like watermelons'.

In the fight near Marash in November 1161, of all Reynald's men taken captive, only thirty of the more valuable knights were spared. All the other captives were killed in cold blood. Perhaps 400 Franks died in the battle and the ensuing massacre. The jubilant Turkish cavalry lopped off the heads of the dead and impaled the grisly trophies on their lances.

The sight must have struck terror into the surviving Frankish prisoners. Reynald and his knights knew that their lives hung on the whim of Nur al-Din. Many crusaders had survived battles, only to suffer a worse fate later on. After an indecisive battle at Hab in 1119, the Turkish emirs, Ilghazi and Toghtekin, had initially spared a sizeable number of their Frankish captives, but this was just to keep them alive for a more grisly death at the hands of hysterical crowds in the streets of Aleppo. Ilghazi put a stop to the slaughter only when he realized how much ransom money he was losing. Often it was simply a matter of luck whether or not a captive survived. Sometimes Muslim leaders introduced cruel variations on this theme, such as encouraging religious men and civilian camp followers to execute captives. These eager but clumsy killers would prolong the victims' death agonies, sawing and hacking at their bodies rather than ending their lives swiftly. The worst example of this was after the battle of Hattin in 1187, when Saladin gave all Templar and Hospitaller captives over to the Sufis and other religious men. Some of these civilians were so useless at their task that they had to be replaced halfway through.

As a mighty lord, Reynald was as safe as could be. Only the most fanatical or most profligate victor could forgo the fortunes commanded by prestigious Frankish captives; Bohemond I, for instance, one of the most feared and renowned of all crusaders, had earned his captors the immense sum of 100,000 bezants. This was the equivalent of untold millions today – the value of the entire island of Cyprus.* But not even great lords could be certain of surviving captivity. In the aftermath of the Field of Blood, Robert the Leper was captured by the Turkish general Ilghazi and pledged a decent ransom of 10,000 gold bezants. This was not enough for Ilghazi, who sent his prisoner to the emir Toghtekin to see if he could frighten Robert into naming a higher price. Toghtekin was a friend and previous ally of Robert, but when the captive appeared, Toghtekin was drunk. The emir stood up, tucked his robe into his belt, drew his sword and decapitated Robert on the spot. Ilghazi later complained to Toghtekin that he had lost a big payday, and that he had only sent Robert over to him to be scared. Toghtekin replied, 'I have no other way of scaring than this.'[1]

And there were other tortures besides slavery or death that a prisoner had to fear. When he captured his mortal enemy, the bellicose Count Joscelin II of Edessa, Nur al-Din ignored all attempts to profit from

---

* Richard the Lionheart later sold Cyprus to the Templars for the same price.

what would have been a substantial ransom. Rather than releasing this dangerous warrior to make more trouble, he preferred to blind Joscelin and keep him chained in ghastly conditions. Joscelin died after nine years of hellish treatment in his hole.

Reynald's concern over his own fate would have been exacerbated by his knowledge that Nur al-Din was a religious zealot who put holy war before earthly profit. He was quite prepared to slaughter prisoners, as he did all those sent to him by his brother, Nusrat al-Din, after he destroyed a Frankish force near the town of Banyas. Such a slaughter was the act of a holy warrior on the infidel enemy – 'a humiliation for them in the present life, and in that to come they shall have bitter chastisement'.

So when Reynald and his men were brought into Aleppo in November 1161, their fate was still uncertain. Their experience as 'sport of the infidels' would have been appalling. In general, the citizens of Muslim towns did not treat Frankish captives well. Typical was the treatment of the Christian prisoners after Nur al-Din's victory at Banyas in 1157, paraded beneath the bloody scalps of their dead comrades:

> They had set the Frankish horsemen in pairs upon camels, each
> pair accompanied by one of their standards unfurled, to which
> were attached a number of skins of their heads with their hair.[2]

The foot soldiers were roped together in threes and fours. They were all then marched through the gloating, mocking crowds. It is likely that the citizens of Aleppo gave an equally horrible welcome to their greatest enemy, the fiendish 'Prince Arnat'. Chained, wounded and filthy with the dust and sweat of combat, Reynald and his men were probably shaved, seated backwards on camels and accompanied by their broken standards and the decapitated heads of the slain. Nur al-Din's men led their living trophies along streets lined by thousands of onlookers, through taunts, jeers, blows, showers of rubbish and faeces. For the proud Prince of Antioch it was a humiliation even more profound – and more perilous – than his submission to the emperor at Mamistra.

Through the maze of Aleppo's markets they wound their way to the city's heart. There stood the great citadel on its vast mound, whose origins date back to prehistory. They passed through the mighty gatehouse, which no Frankish warrior had ever breached. And there, in the mighty fastness of Nur al-Din, Reynald's story is plunged into darkness.

The Citadel of Aleppo, 29 June 1170

Reynald de Chatillon started his day as he had every day for just over eight years and seven months: in the dungeons of Nur al-Din.

That day his routine was probably no different from normal. He may not even have known that it was a Monday, or that it was 29 June, the feast of St Peter and St Paul, the patron saints of Antioch. At about nine o'clock that summer morning, as the worshippers in the churches across Syria celebrated mass in honour of the apostles, their rituals – and Reynald's routine – were violently interrupted.

Suddenly the earth began to tremble.

The walls of Reynald's prison shook. The ground rocked like a ship on the sea. There was a roaring like heavy thunder from underground. Reynald was tossed from side to side.

All over the ancient citadel of Aleppo, walls, towers, roofs and tunnels collapsed in clouds of debris. The sun appeared to rise and set all at once. The earth turned inside out, and from great cracks it vomited forth a black liquid, which poured down through the town.

It was a 'great and terrible earthquake, far more violent than any other within the memory of men now living'.[3] The initial, devastating shock was followed by a series of severe after-tremors. After a long while the traumatized survivors, Reynald among them, rose fearfully to their feet, surprised and thankful to be alive. 'Contrary to expectation,' wrote Michael the Syrian, 'we returned as from the grave, and then our eyes like those of a man who is woke up from sleep, began to shed tears and our tongues give praise.'

The astonishing extent of the damage across all of Syria quickly became clear. 'Strongly fortified cities dating from very early times were completely demolished. The inhabitants, caught in the ruins of their homes, were crushed to death.' Homs, Hama, Shayzar, Antioch – Muslim and Christian cities alike – were affected. In Antioch the cathedral collapsed on the congregation, killing them all.

In Aleppo thousands died, crushed by rubble or drowned in the deluge of liquefied mud. Nur al-Din's capital was the worst hit of all the Muslim cities. 'The quake destroyed it utterly and the survivors were totally terror-stricken. They were unable to shelter in their houses for fear of after-shocks.' Michael the Syrian saw this as divine vengeance on Aleppo, because in the markets there they 'sold Christians like beasts'.[4]

The Frankish lords in captivity were all lucky to survive. Once he realized he was safe, Reynald might even have wondered for a split second whether the cataclysm had opened a road to his escape.

It had not.

As the cries of the wounded and the wails of the bereaved rose over the devastated city, Reynald remained trapped.

Chapter 10

YEARS OF DARKNESS

Captives were most barbarously cast into foul prisons. And ransomed for excessive prices.

Fulcher of Chartres

Rearing up from the heart of the white city of Aleppo, the great limestone citadel rings a conical hill. The core of the hill is natural, but most of it is now a tel, a man-made mound, composed of layer upon layer of ancient cities, built, destroyed, covered by earth and then built on again, over millennia. It is said that Abraham grazed his flocks on the hill and dispensed their milk as alms.* The mound and the gigantic, sloping glacis below the walls are riddled with wells, secret passageways, caverns and dungeons. Some are as small as individual cells, while others are echoing caverns large enough to act as immense storehouses or communal prisons for dozens of prisoners.

Reynald and his fellow captives were held in these pits in the bowels of the hill, so the earthquake of June 1170 would have been a terrifying

---

* Hence the name of Aleppo, *Halab*, which means 'milk' in Arabic.

experience. Their survival was a stroke of luck. In 1115, the Armenian Prince Constantine of Gargar, captured by the Franks, was a prisoner in the fortress of Samosata when he was 'swallowed up' by an earthquake.[1]

Reynald may well have been held in a number of different cells during his years of captivity, though we cannot be sure which ones. It is unlikely that a prisoner of his value and daring nature would have been held under house arrest, but if so, his freedom would have been severely circumscribed. It is possible that prisoners were sometimes allowed out for air or for hard labour. Saladin later routinely used prisoners of war for construction, including the fortifications in Acre and the citadel of Cairo, but these were ordinary prisoners, not princes. If Reynald were ever allowed into the open, it would have been in chains. Frankish territory was only a few hours' ride away and he was far too valuable to allow him any risk of escape. The likelihood is that he was permanently in chains, whether in a deep dungeon or not.

And the conditions in those dungeons were foul and terrible. Fulcher of Chartres wrote that inmates were:

> *tormented by three evils, namely hunger, thirst, and cold, and secretly put to death.*[2]

The great Arabic historian Ibn Khaldun also saw prison as a terrible fate:

> *People who go down into deep wells and dungeons perish when the air becomes hot through putrefaction, and no winds enter these places to stir the air up.*[3]

Imprisonment in Aleppo was regarded as especially tough. Nur al-Din treated his prisoners with 'unheard-of inhumanity', as he demonstrated with his torture of Count Joscelin II. Reynald's treatment was also harsh;

William of Tyre described it as 'hard captivity'. But clearly Reynald had a remarkably resilient constitution. Many men were broken in captivity, like Alfonse Jordan and thousands of the pathetic survivors of the Second Crusade released by Nur al-Din in 1159. Though no doubt he suffered, as any long-term prisoner suffers, Reynald did not break. Nor did he yield to temptations such as the pressure exerted on captives to convert to Islam. Reynald would not have been tempted by this offer.

One vital support to prisoners is human contact. Apart from his jailers, companionship may have been rare for Reynald, and unless the Frankish leaders were indeed kept in communal cells, contact with fellow Christians may have been even rarer. Priests were allowed to administer the last rites to captives – Joscelin II received extreme unction from the Jacobite Bishop of Aleppo – but it is not known what access there was to priests or to Christian sacraments at other times.

Part of Reynald's misery must have been fear for his family and his principality, and he would have been right. Nur al-Din took advantage of Reynald's capture to ravage Antiochene territory, attacking the coastal town of Latakyeh and taking thousands of prisoners. King Baldwin III was forced to march north from Jerusalem to take charge of Antioch again. Princess Constance had once more been deprived of a husband by the never-ending war with Nur al-Din. Shaking off the shock of losing Reynald, she made an attempt to rule in her own right, but King Baldwin and Thoros the Armenian thwarted her. They placed her fifteen-year-old son, Prince Bohemond III, known as 'the Stammerer', on his stepfather's throne. The young prince, who was not quite old enough to rule in his own right, and in any case showed little promise, was to be guided by the indefatigable Patriarch Aimery, who returned as regent.

The relationship between Bohemond and his stepfather is not clear, but it does not appear to have been close. There may well have been the sort of tensions and resentments found in many step-families.

Perhaps Bohemond's stammer and doubtful character were the result of psychological traumas in childhood? The question arises as to whether his stepfather had something to do with this, especially as Reynald would later have another stepson who stammered and was widely regarded as a weak personality. This pattern would fit with an impatient, demanding father imposing impossibly high expectations on his (step-) children. Whether Reynald was a good parent or not, little of his charisma or his machismo rubbed off on his stepsons.

With Bohemond there would no doubt have been additional political tension between stepfather and son; Reynald was, after all, occupying the post that was Bohemond's by birth. Certainly Bohemond's accession to the princely throne does not seem to have increased Reynald's chances of release. The new prince had no political incentive to ransom his renowned and intimidating predecessor, nor would Patriarch Aimery be likely to advise the ransom of the man he loathed.

With Bohemond enthroned as prince and Princess Constance sidelined, Reynald had no further claim to power in Antioch. His irrelevance was finalized in 1163, when Constance died. When the news reached him, Reynald must have been deeply grieved. For more than ten years, secretly and then openly, she had loved him. She had borne his children and risked her realm and reputation when she stooped from her pedestal to marry him up out of obscurity. Reynald may well have felt increased frustration and anger at his captors – it was their fault he had been unable to help his wife, unable to comfort her as she died.

Along with the emotional distress, Reynald would presumably have regretted his consequent loss of status; with Constance dead, any hope Reynald may have had for regaining a position in Antioch, where his stepson now ruled, had also died. Another concern might have been for the safety of his surviving children by Constance, Agnes and Baldwin, who were now unwanted potential complications to the dynastic succession in Antioch. Prudently, for the children's well-being,

Reynald's remaining allies in the city dispatched the children to the imperial court in Constantinople, where their half-sister Maria was now empress. Like his father, Reynald's son, Prince Baldwin, would soon show military promise.

The year 1163 also saw the death of King Baldwin III of Jerusalem. He left no children, and Nur al-Din was urged by his emirs to take advantage of the interregnum to invade the Latin states. Nur al-Din is said to have refused because of his respect for Baldwin, saying, 'We should sympathize with their grief and in pity spare them, because they have lost a prince such as the rest of the world does not possess today.'[4] Baldwin's successor was his capable brother, Amalric, who soon found his resources stretched to the limit by Nur al-Din.

In 1164, the *atabeg* resumed his holy war against the Franks, and this offensive soon brought Reynald illustrious company in the cells of Aleppo. At Harim, near Antioch, Nur al-Din won a great victory against a combined Greek-Armenian-Frankish army. The captives were a *Who's Who* of the Christian East. They included Joscelin de Courtenay, titular Count of Edessa; the Byzantine general Constantine Coloman; and Reynald's rival, Raymond III of Tripoli. Antioch was also left leaderless, as the recently elevated Prince Bohemond III joined his stepfather in the dungeons. It was common for prisoners to be kept in communal pits – for example, King Baldwin II and Count Joscelin I had been held together in the pit of Khartpert – so all these VIPs may have been incarcerated together with Reynald. It is possible that some of the new arrivals were not altogether welcome to Reynald. Count Raymond would not have forgotten Reynald's role in negotiating the imperial marriage that ruined his sister's life. The relationship between Bohemond III and his stepfather may also have been strained. Still, after three lonely years in captivity, news from outside and contact with his peers – albeit rivals – would likely have been a blessing. Brian Keenan, who was imprisoned by Islamic Jihad in Lebanon for four and a half years in the 1980s, wrote that 'being alone is the most difficult situation to deal with as a hostage'. But when he was first joined by other prisoners, his feelings were mixed: 'The warmth, the intimacy and companionship which came flooding to us both at that first meeting was always undermined by something deeper... a curious wariness that each felt for the other person with whom he had to share his life.'[5]

Any pleasure Reynald felt would also have been counter-balanced by the terrible defeat the Franks had suffered. The strategically critical castle of Harim, previously captured for Antioch by Reynald, had fallen to Nur al-Din. The Franks would never recapture it, nor would Antioch ever fully recover its military might.

A couple of the new prisoners were not around for long. Still wary of angering the Emperor Manuel, Nur al-Din quickly released Constantine Coloman, the Greek general, for the token payment of 150 bolts of cloth. It then took less than a year to agree the release of Reynald's stepson. Bohemond's sister Maria had been empress since 1161 and Nur al-Din knew it would be unwise to hold on to the emperor's brother-in-law. The *atabeg* was also prepared to release the callow Bohemond because the boy was not seen as much of a threat. Keeping him hostage ran the risk of a more effective leader taking charge in Antioch – it might even have brought direct rule from Byzantium itself. Bohemond the Stammerer was released for the huge sum of 100,000 bezants. His stepfather remained languishing in prison.

Quite soon after Reynald's capture, it must have become clear that Nur al-Din was not going to ransom him. Prince Reynald was just too dangerous to release. The negotiations around the liberation of Coloman and Bohemond provided an opportunity for new efforts to secure a ransom for Reynald, but still Nur al-Din refused to let him go, no matter how huge the sums on offer. Nor did he free Raymond or Joscelin. Cruelly, the miserable Joscelin was thrown into the same pit in which his father had died.

The Emperor Manuel had guaranteed Prince Bohemond's ransom and, as soon as he was freed, Bohemond travelled to Constantinople to say his thanks and get hold of the treasure needed to pay Nur al-Din. The emperor provided the money, but there was a catch. With the weak Bohemond as Prince of Antioch, Manuel saw his chance to make a strong statement of Byzantine dominance. When Bohemond returned to Antioch, the Greek patriarch Athanasius accompanied him. The controversial 'Patriarch Clause' was finally being exercised. For the first time in more than sixty years[*] a Greek bishop would preside in the Cathedral of St Peter. This was doctrinally unacceptable to most Latins, who regarded the Greek Church as schismatic. More importantly, it was politically unacceptable to the Latins, embodying as it did Greek supremacy over Antioch.

Antioch's Latin patriarch, Aimery of Limoges, was outraged. He retaliated by placing Antioch under interdict, forbidding the sacrament to worshippers. He then took refuge in one of his castles at Cursat. There he again seethed and schemed in exile until the terrible earthquake of 1170, when the Cathedral of St Peter fell down on top of Athanasius and all the Greek clergy. Prince Bohemond and the populace begged Aimery to return, believing that his curse had brought the disaster upon the city. Aimery agreed and lifted the interdict, on the condition that the Greek patriarch be 'ignominiously expelled'. Even though Athanasius lay fatally injured from falling masonry, Aimery insisted on his eviction from the city. In his death throes, the Greek patriarch was dragged out on a litter and dumped beyond the walls.

Amidst the ruins of Aleppo, in the wake of that same earthquake, Reynald's ordeal continued. He would then have been in his mid-forties and had already suffered almost nine years of harsh imprisonment, with no end in sight. Long-term captivity has different effects on prisoners.

---

[*] Soon after his capture of Antioch in 1099, Bohemond of Taranto had expelled the Greek patriarch John the Oxite, leaving just a Latin patriarch.

Some reach accommodation with their captors. Some plunge into depression and thoughts of suicide. Others turn to anger and resistance. Over many years the same prisoner may experience all of these reactions. For American prisoners of war in Vietnam, for instance:

> The battle was not only a fight for daily survival, but also a
> fight against psychological coercion, physical torture, boredom,
> humiliation, feelings of helplessness, and oftentimes extreme
> mental depression.[6]

Common to start with is an initial period of denial. Once he had realized that Nur al-Din was not going to release him, and the reality of his predicament began to set in, Reynald may well have found anger to be an effective survival strategy. His warrior's mind, we can be sure, would have turned to defiance. As Keenan wrote, 'the fury of life is stronger than the compulsion of death. Something in the human spirit seeks a way to overcome such oppression. There is always something in us that will not submit.'

It is also very likely that Reynald would have planned to escape; early in his captivity he may well have felt this was not impossible. Usama Ibn Munqidh tells how a resourceful Bedouin freed a Muslim captive from Frankish custody by digging a tunnel into his cell. But tunnelling through the mound of Aleppo was impossible.

Rescue plans were probably discussed by Reynald's Frankish friends, but without much real intent. Such efforts did not have a good record of success. In 1123, King Baldwin II was freed from his prison in the citadel of Khartpert by a daring raid in which his Armenian rescuers disguised themselves as monks and merchants to infiltrate the city. Once inside, they killed the Turkish garrison and freed Baldwin. Unfortunately they were then trapped in the citadel by Muslim reinforcements and slaughtered to a man.* Baldwin would later ransom himself for 80,000 dinars, which were handed over; and for some castles, which were not. But Aleppo was a different proposition, being many times the size of Khartpert, with a garrison as big as an army. Reynald would soon have realized there was no realistic chance of a rescue from outside, though this might not have stopped him dreaming up escape plans, something that prisoners of war in all epochs have used as a strategy of mental resistance.

As the hopes of escape faded, Reynald would have begun to accept his lot and fall into a routine. Confinement must have been torture for a man of action like him, a man of adventure and impatience. It may have been especially tormenting for crusaders like Reynald, who were more psychologically prepared for victory or death than for captivity.[7] The terrors of being held in dark pits, perpetually in chains, and the fear of death, the powerlessness, the pain of beatings, the humiliations, the privations of hunger and cold – all these horrors, typical of long-term imprisonment in the Levant, Reynald may have suffered. And open-ended captivity preys on the body and the mind. As Brian Keenan described: 'The days chased each other and the future stood before me grey as my walls and as invincible.' Recent medical research on such experiences has shown increased rates of Post-Traumatic Stress Disorder among long-term POWs. Sometimes the torment can drive you mad. Keenan again:

> All order has gone from my world, I am invaded at random
> by unwanted and unknown images. In this place where there
> is nothing, full-fed fantasy and craziness are my frequent
> tormenting visitors.

---

* Any women who had helped the rescue attempt were also killed, being thrown over the ramparts.

These effects are multiplied by time, and Reynald became one of the longest-held prisoners of the crusades.*

Reynald resisted the lure of madness, but the question remains as to how the experience of prison affected his thinking. Historians have tended to argue that during his captivity Reynald developed a strong animosity towards Muslims. In her thoughtful review of Reynald's time as a prisoner of war, Professor Carole Hillenbrand wrote:

> *Reynald's attitude to Islam and to his Muslim captors, no matter what survival strategies he may have developed, must have been one of profound and settled hatred.* [8]

This may be overstating Reynald's view, but it is certain that captivity did nothing to soften his heart against the Muslims. Over the years he would have developed a much deeper understanding of Islamic society, of its seasons and rhythms, its festivals and values. He would have learned more about the different cultures of the Muslim peoples of Syria, the Turks, Kurds, settled Arabs and Bedouin. Prison may also be where he picked up his knowledge of Arabic. [9]

Whether hatred festered, along with the frustrations and fears of such a long imprisonment, we cannot be sure. But Reynald would have experienced at first hand the Muslims' unshakeable hatred of the crusaders. In the city of the holy warrior Nur al-Din, he would also have learned more about the jihad, and how it motivated the thousands of religious fanatics who volunteered from all over the Islamic world to fight the crusaders. Reflecting in his cell, the imprisoned warrior may well have concluded that, in the long term, there would be no peace

---

* His stint was less than half that of the record-holder, a knight called Gauffier. Captured by the Egyptians at Ramleh in 1103, Gauffier turned up again in Jerusalem thirty-four years later. In the meantime the Jacobite Church had claimed his lands. The astonished Jacobites confirmed Gauffier's identity and paid him 300 bezants in compensation.

with the Muslims, certainly not under the leadership of the *mujahid* Nur al-Din.

His fellow captive, Raymond III, appears to have responded to his captivity very differently. Raymond seems almost to have contracted a kind of Stockholm Syndrome,* becoming fluent in Arabic and growing very close to his Muslim captors. Later he would even be tempted to embrace Islam. This sympathy with the crusaders' foes would become a major point of contention with Reynald de Chatillon. In the long run it would lead to tragic consequences. We may wonder whether the rivalry between Reynald and Raymond, which later became so bitter, festered during the years of whispers in the dark cells of Aleppo. In the enforced intimacy of such captivity, people's fundamental strengths and weaknesses, their worst fears, their deepest desires are relentlessly exposed. It can go both ways: shared suffering led to lifelong friendship between Reynald and Joscelin de Courtenay. What Reynald and Raymond learned about each other through the long years in chains appears to have had the opposite effect.

Reynald must have fretted constantly at his helplessness. He had entered prison aged around thirty-six and his prime years were passing by. He must have been desperate, throughout his incarceration, to return to the fray and inflict some payback on his enemies. But even in confinement, his status as prince and his reputation as a warrior meant that he was not wholly absent from the political scene. Throughout the years of his enforced absence, crusader leaders wrote reams of letters to European monarchs pleading for aid. In these desperate missives the plight of the Prince of Antioch features frequently, as one of the abominations suffered by the Christians of the East that needs to be righted by a new crusade.

There would have been attempts to ransom Reynald over the years,

---

* Stockholm Syndrome is so called because of a botched bank raid in Stockholm in 1973, when the hostages came to sympathize very strongly with their captors.

and we can be sure that Reynald himself kept agitating to be released. His character was not one to passively accept his fate. But Nur al-Din refused to ransom Reynald with his stepson in 1164 and this would be his stance for another decade. The great Frankish lords in his prisons were potent symbols of his superiority over the unbelievers. 'He gained great glory from holding our rich men in his prison,' wrote William of Tyre. Of the other long-term prisoners held with Reynald, Hugh de Lusignan was released by death, and Raymond III was freed in the early 1170s, having spent more than 'eight years as a prisoner in beggary and in chains'.[10]

Reynald somehow survived the inevitable strains on his sanity. And we can be sure that he kept his mind active. We hear that he learned 'some reading and writing',[11] for instance. As with many modern convicts, it took jail to finally teach the unlettered Burgundian knight to read. News from outside would have been another vital ingredient for a healthy mental state, and through the years he would have heard both good and bad. Perhaps he knew that in 1172 his daughter Agnes became Queen of Hungary through her marriage to Bela III, a protégé of the Emperor Manuel. He may also have learned of the birth of Emeric, his first grandchild, in 1174.

From his jailers or newly arrived prisoners he would have learned how Nur al-Din had steadily increased his power in Syria. He would have heard echoes of the great battles for Egypt and, sometime after 1168, he would have received the chilling news that the Kurdish general Shirkuh and his nephew Saladin had finally conquered that fabulously wealthy and populous country in Nur al-Din's name. No longer a simple emir or *atabeg* of Aleppo, Reynald's captor was now known as *malik* (king), or even 'sultan' of Syria and Egypt.

Many times over the years, as hopes were raised and then dashed, as earthquakes hit and then passed, as fellow captives were killed or released, Reynald might have surrendered, in body or spirit, to the lure of despair or the ravages of disease or malnutrition. But he did not. Then, after fifteen years in the dungeons of Nur al-Din, the lands of Syria were thrown into turmoil once again.

This time the earthquake was political.

The Citadel of Damascus, 15 May 1174

The doctors bustled in and out, but their patient in the small, dark prayer room did not move. Though he was lying down, hardly breathing, you could still make out that he was a tall, strong man. He was handsome too, swarthy with a wide forehead and charming eyes.

The Sultan Nur al-Din Mahmud, Son of Zengi, was in the grip of a strangling quinsy in his throat. He had not moved from the tiny chamber since the sickness took hold. His doctor remonstrated with him and advised that he should be bled.

'A sixty-year-old is not to be bled,' he said. His voice was barely audible. The swelling abscess was slowly poisoning and suffocating him. They tried to move the sultan to a light and airy place and give him other treatments, but nothing had any effect. God had 'whispered to him the command that cannot be shunned'.[12]

A few days before, one of his friends had bidden Nur al-Din farewell, saying, 'Glory be to him who knows whether we shall meet here next year or not.'

'Do not say that,' replied Nur al-Din. 'Rather glory be to Him who knows whether we shall meet in a *month's* time or not.'[13]

Eleven days later, Nur al-Din – master of Egypt and Syria, the ardent champion of jihad and scourge of the Franks – was dead. He was laid to rest in the citadel, but afterwards his body was moved to the religious school that he had built in Damascus in the Market of the Palm Leaf Sellers.

By then his empire was already disintegrating. His son and heir was the pawn of ambitious courtiers, his cousins were at war.

146 ✛ GOD'S WOLF

Biding his time in Cairo, waiting for the chance to strike, was another claimant to Nur al-Din's legacy: his vizier in the great realm of Egypt, the brilliant and ambitious Saladin.

The world had changed and it meant a glimmer of hope for Reynald.

Chapter 11

PHOENIX

After fifteen years… he emerged, like purified silver or pure gold, from the furnace of captivity.

Peter of Blois[1]

Nur al-Din Mahmud, son of Zengi, was deeply mourned. Saladin referred to his passing in May 1174 as 'an earthquake shock'.

For the Muslims, Nur al-Din had been a widely revered and committed leader. He was also a brilliant soldier who had continued the reunification of Islam against the Frankish invaders, a process begun by his father. By the time of his death, Nur al-Din had encircled the Franks by uniting Syria and Egypt. His next step would have been to crush them. But the noose had not yet been drawn tight around the Franks because Egypt was not directly controlled by Nur al-Din; it was ruled by the man who was ostensibly Nur al-Din's viceroy – the remarkable Saladin.

A Kurdish nobleman whose father had saved Zengi's life, Salah al-Din Yusuf was a daunting, cunning and ruthless enemy, attracting admiration from Christian and Muslim alike. William of Tyre described him as being 'of keen and vigorous mind, valiant in war, and of an extremely generous disposition'.[2]

Saladin first won Frankish respect during King Amalric's campaigns in Egypt in the 1160s. This period ended with Saladin's uncle, Shirkuh, taking control of Egypt in Nur al-Din's name in January 1169. The young Saladin had particularly distinguished himself in robustly defending Alexandria against the crusaders. After that battle he even lodged for a while in the crusader camp. As time went on, stories grew up around Saladin's relations with the Franks. There were tales that he had been a captive in the castle of Kerak during his youth, that he had been schooled in the ways of Christian chivalry, even that he had been dubbed a knight. Saladin's true character was rather less glossy than the myths: when Shirkuh died after just two months as ruler of Egypt, Saladin used astute politicking, imprisonment and assassination to eliminate all challenges to his authority.* He also quietly extinguished the line of Shi'ite Fatimid caliphs who had ruled Egypt since the year 969. The official version was that in 1171 the last Fatimid caliph conveniently died and the rest of his family lived out their days in seclusion in the palace. William of Tyre reports a different story:

> It is said that at the very beginning of his [Saladin's] rule, when he visited the caliph…he struck his lord to the ground with a club which he held in his hand and slew him. He then put all the caliph's children to the sword…[3]

In parallel with the demise of the Fatimid dynasty, Saladin began to change the official Islamic sect of Egypt from the minority Shi'ite

---

* Saladin detained the Egyptian vizier Shawar and, according to at least one chronicler, personally cut his throat. This is one of only three occasions that I can find when Saladin himself is said to have drawn blood with his weapon. All three involved helpless victims, the last a much more famous prisoner than Shawar, almost thirty years later.

LEFT: The contents of the FedEx package sent by Al-Qaida in 2010, addressed to Reynald de Chatillon. The printer contained a bomb made of the explosive PETN, programmed to detonate over Chicago, Illinois.

BELOW: The powerful and beautiful Eleanor of Aquitaine. She went on the Second Crusade (1147–49) with her husband King Louis of France, bringing romance and scandal along with her. Fresco from the Chapel of St Radegund in Chinon, France (13th century).

ABOVE: Knights setting out for Outremer on the Second Crusade. Cressac Chapel fresco (12th century).

LEFT: The leaders of the Second Crusade argue at the council of Acre, June 1148 (*top*). The crusaders then make their ill-fated attack on the Muslim city of Damascus, July 1148 (*bottom*). From the manuscript of William of Tyre's *History of Deeds done beyond the Sea* (late 12th century).

BELOW: Reynald de Chatillon's seal as Prince of Antioch. One side shows Reynald as a mounted knight. The other shows St Peter and St Paul, both closely associated with Antioch.

ABOVE: Reynald tortures the patriarch of Antioch on top of a tower, *c.* 1154. From the manuscript of William of Tyre's *History* and its *Continuation* (13th century).

ABOVE: *View from across the Orontes river* by J. Redway (1841). This engraving shows the daunting defences of the great ancient metropolis of Antioch.

The impregnable might of Reynald's stronghold at Kerak in Oultrejordan. For the Muslims it was 'a wolf placed in the valley' to hamper their communications and prey on caravan traffic.

The strategic Muslim stronghold of Shayzar on the frontiers of Antioch resisted crusader assaults for half a century. In 1157, a coalition forged by Reynald de Chatillon captured the lower town and had the upper fortress at its mercy.

The citadel of Aleppo, Syria, crowns its towering tel – a mound made up of cities dating back to prehistory. In the twelfth century, Reynald was among many crusader prisoners who languished for years in its deep pits and dungeons.

The castle on the Ile de Graye off Aila (Eilat) in the Red Sea. It is now known as Saladin's Island, and is Egyptian territory. Reynald besieged this fort with two galleys during his raid of 1182/3.

Reynald's bitter enemy, the astute and ambitious Muslim leader, Saladin (1137–93). Reynald dealt Saladin his worst military defeat and at least twice Saladin swore he would personally kill Reynald. Portrait after a contemporary miniature (c. 1180).

Reynald's seal as Lord of Oultrejordan showing his swan symbol. He retained the title of prince.

Manuel I Comnemos, Byzantine emperor from 1143–80, with his second wife
Maria of Antioch, stepdaughter of Reynald de Chatillon. Reynald's role in this
marriage may have had damaging long-term consequences for the crusaders.
Image from a facsimile of a manuscript from the Vatican Library.

RIGHT: Christianity's Holy of Holies, the Church of the Holy Sepulchre in Jerusalem. This is the view of the twelfth-century crusader façade. Here, in 1186, Reynald's power in the Kingdom of Jerusalem reached its zenith.

LEFT: The Horns of Hattin in Galilee, Israel – site of the momentous battle of 1187. From the Horns you can look eastwards down to the Sea of Galilee in the distance.

ABOVE: Crusaders and Saracens fight over the Holy Cross at the Battle of Hattin, 1187. From the *Chronica Maiora* by Matthew Paris (13th century).

Islam of the Fatimids to the Sunni orthodox mainstream. In this he was initially following the direct orders of his master, the devout and strictly Sunni Nur al-Din, but Saladin soon saw that the policy was very popular with the Sunni Muslim majority. He then embraced the mission enthusiastically, thoroughly rooting out Shi'ite 'heresy' in Egypt. An important part of Saladin's image, both during his lifetime and in posterity, was built on this reputation as a Sunni champion. During his reign, support from influential Sunni figures such as the Qadi* Al-Fadil would be one of the main pillars of his power.

While maintaining a veneer of obedience to Nur al-Din, Saladin had actually steadily distanced himself from his overlord. From Syria, Nur al-Din had watched his protégé's growing independence with anger and alarm. To teach him a lesson, Nur al-Din prepared to invade Egypt in person. Fortunately for Saladin, Nur al-Din's plans were interrupted by his final illness. His successor was his son, Al-Malik al-Salih, who was just eleven years old. Al-Salih quickly became the pawn of competing emirs, and Nur al-Din's patient unification of Islamic Syria was undone in a moment, as his dominions fragmented. With the vast wealth and population of Egypt at his disposal, Saladin was left as the most powerful Muslim ruler in the region.

His luck was in again soon afterwards, when in July 1174 King Amalric of Jerusalem also died, succumbing to a combination of dysentery and over-eager bleeding from his Frankish doctor. Aged just thirty-eight, he had ruled for eleven years and had been an effective, aggressive and energetic leader who had tirelessly taken the fight to his Muslim foes. His loss was a great blow to the Latin states at an unfortunate moment. The crusaders urgently needed a strong ruler to exploit Nur al-Din's death and combat the growing menace of Saladin,

---

* A Qadi is an Islamic judge, but the term is used more loosely for a religious authority or administrator.

but Amalric's heir was his son Baldwin IV, who was just thirteen years old and was afflicted by a grave and mysterious illness.

Baldwin was a handsome and able youth of great promise, but when he was nine years old, the young prince's tutor, William of Tyre, had noticed something unusual about him:

> He was playing one day with his companions of noble rank, when
> they began, as playful boys often do, to pinch each other's arms
> and hands with their nails. The other boys gave evidence of pain
> by their outcries, but Baldwin, although his comrades did not spare
> him, endured it altogether too patiently, as if he felt nothing…
> I discovered that his right arm and hand were partially numb,
> so that he did not feel pinching or even biting in the least.[4]

These were the first signs of a terrible and incurable disease. As the boy-king grew older, the symptoms became worse and more visible, as the extremities of his face and limbs began to rot. By the time he was fifteen it was clear that Baldwin was suffering from the disfiguring and debilitating effects of a virulent strain of leprosy.

Politics adores a power vacuum. Competing barons were soon jostling for pre-eminence around the ailing young king. Foremost among these was Miles de Plancy, lord of the great fief of Oultrejordan, the lands beyond the Jordan River. Miles held the powerful post of seneschal, effectively the king's deputy. He had been King Amalric's closest friend, but with Amalric gone, he was proving increasingly unpopular with the baronage. The other contender for power was Count Raymond III of Tripoli, recently ransomed from prison in Aleppo for 80,000 bezants. Raymond was not satisfied with ruling his county of Tripoli; he wanted more. While his nemesis Reynald chafed in prison, Raymond – hungry for power – was assiduously building up his influence in the Kingdom of Jerusalem. Raymond was not only the boy-king's closest male relative, but was now also Prince of Galilee, making him the kingdom's most powerful magnate. He had gained this status by marrying Princess Eschiva of Galilee, the widow of Reynald's old comrade-in-arms, Walter of St Omer. On these grounds the ambitious and able Raymond now claimed the regency. In late 1174, at the crusader port of Acre, Raymond's claim was put before a grand assembly of the nobles of Jerusalem. He won enough support to force Miles de Plancy to give way, and Raymond was officially declared regent. A few nights later, persons unknown murdered Miles in an Acre street.

While the Franks were paralysed by internal rivalries, the Syrian domains of Nur al-Din splintered into competing statelets. Damascus and Aleppo fell under the control of ambitious emirs. The Zengid Saif al-Din, ruler of Mosul in neighbouring Mesopotamia, seized some Syrian territory but did not have the power or the daring to unite the squabbling city states against the menace of Saladin. The political turbulence would have percolated to Reynald and his fellow prisoners. They must have been given some hope that the changes would bring their release. On Nur al-Din's death, new efforts at ransom negotiations would have begun very quickly between the Franks and the various emirs jockeying for power in Aleppo. The disappearance of Nur al-Din meant that weaker, greedier Muslim leaders might now be tempted to cash in on the valuable but wasting assets languishing under the citadel.

The politician who emerged from the pack in Aleppo was Gumushtekin, a eunuch of Frankish origin. He soon brought Nur al-Din's son and heir, Al-Salih, to Aleppo, to rule as figurehead. Afraid that Gumushtekin would attack their city, the people of Damascus demanded protection. Messengers were sent to Egypt to summon the one man powerful enough to help: Saladin.

Saladin needed no second invitation. He set off from Egypt with just 700 cavalry and travelled swiftly along the desert fringes, taking the direct route through the Frankish territory of Oultrejordan. Late in

October 1174 he entered Damascus and was acclaimed by the populace. Still pretending loyalty to the legitimate Zengid dynasty, Saladin took power in the name of Al-Salih. He maintained this flimsy cover story when he marched north, taking the cities of Homs and Hama, though the citadel of Homs held out. In late December 1174, the murmurs of war may have carried all the way through the stone-clad castle mound to Reynald in his prison, as Saladin laid siege to Aleppo itself. Al-Salih did not fall for Saladin's empty professions of obedience and, in a rousing speech, inspired the people of Aleppo to resist. 'This wicked man,' he told the assembled citizens, 'who repudiates my father's goodness to him, has come to take my lands. He respects neither God Almighty, nor his creatures.'[5]

Aleppo rallied to its young leader and defied Saladin, but the city's forces were too weak to hold him off on their own. Just as Damascus in previous times had allied with the Franks against the power of Nur al-Din, so Aleppo now turned to third parties to prevent Saladin from dominating Syria. First Gumushtekin engaged the leader of the Assassins sect, Rashid al-Din Sinan, the 'Old Man of the Mountain', to take care of the sultan. Rashid al-Din was happy to help. Desperate to remain independent from orthodox Islamic rule, the Assassins were deeply concerned about Saladin's tightening grip on Syria.

Rashid al-Din ordered a squad of his devoted followers to carry out the hit. One night they infiltrated Saladin's camp. They were just outside Saladin's tent when a member of the sultan's entourage happened to recognize one of the killers. Saladin's guards turned out and cut down the Assassins a few feet from their target. Gumushtekin then turned to the Franks, calling on the recently released Raymond of Tripoli to intervene. Raymond obliged by moving half-heartedly towards the city of Homs in the territory of Damascus. This forced Saladin to raise the siege of Aleppo and move south. Raymond, however, then threw away his advantage. In an early sign of his dangerously accommodating attitude to Saladin, he agreed on a dubious deal: Saladin would forgive Raymond his (substantial) outstanding ransom debt, while Raymond would give Saladin a free hand in Syria. Even according to Raymond's supporter, William of Tyre, this agreement was 'decidedly detrimental' to the Franks, because 'Saladin should have been resisted to the utmost'. Instead Saladin realized he could buy off the Franks – or Raymond, at least – and rely on their inactivity. After Raymond withdrew, Saladin captured the citadel of Homs and completed his conquest of the city.

Sold out by Raymond, Al-Malik al-Salih and the other Zengids (including Saif al-din, Lord of Mosul) then tried a united front against Saladin, but in a battle near Hama, Saladin defeated the combined forces of Aleppo and Mosul. He took advantage of his triumph to abandon his empty professions of loyalty to Al-Salih and began striking coinage in his own name, styling himself 'sultan'. In May of 1175 the caliph in Baghdad sent Saladin robes of office, legitimizing his authority.

The following year the Zengids tried again to repel the upstart. In March, Saif al-Din led a substantial army into Syria from Mosul. Battle was joined at the Hill of the Sultan near Aleppo. The outcome hung in the balance, until Saladin charged in person and won a decisive victory. He was generous and merciful to his opponents in defeat, winning a lot of admiration in the process. As well as controlling Egypt, Saladin was now firmly in charge of almost all of Syria.

Only Aleppo remained loyal to Al-Salih, and to replenish his treasury and shore up his alliance of convenience with the Franks, Al-Salih's minister Gumushtekin began a policy of releasing the prominent Frankish prisoners in Aleppo's jails. Count Joscelin de Courtenay, without a county since the eradication of Edessa, was freed after more than eleven years of captivity, for a hefty ransom of 50,000 bezants. He made straight for Jerusalem, where his sister Agnes, mother of the young King Baldwin IV, wielded increasingly wide-ranging powers. Joscelin's arrival boosted the hold of the Courtenay faction at court and he was soon given the plum job of seneschal, becoming the king's deputy and controller of the kingdom's treasury, *La Grande Secrète*.

As well as finally achieving a profit on their long-held assets and showing gratitude to the Franks for their aid, Gumushtekin hoped the warriors he released would help the Franks mount an opposition to Saladin. In Reynald de Chatillon, this hope was realized. Over the next decade he would become Saladin's most resolute and effective opponent. In the end, though, the prisoner-release policy backfired for Gumushtekin. Freeing the Frankish devils proved unpopular with the people of Aleppo, who felt that the eunuch vizier was too sympathetic to his Western roots. Al-Salih used this as one of the grievances against his vizier when, soon afterwards, he seized personal control of Aleppo. Al-Salih then forced Gumushtekin to surrender his castle of Harim. When the garrison refused to oblige, Al-Salih hung his former vizier upside-down outside the castle walls and tortured him to death.

In the spring of 1176, the last of all the big beasts to be released, Reynald de Chatillon stepped blinking into the blazing Syrian sunlight. It took the biggest ransom ever paid to free him – 120,000 gold bezants. The amount was literally more than a king's ransom; it had only cost 80,000 to ransom King Baldwin II in 1124. The magnitude of the ransom reflects Reynald's awesome reputation amongst the Muslims. The fact that it was paid proves his equally legendary status amongst the crusaders, to many of whom he would have been no more than a revered name from a different age. William of Tyre says that Reynald's friends raised the vast sum. Who they were we do not know: what was left of Reynald's old cohorts in Antioch perhaps. Joscelin might have helped – it appears that he and Reynald became very close while confined in Aleppo – but the new seneschal had tapped out his connections to fund his own ransom. Most likely the ultimate source of the 120,000 bezants was Emperor Manuel. At the Byzantine court Reynald's stepdaughter, the Empress Maria, presumably had her husband's ear, while Reynald's son, Baldwin, had impressed Manuel enough to be trusted with a senior military command. Reynald's daughter Agnes was queen of Byzantium's client regime in Hungary. Whoever raised the funds, Reynald was thought to be worth the largest sum ever paid in eighty years of crusading ransoms.*

When Reynald de Chatillon was captured he had been in his mid-thirties. By his release he was probably over fifty and past his prime. He was remarkably durable, however, and emerged brimming with drive and intensity. Inevitably his ordeal had left its mark: 'Although still young,' lamented Peter of Blois, 'his whole head was sprinkled with untimely grey.' But neither age nor imprisonment had withered him, and Reynald would soon prove his worth to the crusader cause. As his ransomers must have hoped, his skills had not rusted through lack of use, and his hand had not forgotten how to grip a sword.

The release of these inspirational leaders was a fillip for the Frankish cause. Peter of Blois wrote that Reynald's 'much-longed-for release' was received everywhere with ineffable joy. But not all his peers in the East were ecstatic to see Reynald back in the crusader ranks. At first Reynald returned to the city where he had initially scaled the heights of power, but he found nothing to keep him in Antioch. He retained the title of 'Prince' for life, but had no rights to position or property in the principality. His wife was dead. His children had gone to Byzantium. The patriarch was still the indestructible Aimery of Limoges, Reynald's sworn enemy. The current prince, Reynald's stepson Bohemond III, was now in his thirties and well established in his rule. He had no desire to see another Prince of Antioch in the city, especially not a predecessor and potential rival with the ambition and awesome reputation of his stepfather. Reynald soon abandoned the state where he had achieved

---

* Only one larger sum would ever be agreed: the ransom of Baldwin of Ibelin in 1180 for 150,000 bezants. This was inflated because Saladin believed that Baldwin was a candidate for the throne of Jerusalem.

his remarkable rise. A landless knight-errant again, endowed with little more than an empty title, he may even briefly have considered returning to Europe. But his tastes, character and abilities were better suited to the precarious luxury, the extreme risks and rewards of the war-torn East. He had already made his name and one fortune in Outremer. His fame, his contacts and his future lay there too, as did, perhaps, the religious motivation to protect the Christian gains in the East. Besides, the years of brooding in captivity may have left him with a strong sense of unfinished business. Of the three Latin states, only one offered Reynald any opportunity. Antioch was barred to him; the county of Tripoli, ruled by his rival, Raymond III, was equally unwelcoming. The ageless adventurer swallowed his princely pride and left Antioch to try his luck in a new realm. Reynald rode south through the territory of Antioch and Tripoli and into the promised Palestine of milk and honey that was the Kingdom of Jerusalem.

Not all the land was as rewarding as God had described it to Abraham. There were foetid, fever-ridden swamps in places and, from the central town of Ramleh southwards, vast tracts of the kingdom were essentially sand. There were areas of plenty, though; port cities like Beirut, Tyre and Acre thrived as trading emporiums between East and West. Plantations of sugar cane and citrus flourished along the humid coast, while olive groves covered the hills inland. And everywhere the land was lush with holy places.

To get to Jerusalem, Reynald might have hugged the coast, then turned east at Jaffa onto the main pilgrim road to Ramleh and up through the hills. Alternatively he could have ridden inland, then south across the uplands of Samaria. Either way, he would have been riding across holy ground. The north included Galilee, with its capital Tiberias on the great lake or 'sea' where Jesus walked on the water. Jesus' home town of Nazareth was nearby, as were the sites of the miracles at Cana (water into wine) and Capernaum (healing the centurion's

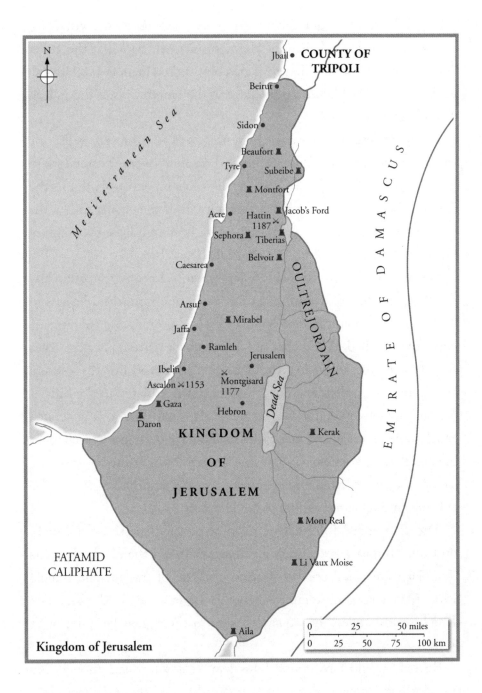

N

COUNTY OF
TRIPOLI

Jbaïl

Beirut

Mediterranean Sea

Sidon

Beaufort

Tyre

Subeibe

Montfort

Acre

Hattin
1187

Jacob's Ford

Sephora

Tiberias

Belvoir

Caesarea

OULTREJORDAIN

EMIRATE OF DAMASCUS

Arsuf

Mirabel

Jaffa

Ramleh

Jerusalem

Ibelin

Montgisard
1177

Dead Sea

Ascalon ✕1153

Gaza

Hebron

Daron

Kerak

KINGDOM

OF

JERUSALEM

Mont Real

FATAMID
CALIPHATE

Li Vaux Moise

Aila

0		25		50 miles
0	25	50	75	100 km

Kingdom of Jerusalem

servant). Conical Mount Tabor with its great monastery was visible for miles. Armageddon, Lebanon, Hermon, Carmel, Samaria, the River Jordan, the Dead Sea – the very geography of the kingdom was biblical; and, at its spiritual heart, on the edge of the barren hills of the Judean Wilderness, lay Jerusalem.

Reynald's destination was the holiest place of all – the very wellspring of the crusading spirit. Pilgrims flocked from all over Christendom to pray nearby at Christ's birthplace in Bethlehem, and to bathe in the Jordan where he was baptized. In the city itself they could follow the stations of his passion to pray at the very holy of holies, the tomb of Christ in Jerusalem's Church of the Holy Sepulchre.

When Reynald arrived in 1176, Jerusalem had been a Christian city for three-quarters of a century. After its capture from the Muslims in 1099, the Jewish and Islamic populations had been massacred and any survivors expelled. As Fulcher of Chartres had written, poor crusaders found themselves living in great mansions. Still, apart from its role as a tourist trap, Jerusalem was not a wealthy town. Isolated in the hills, it lay on no trade route, nor was it strategically sited. The ports generated much more revenue, and many sites would have been more convenient as capital, but Jerusalem was supreme through its holy associations. The main business of Jerusalem was power – it was a military base and the spiritual and temporal capital of the kingdom.

The Patriarch of Jerusalem ruled over the Palestinian Church, and the Military Orders were also headquartered there. The Knights Templar were based on the gigantic platform of the ancient Temple Mount, in Solomon's temple – actually the mosque of Al-Aqsa. The Knights Hospitallers' headquarters were in their great Hospital of St John.

Reynald would have found Jerusalem weakly fortified, though. No invader had threatened the city for decades, and the walls were in a decrepit state. Only the powerful citadel, the Tower of David, was in good repair. It was an appropriate place for Reynald to celebrate his freedom, though; with a lot of pilgrim tourists and soldiers around, the capital had a reputation as a decadent, licentious party town. We don't know how fully he took advantage of the entertainment on offer, but we do know that at court he walked into a snakepit of intrigue.

Rumour and conspiracy swirled around the boy-king Baldwin IV. The immediate incentive was who would govern when King Baldwin's leprosy made him too sick to rule. A little further ahead, ambitious nobles like Raymond of Tripoli saw an even greater prize on offer – the succession itself. Baldwin would not live long. He could not father children, and there was no clear heir apparent. Two main cliques had coalesced in the contest for power; and Raymond of Tripoli headed one of these factions. Through Baldwin IV's minority, Raymond had been too passive as regent. He had appointed the brilliant Archbishop William of Tyre as chancellor and had managed to hold the realm together, but he had signally failed to inhibit the inexorable rise of Saladin. Raymond had recently surrendered the regency when Baldwin came of age, but he was left with a taste for high office and harboured ambitions for the very summit. His support came from numerous barons, especially the influential Ibelin family, led by the prominent knight Baldwin of Ibelin and his younger brother Balian. Critically for Reynald's subsequent reputation, the historian William of Tyre was of this faction, as was the chronicler Ernoul, the squire of Balian of Ibelin.

Until the return of Reynald, the second 'royal' faction had no clear leader. It was centred on the king's mother, Agnes de Courtenay, and her brother, Count Joscelin de Courtenay, titular Count of Edessa and Reynald's long-time companion in prison. They were deeply suspicious of Raymond's regal ambitions. Their allies included a group of pushy newcomers from Poitou in France, led by the de Lusignan family. The leading churchman in their group was the Archbishop of Caesarea, Heraclius.

On his arrival, Reynald may well have met with hostility from Count Raymond, stemming from their time as POWs. And Raymond could still have harboured rancour for Reynald's part in the jilting of his sister Melisende. Even without any personal animus, Raymond and his baronial supporters would have been very wary of the prodigal Prince Reynald as a dangerous new rival on the scene. And rightfully so.

The forceful and ambitious Reynald was a formidable recruit for the royal Courtenay clique at court. In Reynald's unswerving loyalty to the crown, Raymond's lust for supreme power would find an insuperable obstacle. For the next ten years and more, the internal politics of the kingdom would be dominated by this struggle between the two men who had suffered for years in the jails of Aleppo – Raymond of Tripoli and Reynald de Chatillon. In their bitter rivalry they would each enjoy spells of pre-eminence, and their final split would come to a head in the most decisive battle of the crusades.

The Muslims had no doubt that Raymond and Reynald were the two most important Frankish leaders. Both were constantly cursed and denigrated, though Raymond was often credited with intelligence, shrewdness and wisdom, while Reynald was not. Reynald, on the other hand, was clearly regarded as the more dangerous opponent and was the more hated, feared and vilified. It was these two leaders whom Saladin's aide, the Qadi Al-Fadil, would ask the sultan to eliminate, because 'victory can only be achieved with their deaths'. From the perspective of domestic Frankish affairs, it is equally clear that Reynald was consistently the most prominent, determined and effective leader of the faction opposing Raymond's designs on the kingdom.

Despite suspicion from some quarters, Reynald returned to a hero's welcome in the Holy City. Even more than the size of his ransom, the phoenix-like resurgence of Reynald's career after his release is proof of the regard that he inspired in his fellow Franks. It is also testament to his remarkable energy and constitution. Unlike so many, who emerged broken from captivity, fifteen years of hard time had not dimmed his health or his capability for energetic and decisive action. Nor had it diminished his swagger, his vaulting ambition or his capacity to be in the right place at the right time.

The first high-level task Reynald was given demonstrates the respect in which he was held and emphasizes an aspect of his character that was clear to contemporaries, but has been almost universally ignored by subsequent historians – his diplomacy. The young King Baldwin IV chose Reynald, stepfather to Emperor Manuel's wife, Maria of Antioch, to head an embassy to Constantinople, to negotiate a strategic alliance with the empire.[6]

In contrast to the kingdom's passive stance under Raymond's regency, Reynald's re-emergence opened the door to a more combative Frankish strategy. Reynald clearly believed that the crusaders should – and, significantly, could – defeat the Muslims on the battlefield. Since the death of Nur al-Din, the Muslim emirates in Syria were weak. The real threat came from the wealthy and well-populated country of Egypt. Under Raymond, the Franks had missed a chance to strike while Saladin was still establishing his rule and they needed to remedy that mistake. Reynald's task was to convince the emperor to join in a combined invasion of Saladin's realm. The Byzantine fleet would attack Egypt from the sea and the Frankish army by land. It was an ideal first assignment for Reynald: a chance to recuperate, grow stronger and enjoy his freedom. The trip must also have been gilded with the anticipation of reuniting with his son Baldwin, now an officer in the imperial army. It is not known whether he was able to meet his daughter, Queen Agnes of Hungary, or his infant grandsons, the future kings Emeric I and Andrew II. Reynald was probably also fulfilling a duty in seeing Manuel and Maria again; if the emperor had indeed underwritten his enormous ransom, perhaps at the urging of his wife, then Reynald needed to express his gratitude. As he approached the Golden Horn and the great sea walls of Constantinople in that autumn of 1176, he must have been in a positive frame of mind, confident that his relationship with the emperor would deliver results.

But Manuel was no longer the man Reynald had bowed to in Mamistra. Earlier that year, in the summer of 1176, the emperor had marched his army into Asia Minor to crush the Seljuks of Iconium once and for all. The sultan, Kilij Arslan, offered generous peace terms, but Manuel, confident of victory, rebuffed him. His monstrous army marched on complacently and, on 17 September, pushed through a narrow pass near the ruins of the fortress at Myriokephalon. The Turks allowed the vanguard to emerge from the pass, then fell upon them from all sides. The units strung out along the trail suffered heavy casualties as they struggled up through a blinding dust storm to join the main battle. Some of the leading divisions were all but annihilated. The defeat was severe. It was not nearly as disastrous as that of Manzikert (at least Manuel had escaped, unlike the Emperor Romanus Diogenes in 1071), but it turned out to be just as significant. Sometime during the battle the iron-willed Manuel's nerve had snapped. He was never quite the same afterwards, and the empire as a whole would never fully recover from the calamity. Kilij Arslan failed to decisively exploit his victory, but it definitively ended Byzantine attempts to restore imperial authority in Anatolia, and left the Greeks permanently on the defensive. In Syria, too, the impact was not immediately felt, but it would not be long before Saladin realized that he was free to act against the Latin states without any real threat of Byzantine military intervention.

When Reynald arrived in Byzantium, the disastrous legacy for Christendom of Myriokephalon had not yet become clear, but its impact on Reynald personally was immediate and wounding. His son Baldwin had commanded a division of the Byzantine army at the battle. When the Turks surrounded them, he led his cavalry in a defiant attack. If better supported, Baldwin's charge might have swung the battle, but

Manuel's leadership and his courage had deserted him. Baldwin died fighting along with all his men, 'displaying desperate courage in their daring and noble deeds'.[7] Reynald could be proud of his son, but what a devastating blow this tragedy must have been to him, still in the first flush of joy at his freedom. Amongst the many things that fifteen years of imprisonment had cost Prince Reynald was the chance ever to know his son as a man.

Despite Byzantium's weakened state and Reynald's personal loss, the mission had a positive outcome. Essentially it reaffirmed the Byzantine protectorate over Jerusalem previously agreed by King Amalric. The terms of the deal are interesting as they reflect those negotiated by Reynald to save his skin back in 1159. Manuel agreed to send his fleet, which was still intact, to conquer Egypt with the Franks. In return, the Kingdom of Jerusalem would recognize Byzantine suzerainty and accept the return of an Orthodox patriarch to the Holy City. The attack on Egypt was set for the campaigning season of 1177. To crown the success of his embassy, Reynald also succeeded in negotiating the betrothal of his stepson, Prince Bohemond of Antioch, to the emperor's great-niece Theodora. Bohemond and Reynald may not have seen eye-to-eye, but when it came to marriage alliances, Bohemond let the master weave his magic.

Reynald's diplomatic accomplishment immediately added to his prestige and further impressed the new generation of nobles in the Kingdom of Jerusalem. Reynald had a princely title and a reputation, but neither would have carried any weight with the cynical baronage without his obvious abilities and their proofs – such as his diplomatic success. The landless Joscelin had risen to the post of seneschal immediately on his release, but he was King Baldwin's uncle, brother of the king's mother, the influential Queen Agnes. Reynald had the support of his old cellmate, but no family connections in Jerusalem. He had no land or wealth to buy support, or vassals to enforce it. He had to walk the walk and exploit his energy and charisma. With his reputation running high on his return from Constantinople, Reynald set his sights even higher.

Of the most powerful political roles in the kingdom, Joscelin had taken the office of 'Seneschal', as we have seen. The chief military post, that of 'Constable', was occupied by the greatly respected Humphrey II of Toron. The greatest prize still on offer was the hand of *La Dame du Crac*, Stephanie de Milly, widow of the murdered Miles de Plancy. Stephanie carried with her the rights to the fief of Oultrejordan and its great fortresses, the *Crac de Mont Real* and the incomparable *Crac de Moab* (Kerak). Reynald again managed to position himself correctly and, just as he had outwitted other suitors in Antioch to marry Constance, so he was selected by the king as the ideal candidate for this job – a critical one for the kingdom's defence. The Prince of Antioch was resurrected as Seigneur of Oultrejordan, Lord of Kerak and Mont Real. The new wife, Stephanie de Milly, came with the territory. His contemporaries were clear about why Reynald was so rewarded:

> *Because he had guarded the Land of Antioch so well, and because*
> *of what a fine knight he was, they gave him the Lady of Kerak*
> *and Mont Real to be his wife.*[8]

We do not know how old Stephanie was when she married Reynald – she may still have been in her twenties – but she was already an old hand at political marriages. Her first was to Humphrey III of Toron, son of the constable, by whom she had two children, Humphrey IV and Isabelle. On her first husband's death in 1173, she was quickly wedded to the seneschal Miles de Plancy, who was murdered in 1174. An intriguer in her own right, she was firmly embedded in the Courtenay clique at court. There is no evidence that she had any particular attraction or emotional attachment to Reynald. Whereas Reynald's first marriage in his twenties was partly romantic, his second at around fifty years of age appears to have been purely political. Reynald was to prove himself a loyal father to his new stepchildren, but he and Stephanie would have no children of their own.

Once again, Reynald had fallen on his feet in a spectacular way, but his resurgence was not universally popular in Jerusalem. Ambitious local barons had hoped to marry the eligible *Dame du Crac*, and would have been miffed at this outsider swooping in and stealing her from under their noses. Raymond and his baronial supporters would have seen it as a significant power shift towards the Courtenay faction. Reynald's marriage to Stephanie de Milly further committed him to this party; Stephanie had no love for Raymond, suspecting him of the murder of her previous husband, Miles de Plancy.

As Lord of Oultrejordan, Reynald added immense wealth and power to his personal strengths. Overnight he became one of the mightiest feudal barons in the country, owing the service of sixty knights to the crown. Oultrejordan's knight-service was exceeded only by the hundred knights owed by Raymond's principality of Galilee, by the lordship of Sidon and by the fief of Jaffa and Ascalon, traditionally granted to a royal prince or husband of a princess.[9]

Reynald's pre-eminence among the barons of the kingdom is quickly seen in the records. From 1177 onwards, Reynald put his signature on many royal documents, always as the first or second of the magnates to sign after the king – a clear indication of his precedence at court. He was certainly involved in the major decisions affecting the realm. The most pressing issue they had to confront was the succession. The ailing King Baldwin would not live long, but as a leper he could not marry. His heirs were his sisters, Sybilla and Isabella. In 1176, to ensure a male successor, Sybilla married the able and popular William 'Longsword' of Montferrat. In the event of Baldwin's death he might have made a good regent and, in time, a good king.

As the year 1177 progressed, King Baldwin's health deteriorated again. A deputy was needed to run the affairs of the kingdom. The obvious choice would have been William Longsword, but in June 1177, struck down by another of Outremer's mysterious illnesses, he died, leaving Sybilla pregnant. King Baldwin then turned to the most reliable and respected of his nobles, Reynald de Chatillon. Reynald was appointed 'Procurator' of the army and the kingdom, effectively the king's executive regent. Raymond of Tripoli and his sympathizers would not have been pleased at this severe affront. It was clear that the king no longer regarded Raymond as the leading man of the realm. Reynald's preferment was an openly critical verdict on Count Raymond's past performance as regent and his unwillingness to take on Saladin. It also demonstrated the desire of the king and the royal faction to distance the power-hungry Raymond from the crown.

Reynald, on the other hand, though ambitious, had no claim to the throne and was extremely loyal. As Professor Bernard Hamilton points out, another reason for choosing Reynald was that any regent would have to work with the Byzantines in the planned invasion of Egypt.[10] Given his many dealings with Manuel, Reynald was best suited to that task. He had offended the emperor, yes; but he had subsequently shown a grasp of realpolitik, understood Byzantine ways and had done his penance. On the other hand, the Greeks may not have accepted Raymond as commander-in-chief of the Franks. Raymond had still not reconciled with the emperor since Manuel condemned his sister to spinsterhood, and his savage revenge raid on Cyprus, unlike Reynald's, remained unexpiated.

Overall there was agreement amongst the barons on the appointment of Reynald. According to William of Tyre, then chancellor of the kingdom, Prince Reynald 'often exercised command in place of the sick sovereign'[11] and was given the honour of executive regent because he was 'a man of proven loyalty and unusual steadfastness of character'.[12]

The lowly Burgundian knight was therefore effectively running the Kingdom of Jerusalem when, in August 1177, the great magnate Count Philip of Flanders arrived from Europe on crusade. The son of the serial crusader Thierry of Flanders, Philip was a ready-made solution for the Kingdom of Jerusalem's internal political divisions – if he could be persuaded to stay and take charge. Philip also arrived with a large troop of knights, a formidable addition to the Frankish field army, now in readiness for the imminent invasion of Egypt. King Baldwin was again unwell and was staying at Ascalon on the coast, for his health. He was carried on a litter up to Jerusalem, where he offered the regency to Philip. This might have been a snub to Reynald, but he never seems to have borne the king any ill will, and his loyalty to the royal party in the kingdom did not waver. In any case, Philip declined the offer. He had no wish to remain in the East as on-off regent while the king's health waxed and waned. King Baldwin then offered him command of the invasion of Egypt, but again Philip demurred. He would not accept the leadership unless he had the right to rule the conquered territories. This was unacceptable to the king and his barons. Just as Philip's father Thierry had found at the sieges of Damascus and Shazyar, the local nobility could not countenance such a great prize falling into the hands of a visitor. Moreover, in this case the Franks had no room for manoeuvre. The treaty with Manuel promised that any Egyptian conquests would become Byzantine territory.

When Philip rejected the post, Reynald was reconfirmed as commander-in-chief. Normally military command would have devolved on the constable, Humphrey II of Toron, but he was also very ill. Again Reynald's appointment had the support of the kingdom's nobility. Unfortunately Philip, recalling Thierry's quarrel with Reynald at Shayzar, categorically refused to serve under the Lord of Kerak.

While the Franks bickered, a magnificent imperial fleet of seventy galleys and their support ships sailed into the port of Acre. The Greek field army may have been shattered at Myriokephalon, but their sea power was still intact and ready to implement the alliance negotiated by Reynald. Among the fleet's passengers was the Orthodox Patriarch of Jerusalem, Leontius, who was to spend an uncomfortable few months in the Latin Kingdom before returning to Constantinople. Weeks passed and the Byzantines watched in increasing impatience and alarm as the invasion plans stuttered and then stalled. Meanwhile Saladin, with ample warning of his enemies' intentions, gathered a huge army to defend the Egyptian frontier.

The machinations of Reynald's rivals lay behind Philip's hesitations. Raymond of Tripoli could not bring himself to fight alongside the Byzantines, or under the orders of Reynald de Chatillon, and his hand was revealed when, eventually, the frustrated Philip abandoned the Kingdom of Jerusalem. He took his men, along with a hundred local knights – the pick of Jerusalem's fighting men – and went north to campaign with Raymond and Bohemond of Antioch. This drove another wedge between Reynald's faction and that of Raymond of Tripoli. Many of the Franks blamed Philip's uncooperative attitude on the intrigues of Raymond and his ally Bohemond, who was also perhaps taking the chance to get one over on his stepfather. According to William of Tyre:

> It was said that they tried to entice him [Philip] to their own lands, hoping with his help to undertake something which would benefit their states.[13]

In the end they achieved nothing more than abortive attacks on Hama and Harim. Philip, like his father, went home empty-handed. He had fulfilled his crusading vows, but had failed to maximize the potential of his military might for the benefit of Christendom.

Meanwhile the Egyptian invasion plan was in tatters. The splendid Byzantine war fleet weighed anchor and sailed back to Constantinople.

A real chance – perhaps the only one the Franks would ever have – to break Saladin's power was over, without ever beginning. The manoeuvrings of Raymond and Bohemond had ruined the kingdom's offensive plans, soured relations with Byzantium and handed its commander-in-chief, Reynald, a perilous strategic position.

In anticipation of the amphibious invasion, Saladin had assembled an enormous, experienced and well-equipped army in the Nile delta. The combination of Egyptian and Syrian squadrons provided him with spectacular armed strength. 'No Muslim leader ever had an army like this,' said Saladin's right-hand man, the Qadi Al-Fadil, after watching a march-past of almost 150 divisions in Cairo. With the departure of the Greek fleet to Byzantium and substantial Frankish forces to the north, the kingdom had been left undefended. Saladin saw the chance to use his incomparable army in attack. He was already suspected of caring more about his own career than the good of Islam. Saladin's Muslim opponents frequently pointed out that he spent far more time fighting them than he did in prosecuting the jihad against the infidel. For the sake of his reputation, Saladin needed a success against the Franks.

Saladin invaded the Kingdom of Jerusalem.

Marching rapidly across the desert, he left his heavy baggage at the ruins of the ancient pharaonic city of Al-Arish and swooped into Palestine with a huge army of around 26,000 men. These were mostly highly mobile horse archers, but also included a seasoned corps of 8,000 heavier Mamluk cavalry and Saladin's elite guard. They ravaged the countryside, capturing, killing and 'tearing to pieces' as they went. Bypassing the powerful fortress at Gaza and its garrison of eighty Templar knights, they appeared before Ascalon on 23 November 1177. The savagery of this incursion is preserved in Michael the Syrian's lurid propaganda story that Saladin sacrificed a captive Frank and then washed in his blood.

Learning of the invasion, the king issued the *arrière ban*. Only used as a last resort in times of utmost need, this proclamation summoned every able-bodied man in the kingdom to arms. Baldwin himself was so ill that his life was despaired of, but with great courage he rode out at the head of his host. Under the generalship of Prince Reynald, the army marched south from Jerusalem in haste and managed to arrive at Ascalon just before Saladin. Underlining the gravity of the emergency, they had marched from Jerusalem with the True Cross, the holiest relic of the Latin East. Covered in gold and encrusted with jewels, it was said to contain wood from the very cross on which Christ was crucified. They had also marched with every knight still left in the kingdom.

When Saladin's army appeared before Ascalon, Reynald led the royal host out in front of the city. The Frankish army was sizeable – around 500 knights, and perhaps a few thousand sergeants and Turcopoles – but Saladin's vast army outnumbered them many times over. The cause was clearly hopeless, and 'those most experienced in war', like Reynald, favoured caution. Skirmishes and single combats took place, but the Franks stood off from the enemy attacks. The Muslim force was too numerous to risk camping in the open, so as night drew in, Reynald ordered the retreat behind the walls of Ascalon. Confident that the relatively small Frankish army posed no threat, Saladin left it in his rear and marched on deeper into Palestine, ravaging the countryside as he went. So sure of victory were the invaders, remembered William of Tyre, that:

> They no longer remained in close array but paraded about in admiration of their own prowess. As though already victorious, Saladin began to allot definite parts of his conquered possessions to his fellow soldiers, and his forces, as if they had already secured all they desired, began to conduct themselves with utter disregard of caution. In scattered bands they wandered freely about and scoured the country in every direction.[14]

While Saladin's men pillaged the kingdom unopposed, no reinforcements arrived for the increasingly beleaguered Frankish army in Ascalon. As the militia levies from around the kingdom hurried towards the coast to answer the call of the *arrière ban*, they were intercepted in droves by Saladin's men and either killed or roped together and sent to the rear, to be sold as slaves. Saladin's forces spread out across the coastal plain as far as Ramleh and the foot of the road leading up through the hills to Jerusalem itself. There was panic in the capital, which the king had stripped of its defenders.

The terrified populace abandoned the city with its rundown walls and crowded into the citadel, the Tower of David. Saladin was on the verge of total victory.

Reynald de Chatillon was faced with a desperate situation. The king was severely ill. There, in the field, Reynald was the acting head of the kingdom and the general of its army. He was the man best versed in the arts of war; the steadfast, valiant leader in whom the barons of the kingdom had put their trust. Now, with Saladin's troops burning, looting and killing in the heart of the realm, and with nothing between them and the capital, he would have to justify that trust.

As Prince of Antioch, Reynald had bitter experience of challenging superior Turkish forces in battle, but as he considered his options that winter's night, he would have realized that, faced with the destruction of the kingdom, he had little choice. He decided to offer battle. Collecting the Templar knights from Gaza, Reynald marched the army north along the coast, then turned inland in search of Saladin's victorious hordes. Marching towards the town of Ramleh, they entered a ravaged landscape covered with drifting smoke and lit by flames from burning villages. Tragic reports of massacres and devastation arrived from all directions, imbuing the Christians with burning rage and a deep resolve. As they advanced, they drove off groups of Muslim looters and skirmishers and then, sometime around midday on 25 November, they sighted the enemy's main force. Saladin's army had lost cohesion and was missing various units that were out scouring the plain, but it was still many times larger than the Frankish army.

Behind their desperately ill leper-king, the Christian host knelt before the True Cross and, weeping and pledging to fight to the death, prayed fervently for divine aid.

Mont Gisard, Palestine, St Catherine's Day, 25 November 1177

Around the middle of that winter day the army of the Kingdom of Jerusalem, led by Reynald de Chatillon, formed their ranks near the long, low hill of Mont Gisard, the tel that hides the biblical city of Gezer.

In front of the crusaders loomed a terrifying sight. The rolling plain was hidden under a roiling, swirling host of thousands of horsemen, their yellow, green and black banners whirling, drums and trumpets sounding as they galloped into formation. The situation looked grim for the defiant warriors drawn up around the True Cross. While there was no room for retreat, a pitched battle carried grave risks. Defeat would mean annihilation, the loss of Jerusalem and of much of the kingdom, at a stroke.

But the experienced military eye would have spotted some confusion in Saladin's manoeuvres. The sultan's army had been caught unprepared. Many of his troops were still out pillaging far and wide. In some consternation, Saladin sent urgently to summon them back to the main force.

Though he had achieved a measure of surprise, Reynald did not rush pell-mell into the fight. Surveying the enemy shrewdly, he drew his forces up in battle array and held his knights in check, waiting for the right moment to deliver the telling charge. Faced with such overwhelming numbers, he knew they might get only one chance. Still unsettled, Saladin's divisions began an intricate tactical manoeuvre to improve their position. This disturbed their formation. Reynald saw an opportunity and made a momentous decision. He attacked.

Yelling their war cries, the heavy Frankish cavalry charged en masse into the heart of the Turkish lines. 'Agile as wolves' and 'ardent as the flame', they swooped down on Saladin's forces 'as an eagle pounces on a flock of partridges'.[15]

The Muslim centre was commanded by Taqi al-Din, Saladin's nephew. A capable general, he held his men together in the face of the ferocious crusader onslaught, and the two armies collided with shocking force. One band of knights cut right through the Muslim ranks to within reach of Saladin himself. He was saved only by the last-ditch intervention of his personal bodyguard.

Leaving carnage in his wake, Reynald plunged into the thick of the fight. That day, as years of pent-up frustration and inactivity boiled over in the rage of battle, he personally performed the greatest feats of valour on the field.

For a while the Turkish centre held off the Franks, with grim slaughter on both sides, but Reynald had judged his tactics well. With the momentum of attack and inspired by holy zeal, the fury of the heavily armoured crusaders at close quarters was simply irresistible.

As the True Cross glowed with a mysterious light, God stirred up a whirlwind against the enemy and St George appeared on the crusaders' side, the fight turned inexorably their way. The Muslims began to suffer a terrible butchery. Despite their massive superiority in numbers, the Muslim ranks wavered, tottered and then collapsed in confusion.

Saladin's proud army turned and fled.

Chapter 12

HERO

… we shall soon see fields strewn with pieces of helmets and shields and swords and saddle-bows and men cleft through their bodies to their girdles, and we shall see horses running wild and many lances in side and breast, and joy and tears and dole and rejoicing; the loss will be great and the gain will be immense.

Bertran de Born[1]

The Franks hounded the routed rabble across the plain. Enslaving and killing without mercy, they harried them for twelve leagues, as far as the swamps known as the Marsh of the Starlings. Only the onset of night saved the Muslims from complete annihilation.

Along with thousands of captives, the booty of horses, tents, weapons and armour was staggering. The Franks captured Saladin's camp and all his treasure on the field. As the Muslim army disintegrated around them, the captive levies from the *arrière ban* slipped their shackles and killed the guards, seizing supplies and remounts. In their flight, the Muslims had discarded anything that weighed them down, and from the sedge and reed beds the Franks dredged out breastplates, helmets, shields and weapons of every sort. 'Roland and Oliver,' wrote Ernoul in reference to the great heroes of the *chansons*, 'did not take so many arms at the battle of Ronceval.' Scattered stragglers and bands of looters were easily rounded up over the next few days. The most enthusiastic of the Frankish pursuers took almost a week to return, leading camels heavy with saddles, rich vestments, coats of mail and more. For weeks afterwards, prisoners were brought in from caves, forests and mountains. Many gave themselves up, preferring captivity to the privations of hunger and cold in the rainy winter weather.

For the Muslim soldiers who escaped the battle, further hardship was to come. Weary and demoralized, without food or shelter, they were beset by ten days of violent rainstorms and bitter cold. Their exhausted horses, already tired and hungry after the desert crossing and days of hard riding across Palestine, could not cope with the return journey. They expired in droves. Worse, as the tattered remnants of Saladin's army struggled back across the wild, rain-lashed wastes, Bedouin Arab tribesmen harassed them mercilessly. The opportunistic nomads also seized the sultan's heavy baggage at Al-Arish. As William of Tyre gloated:

> Thus those who thought they had escaped from us fell into [the Bedouin's] hands as prey, so that the prophecy seemed to be fulfilled which says, 'that which the locust hath left, hath the canker-worm eaten.'[2]

Saladin himself, having only just escaped the battlefield unscathed, barely evaded the Bedouin's clutches. He made it back to Egypt on a camel, with just a small group of retainers.

The battle is usually quickly passed over in modern histories, but Mont Gisard in November 1177 was perhaps the greatest victory won by a Frankish army in the history of crusading in the Levant. It certainly ranks with the decisive battles at Doryleum and Antioch during the

First Crusade. To look at it from another point of view, a Frankish defeat on this scale would have precipitated the fall of the kingdom. Even where the impact of the battle is pointed out, it is routine for historians to give all the credit for the triumph to the brave boy-king Baldwin and to gloss over the fact that Reynald was the victorious general. Some contemporary historians were guilty of this as well. Typically, William of Tyre minimizes Reynald's contribution, just as he passed over Reynald's deeds at Ascalon in 1153. Describing the battle of Mont Gisard, the usually thorough historian simply mentions Reynald's presence as the leading lay baron, but cannot stretch to praising his political rival. Luckily we have Muslim and other Christian sources to confirm Reynald's role. Ernoul says simply: 'It was Reynald, Lord of Kerak, who fought with the greatest prowess in the battle of Mont Gisard.'[3] Baha al-Din, Saladin's biographer, confirms that: 'The commander of the Franks was Prince Reynald, who had recently been ransomed at Aleppo.'[4]

Not much of this campaign fits with the received caricature of Reynald. His appointment as general for loyalty and steadfastness, his prudent tactics at Ascalon, his clever decision to march up the coast and surprise the enemy – none of it matches the image of the irresponsible robber baron. One act does fit: the final, all-or-nothing battle against the odds. But Reynald was well versed in warfare. He knew how to even the game in his favour; knew the capability of his troops and that of his enemy. On this occasion, with an inspired, unified force, well led and fighting with rage and determination, Reynald took the hard choice to fight. A defeat would have meant annihilation and the loss of the kingdom. Reynald won.

The Lord of Kerak did not deliver a painless triumph. Mont Gisard was a costly victory for the Franks. Casualties were heavy in their ranks as well, sustained mainly in the bitter mêlée against the staunch divisions of Saladin's yellow-clad Mamluk bodyguard under Taqi al-Din, whose son was killed in the struggle. The crusader dead numbered more than 1,000 men. The Knights Hospitaller in Jerusalem took in 750 wounded. Still, King Baldwin returned to Jerusalem in triumph, laden with the spoils of war. To commemorate the victory on St Catherine's Day, Baldwin later built a monastery on the site, called 'St Catherine of the Battlefield'.

Although Saladin's propagandists tried to minimize the damage, the defeat was a major setback and a profound humiliation for the sultan. According to Michael the Syrian, '[Saladin] was covered in shame… he put on robes of mourning, shut himself in a room and imposed on himself several days in the dark, as penance'.[5]

Almost a decade would pass before Saladin could win a victory great enough to erase the ignominy of Mont Gisard. The battle was also the first of many occasions on which he had cause to regret the presence of Reynald de Chatillon in his enemy's ranks. Neither man knew it then, but Mont Gisard was the beginning of a monumental struggle to the death. Just as Reynald's contest with Raymond dominated the Franks' internal politics, so his confrontation with Saladin would frame Christian–Muslim relations for the next decade. At Mont Gisard, Reynald announced his reappearance on the military stage in the most stunning fashion.

It was a great victory, but even in their triumph the Franks may have seen fateful signs. Despite the obliteration of Saladin's army, the resources of Egypt – in riches and manpower – were limitless, and the defeat had hardly dented the Muslim forces of Syria. While the crusaders did not have the military resources to follow up their victory, within months Saladin's armies were up and moving again. For the Franks to deal a knockout blow against their Muslim enemies was virtually impossible, but to survive they had to keep fighting. Their task was to reduce Saladin's resources and at all costs prevent his complete domination of Syria as well as Egypt.

In this strategic battle, Reynald and his fief of Oultrejordan would form the front line.

Chapter 13

LORD OF
LA GRANDE BERRIE

Kerak is the anxiety that blocks the throat, the dust that obscures sight, the obstacle that strangles hopes and lies in ambush to overcome heroic resistance. This fortress is a wolf placed in this valley by fortune.

Al-Qadi al-Fadil

Raids are our agriculture.

Bedouin proverb

In the wake of the battle of Mont Gisard in November 1177, Reynald's reputation was stratospheric. There is no doubt that he continued to play a leading role in the affairs of the kingdom, and he was present in all the major confrontations involving the army of Jerusalem. But beyond that, the chroniclers are quiet as to his exact whereabouts. Presumably whenever the young king's health recovered enough for him to take day-to-day charge of events, the need for an executive regent faded and Reynald would repair to his domains in Oultrejordan. In his new frontline fief, as in Antioch, he would spend more time in armour than in his court finery.

The strategic importance of Oultrejordan to the Kingdom of Jerusalem far outweighed its feudal obligations. King Baldwin I had recognized its value in the earliest days of the Latin Kingdom and had laid the foundations of the fiefdom in a series of daring and far-reaching raids into the unknown. He made his first crossing of the Jordan River in 1101, and in 1107 evicted a Turkish army from the ancient Nabatean city of Petra. In 1116 he campaigned far out across *La Grande Berrie*, the great southern desert, and captured Aila (the modern Eilat or Aqaba), the port at the tip of the Red Sea and a staging post on the desert trail between Egypt, Syria and Arabia.

To dominate these vast territories, the Franks built lonely outposts in the void. Reynald's tours of his far-flung dominions would have included the oasis of woods and crops at Shawbak, where Baldwin founded Oultrejordan's first castle, the imposing *Crac de Mont Real*, in 1115. A day's ride south lay the imposing ruins of Petra, where a stone castle was erected on a steepling crag at *Li Vaux Moise*, the Valley of Moses. The castle was perched on the edge of a precipitous chasm, reachable only by a narrow bridge to a gateway hollowed from the rose-red rock itself. Nearby were other small castles such as Al-Habis and, further south looking over the Wadi Araba, the fort of Hormuz.

The greatest stronghold of Oultrejordan was further to the north, at the top of a canyon running down to the Dead Sea. The capital of the biblical Moabites, it was called *Petra Deserti*, 'Rock of the Desert', or *Crac de Moab*, 'Fortress of Moab'. The Muslims called it the 'Castle of the Raven'. Most commonly, in view of its incomparable might, it was known simply as Kerak, meaning 'Fortress'. The Muslim traveller Ibn Battuta described it as:

one of the most marvellous, impregnable and celebrated of
fortresses. It is surrounded on all sides by the riverbed and has but
one gate, the entrance to which is hewn in the living rock.[1]

Construction of Kerak had begun under the Frankish knight Pagan
the Butler in 1142. Successive lords had added to its defences, and by the
time Reynald became its master in the late twelfth century, Kerak was one
of the most powerful fortresses on earth. It was the final element in the
domination of the biblical lands of Idumea and Moab. In his vast fief and
stupendous fastnesses, the Lord of Kerak was effectively an independent
ruler in his domain, something Reynald would have appreciated. His High
Court was the final authority, from which there was no appeal. As early
as 1177 he was signing charters in his fief using his own name, without
mentioning his wife Stephanie: *Ego Raynaldus, quondam Antiochaie*
princeps et nunc, per Dei Gratiam, Hebronensis et Montis Regalis Princeps
('I, Reynald, onetime Prince of Antioch and now, by the grace of God,
Prince of Hebron and Mont Real'). Like a king in his realm, Reynald
was lord in his, by the grace of God. It was also the first time that a Lord
of Oultrejordan styled himself as 'Prince'. Reynald would accept no step
down from the status he had enjoyed in Antioch.

And though Oultrejordan could not compete with the delights of the
ancient metropolis, Reynald would still live in greater splendour than a
monarch in the rough and ready West. The great castles were princely
residences and administrative centres as well as military bases. They
had bathhouses, gracious chapels, luxurious bedchambers and grand
public rooms hung with damask and tapestry, decorated with painted
ceilings, bright murals and intricate carvings in marble and polished
wood. Carpets covered the floors, and the sumptuous meals of the lords
of Kerak, rich with rare spices, were served on platters of precious metal
and porcelain from China. The Franks – both men and women – wore
robes of silk embroidered with golden thread and hung with gems.

Outside the castles, the desert brooded. Enemies lurked in the endless wastes, and wolves, hyenas and lions prowled. In winter it was cold, and snow swept the high ground and drifted deep in the barren canyons plunging to the Dead Sea. In summer the burning *khamsin* winds buffeted the walls. Still, in the region of Kerak and Shawbak, this was wealthy country. Planted with grapes and olives, the land was 'pleasant, healthy and very fertile in wheat, wine and oil'. There were fruitful cornfields and cane plantations producing the famous 'sugar of Kerak', which was exported as syrup or crystal.[2] Kerak also controlled the 'Sea of the Devil' – the Dead Sea – with its saltpans and its rich trade in asphalt. The asphalt, known as 'the stone of Moses', bubbled to the surface in vast floating blocks. 'The people gather it and sell it to all cities and countries round,' recorded the Persian traveller Nasir-i-Khusrow. Its main uses were for waterproofing, medicaments and fuel. 'When you light this rock,' wrote the thirteenth-century Syrian geographer al-Dimashqi, 'it burns like wood.'

The most productive revenue-generator was the passing caravan traffic of merchants and pilgrims. Some of these caravans could be huge, numbering thousands of camels.* The caravans were there to trade with, to be tolled or, as any self-respecting frontier baron like Reynald would have appreciated, to be raided. In every case, the Lord of Oultrejordan had to compete, or cooperate, with the Bedouin, the true lords of these desert lands. Tribes like the Banu Fuhayd and the Banu Ubayy may have been Muslim in name, but they owed allegiance to no earthly power and preyed on Christian and Muslim alike. As the State of Israel was to do 800 years later, the Franks struck up a good relationship with the Bedouin. The kings of Jerusalem co-opted the nomads as allies, giving them rights to extensive grazing lands in the Negev desert in the south of the kingdom. Just as he had proved able to work with the

---

* For instance, William Clito, grandson of William the Conqueror, captured a caravan of 4,000 camels while on crusade.

different native communities in Antioch, Reynald de Chatillon did the same in Oultrejordan. Again belying his unjustified reputation as an unadapted and incomprehending newcomer, he built up an effective alliance with the Bedouin, who proved to be useful spies, guides and auxiliaries. Saladin and his allies despised these opportunistic Muslim tribesmen as traitors. Saladin's secretary, Imad al-Din, complained that:

> He [Reynald] had with him a troop of people without shame, a
> disgrace to our religion. They lived around the route to the Hejaz,
> and for them the pilgrimage was nothing but a metaphor.[3]

Reynald may even have travelled into the wilderness of Sinai. This biblical landscape also, in theory, fell under the rule of the Lord of Oultrejordan, though in reality it was no-man's-land. He may well have visited the great Monastery of St Catherine at the foot of Mount Sinai itself. Completing the tour of his vast domains, he would have taken in the Lordship of Hebron, west of the Jordan in the Judean hills. This prestigious territory had been added to the fief of Oultrejordan as another recognition of Reynald's stature. Here, in the town of Hebron itself, the crusaders had raised a great church on ancient Herodian foundations of gargantuan limestone blocks. Beneath the church were caves containing the venerated tombs of Abraham, Isaac and Jacob, along with their wives. This holy site attracted thriving and profitable pilgrim traffic.

For Saladin, the wedge of Frankish territory jutting east of the Jordan and down across the desert was always an irritation and sometimes a serious strategic problem. Reynald's fief throttled trade, cut communication between Egypt and Syria, hampered the movements of Muslim armies and made the pilgrim route to western Arabia and the Muslim holy cities in the Hejaz impassable or, at least, very costly. As Saladin's biographer, Baha al-Din, recorded, Oultrejordan was:

an obstacle on the route of everyone travelling to Egypt. No
caravan was able to get through unless he [Saladin] went out in
person to convey it through the enemy's lands.[4]

Reynald's men could intercept Saladin's couriers, and any travel between Egypt and Syria risked attack by the Franks. In oases and in ravines like al-Jafr and Muwailih, they would lie in wait for any prey that took their fancy. In 1154, for instance, the Egyptian vizier Al-Abbas had fled across the desert with a vast hoard of treasure. The Franks ambushed him at the oasis of Muwailih, killing Abbas along with one of his sons and stealing all his wealth. Usama Ibn Munqidh, travelling with the vizier, managed to escape, but having eluded the Franks, he almost fell into the clutches of the Bedouin Banu Fuhayd, who killed any stragglers they could find. To avoid the Frankish depredations, many Egyptian pilgrims now took the risky crossing of the Red Sea from the port of Aydhab to the Hejaz. Coming from Syria, pilgrims and military expeditions had to take the longer route via the Darb al-Hajj, the pilgrim road across the desert fringes, or move even further out into the deep desert along a line of remote oases.

This was the key fief that the king had assigned to the noble most likely to keep his foot on the Muslims' throat – Reynald de Chatillon. From now on, unlike during the first part of his career, Reynald fought exclusively against Muslims. The modern historian of Baldwin IV's reign, Bernard Hamilton, suggests this was because of a change in his mentality in prison, making him a more responsible member of the crusading fraternity, focused on the common good rather than his own quarrels. It also fits with Professor Carole Hillenbrand's contention that Reynald developed a 'profound and settled hatred' for Islam while in prison. However, the great change between Reynald's wars before and after his imprisonment can best be explained by geography. As Prince of Antioch, he had to maintain the principality against Armenians and Byzantines as well as Muslims. He fought them all. Later, as Seigneur of Oultrejordan, his task was to protect his fief and impede communications between Egypt and Syria. Here all his enemies were Muslim. He fought them all, too. One thing he was prepared to do in Antioch, which he would not do in Kerak, was bow to a more powerful enemy. Reynald subjected himself to the suzerainty of the Christian emperor of Byzantium. He would never do the same to the Muslim sultan of Syria and Egypt. On the contrary, whatever danger it exposed him to, Reynald would do anything he could to make Saladin's life more difficult.

With Reynald *in situ*, the Franks in Oultrejordan would only become more of a menace to Saladin's plans. Under the predatory Reynald, wrote the Qadi Al-Fadil, the castles of Kerak and Mont Real were like wild beasts: 'There was not a day which passed when they did not devour the flesh of men or drink their blood.' Given its importance, this territory was subject to repeated invasions by Muslim powers. Nur al-Din had attacked Kerak in 1170. Saladin had captured Aila in 1171 and attacked Kerak as early as 1172, aiming to 'widen and improve the road so that the regions might be in contact with one another, and to make things easier for travellers'.[5] With the bellicose Reynald as lord, many more attacks were to come.

In April 1178, Saladin moved to Syria with a substantial army, using the longer desert route. Reynald was unable to impede his progress, but once Saladin had passed by, Reynald struck at the Saracen desert fort of Qalat Guindi. This guarded the oasis one marching stage before Aila on the trail from Egypt.[6] Though the attack failed, it showed Reynald's more militant intent and was one of the few aggressive military actions by the Franks in 1178, which was on the whole a peaceful year in the Levant. Saladin was unwilling to risk another defeat on the battlefield, and the Franks too preferred to lick their wounds and repair their fortresses, including the walls of Jerusalem, which had been found so wanting when menaced by Saladin's invasion.

In the spring of 1179, King Baldwin IV had recovered sufficiently from his illness to raid the herds of Damascus near Banyas. Surprised by the Turks, the king managed to escape, but in a blow to the kingdom, the revered constable Humphrey II of Toron was killed. In a coup for Reynald's faction, Amalric de Lusignan was appointed constable in his stead. He was one of the leading Poitevin knights at court, and reputedly a lover of Queen Agnes. Soon afterwards Saladin won another sharp encounter at Marj Ayyun. Once more the young leper-king barely got away. Unhorsed during the battle, Baldwin was incapable of remounting by himself. A knight had to carry him to safety on piggyback. Baldwin was again becoming very ill. As he wrote to King Louis VII:

> *To be deprived of the use of one's limbs is of little help to one in carrying on the work of government. If I could be cured of the disease of Naaman, I would wash seven times in the Jordan.*[7]

Baldwin asked Louis VII to choose one of his great French barons to marry his sister Sybilla and take over the kingdom. The crusaders' preference was Hugh of Burgundy. Baldwin was now so ill that he expressed a wish to abdicate in Hugh's favour. But Hugh never came. Sybilla meanwhile had borne her dead husband, William of Montferrat, a posthumous son, also called Baldwin. Officially he was heir to the leper-king's throne, but as he was still an infant, the succession remained very much in the balance.

The inevitable factionalism was not long in reappearing. At Easter 1180, with all to play for, Raymond of Tripoli made his move. Supported by Bohemond of Antioch, he approached the kingdom with a substantial force. William of Tyre says that King Baldwin, fearing a *coup d'état*, refused them entry to the kingdom:

> *At that time the lord Prince Bohemond of Antioch and the Lord*
> *Count Raymond of Tripoli, entering the Kingdom with an army,*
> *terrified the lord king who feared lest they should attempt to*
> *organise a revolution by deposing the king and laying claim to the*
> *kingdom for themselves.*[8]

To head off this attempted coup, Baldwin and the Courtenay faction quickly needed to find a viable, adult male heir. Perhaps partly following Sybilla's personal preference, they turned to a surprising candidate, a handsome young knight from Poitou, Guy de Lusignan, brother of Constable Amalric. Reynald would have well understood the consternation that accompanied the king's choice of this little-known knight. William of Tyre was even more critical of Guy than he had been of Reynald on his marriage to Constance a generation earlier. He said that Guy, who had taken the cross to expiate his murder of the Earl of Salisbury, was 'an obscure man, wholly incapable and indiscreet'. Archbishop William, a partisan of Count Raymond, thought the king had made a hasty error of judgement:

> *Although there were men in the kingdom who were more noble,*
> *more brave and more wealthy… to whom [King Baldwin] might*
> *more fittingly for reasons of state have given his sister's hand, he*
> *did not give sufficient weight to the maxim that 'acting on impulse*
> *causes harm to everything.'*[9]

The powerful Ibelin clan, with lands throughout the kingdom, was also disgusted with the choice of Guy as heir to the throne. This was partly because the head of the family, Baldwin of Ibelin, had fancied a royal title and aspired to marry Sybilla himself. Reynald, as a member of the royal 'Courtenay' faction in opposition to Raymond and the Ibelins, was naturally a key supporter of Guy.

This debilitating factionalism is the background to the two-year truce that was agreed with Saladin around May 1180. Reynald was presumably involved in the decision, but not as executive regent. He could not have retained that post after Guy's marriage into the royal family; that would have suggested Guy was unfit for his role as king-in-waiting. This truce, however, was a humiliation for the Franks. It was on equal terms and so, for the first time ever, the Muslims had the benefit of an armistice without paying for the privilege. It was stark proof of Frankish disunity and weakness. Saladin was now free to extend and consolidate his domains in Syria and Mesopotamia without interference from the Latin states.

Saladin's freedom of manoeuvre was further increased later in the year when, on 24 September 1180, the *basileus* Manuel Comnenos died. Last of the three great Comnenos emperors, he was succeeded by his eleven-year-old son, Alexius II, whose mother, Maria of Antioch, became regent. Maria continued her husband's pro-Latin policy, as her stepfather Reynald would have wished, but she had little real opportunity to provide concrete help to the crusaders. Byzantine power was waning, and a virulently anti-Latin movement was swiftly building momentum in Constantinople.

By now Reynald was probably well into his fifties. He had retained a young knight's capacity for violence and love of drama, but he had learned to cloak it well, if need be. The intervening years had added patience, an appreciation of the broader picture and the capacity for planning ahead. Secretly he took advantage of the truce to lay the groundwork for a series of momentous military strikes against Saladin.

On the surface he was acting sensibly, steadily building his power; occupying himself with administration of his great fief, alliance-building and diplomacy. Amongst other acts, he confirmed grants to the Knights Hospitaller in Petra and Mont Real. Then in October 1180, yet again showing his grasp of advantageous marriage alliances, Reynald oversaw the betrothal of his stepson Humphrey IV of Toron to King Baldwin IV's younger sister, Princess Isabella. This match, which he pursued 'with much ardour', further enhanced Reynald's prestige and tied him even more closely to the royal party. It also put Humphrey in line as a possible contender for the throne in the future, via the claims of his royal wife. That meant Reynald was stepfather to a potential future King of Jerusalem. Isabella was only twelve, however, so the actual nuptials were postponed until she reached fifteen, the canonical age for marriage.

The other important political development of 1180, and one that is fundamental to our appreciation of Reynald, was the election of a new Patriarch of Jerusalem. The election result is relevant to Reynald's story because one of the two candidates was the great historian, William, Archbishop of Tyre. The principle support for William came from the faction of his patron, Raymond of Tripoli, who had appointed him chancellor. William's rival for the post was Heraclius, Archbishop of Caesarea, who was backed by Queen Agnes and her faction, headed by Prince Reynald. The good-looking Heraclius was a controversial figure who openly kept a mistress, the flamboyant Pasqua de Riveri. Although she was only a lowly shopkeeper's wife, one chronicler wrote that her lover decked her with so many gems and precious garments that you might have thought her a baroness. So blatant was their affair that she was sarcastically known as *Madame La Patriarchesse*. Heraclius was also rumoured to have had an affair with the king-mother, Agnes. 'She loved him because of his beauty,' according to the gossipy Ernoul. Largely thanks to Agnes' influence, Heraclius was elected. This was despite the ominous prophecy, which Ernoul puts into the mouth of William of Tyre, that, just as a Heraclius had once recovered the True Cross, so a Heraclius would lose it.*

---

* The Byzantine Emperor Heraclius had won the True Cross back from the Persians in AD 628.

In his history, William recorded his painful defeat very tersely, simply recording that after the Patriarch Aimery died, 'less than ten days later, Heraclius, Archbishop of Caesarea was elected in his place'.[10] In reality William was devastated. His bitterness emerged in the disparaging portraits of his enemies. The queen, Agnes of Courtenay was 'a most grasping woman, utterly detestable to God'. The cabal of close advisers around the king, such as Joscelin and Reynald, who advised Baldwin to beware of Raymond's ambition, were 'sons of Belial... troublemakers... wicked men'.

Ernoul is equally unsympathetic to the Courtenays and their allies. Thanks to the debauched and adulterous example set by Heraclius, he claims that 'you could hardly find a respectable woman in the whole of Jerusalem'.[11] It should be remembered that Ernoul's patrons, the Ibelin family, were allied with Raymond of Tripoli against the queen's party, and therefore against Heraclius and Reynald as well. Unfortunately for William, he never made his peace with Heraclius and his faction. The new patriarch excommunicated William, who travelled to Rome to clear his name. Around the year 1184, William died. He was poisoned, some alleged, on the orders of Heraclius. William's critical portrait of Reynald in his work is tainted by bitterness at his electoral defeat. If William had become patriarch, he might well have left us a much more generous record of Reynald's deeds.

William does record that Reynald was needed again for his diplomacy in the winter of 1180. After Emperor Manuel died, Prince Bohemond of Antioch swiftly repudiated his Byzantine wife Theodora and married a woman called Sybille. She was not a popular choice. Christian chroniclers call her a witch and a prostitute, but as Muslim sources reveal, the reality was much worse; she was actually an agent of Saladin:

> The wife of the prince of Antioch, called dame Sybille, had taken the sultan's side, spying on his enemies... in return, he showed her consideration and sent her rich gifts.[12]

Reynald's old enemy, the Patriarch Aimery, excommunicated Bohemond for adultery. Bohemond retaliated by seizing Church property. True to form, Aimery put the principality under interdict and took refuge once again in his stronghold of Cursat. Bohemond's actions towards the Church were described in similar terms to Reynald's, more than twenty-five years earlier:

> [Bohemond] treated the patriarch, the bishops, and other
> prelates of the church in that land as enemies and laid violent
> hands upon them. He violated the precincts of sacred places,
> both churches and monasteries, carried off their sacred objects,
> and, in a wicked spirit of presumptuous daring, disturbed their
> possessions.[13]

But Bohemond never tied his victims naked to a turret, daubed with honey, and so his image has not suffered as a result. However, his actions were still extreme enough to drive powerful barons like Renaud Mazoir to side with the patriarch. The spectre of civil war loomed.

King Baldwin IV then sent a delegation to Antioch to negotiate a settlement. Reynald was the only lay member of the group, which also included the Patriarch Heraclius and the Masters of the Templar and Hospitaller Military Orders. As they passed through Tripoli, they recruited Bohemond's friend Count Raymond as well. Reynald, as Bohemond's stepfather, would have been important in the negotiations, which successfully ended the crisis. Bohemond agreed to return Church property and to go back to his first wife. He did the former, and was forgiven by Patriarch Aimery, but he never got back together with Theodora. Sybille remained his consort for life, presumably influencing Bohemond to follow her master's wishes, and keeping Saladin up to date with Antioch's state secrets the entire time.

Reynald took advantage of his trip to Antioch to wrap up another piece of diplomacy – arranging the marriage of his stepdaughter Isabelle of Toron, daughter of Stephanie de Milly and her first husband, to the Armenian prince Roupen of Cilicia. Amongst other things, this alliance may well have improved relations between the Armenians and the regime of Reynald's stepson Bohemond in neighbouring Antioch. We are told that Reynald, indulging one of his favourite talents – matchmaking – for the last time, negotiated this marriage with his customary enthusiasm.

Then, in November 1181, the Zengid ruler of Aleppo, Al-Malik al-Salih, died from a sudden illness. Poison was suspected. With the death of the rightful heir of Nur al-Din, the way was open for Saladin to overwhelm the Zengid forces and finally capture Aleppo. Frustratingly for the Franks, they had a truce in place with Saladin and were in no position to hinder his movements.

But Reynald cared little for truces. He had other ideas.

The Pilgrim Road, Arabia, December 1181

Near the oasis of Tabuk, where the Syrian Desert blends into the Arabian, wormwood into tamarisk, a column of mailed horsemen moved purposefully down a wide trail. They were heading south along the Darb al-Hajj, the pilgrim road. The path is easy to follow, a wide, darker-brown rut in the arid waste, worn down by the shuffling tread of pilgrims and their caravans since the foundation of Islam.

Bedouin guided this party, but fell horsemen like these had never been seen on the Hajj route before. They were infidels, Christians, knights. At their head, on his warhorse, swaying easily in the saddle, rode Reynald de Chatillon.

Already his raiders had taken prisoners and booty, weighing down their baggage camels. Now they were hunting richer prey – an immense caravan not far ahead on the trail.

As they rode through the landscape of rock and sand, across the tracks of ostrich and oryx, Reynald's thoughts ranged still further ahead. The guides had told him that the road beyond Tabuk was long and hard, but he knew that it lay open, unprotected, all the way to Tayma, the gateway to the Hejaz and to the Holy Cities of Mecca and Medina.

Prince Arnat was breaking the truce, and in a way that no Muslim could ignore.

Chapter 14

DESERT RAIDER

And I do not care for Monday, or Tuesday, or weeks or months
or years, nor for April or May do I stop planning how harm may
come to those who do me wrong.

Bertran de Born

Restlessness is one of the many character traits that is consistent between the pre- and post-prison Reynald. As long as he was at liberty, the prince was never one to sit quietly in his lair. In the winter of 1181–2 he launched his startling raid down the pilgrim trail, deep into that desert 'of which the saying goes: "He who enters it is lost, and he who leaves it is born"'.[1]

Unusually heavy rains had carpeted the dry country with grass, providing enough grazing to support the Frankish horses, even in the deep desert. And so, led by his Bedouin allies, Reynald struck south into *La Grande Berrie*, further than any Frankish force had ever dared. They plundered at least as far as Tabuk, 130 miles beyond Aila. Tayma, 'the vestibule of Medina', was only a few days' ride along the trail.

When the shocking news reached Damascus, Saladin's governor,

Farrukh-Shah, was obliged to hurry south with a large force to the southern borders of the Frankish territories. They ravaged some of Oultrejordan, then took up positions across Reynald's line of retreat from Arabia. Reynald in turn abandoned his raid and turned back to protect his fief.

Why would Reynald have launched this *chevauchée*, possibly breaking a truce in the process and exposing the kingdom to Saladin's retaliation? The obvious motive – one that came naturally to Reynald – was to win booty, but this raid was not simply the act of a short-sighted robber baron. With Saladin's forces poised to seize Aleppo for the sultan, Reynald realized that prompt action was called for. Respecting the truce would have left the Franks powerless to interfere. This was the moment Reynald chose to launch his raid. Bernard Hamilton sees this operation as a strategic move to divert Saladin's forces from Aleppo.[2] And, indeed, when the sultan ordered his army from Damascus to Oultrejordan, Saladin's rival, the Zengid Izz al-Din, was able to take charge of Aleppo unopposed. Reynald's strategy of keeping the military pressure on Saladin was roundly justified.

The raid also had considerable impact beyond the military sphere, and maybe we see here the fruit of many years of Reynald's imprisonment. If not evidence of a profound hatred of Islam, it feels very much like the beginnings of a long-planned revenge. Certainly the raid should be seen as a conscious strike at the Hajj, the annual pilgrimage to Mecca, which is one of the five pillars of the Islamic faith. This was certainly how the Muslims saw it. Arnat's 'evil plan', wrote the great Muslim historian Ibn al-Athir, was 'to march overland to Tayma and from there to the City of the Prophet [Medina]'.[3] Muslims were appalled that: 'The insolent master of [Kerak] dared to invade the Hejaz and spread his impious nets across the pilgrim route.'[4]

Reynald well understood the significance of the pilgrimage to Muslims. He knew that this incursion would require a response and would call into question Saladin's religious credentials, which were key to his prestige. A vital component of these credentials was how well the sultan protected the Holy Cities and the pilgrimage routes that led towards them. By attacking the Hajj, while Saladin remained focused on his contest with the Muslim Zengids, Reynald raised questions about Saladin's dedication to Islam and the jihad, as opposed to his own dynastic interests.

The raid was a spectacular success. It had the strategic effect of keeping Aleppo out of Saladin's grasp, won substantial booty, damaged the sultan's authority and disrupted the Hajj. The overland route to the Holy Cities had been blocked. Ibn Jubayr, who made the Hajj in 1183, was not able to reach Mecca by land. He complained that the road from Egypt to Mecca was via Aila, but that Reynald had barred the route: 'the Franks have near to it a garrisoned castle which prevents men from passing it'.[5]

So the attack struck home, shaming and enraging Saladin. Even for some Franks it was too much provocation. The chronicler Ernoul's version of this period describes how Reynald plundered a great caravan in violation of the truce, and that this was the cause of Saladin's subsequent attacks on the Latin Kingdom. Ernoul adds that the booty from the raid added up to a staggering 200,000 bezants. Saladin complained to the King of Jerusalem, demanding restitution, but when Baldwin asked Reynald to release his prisoners and return the spoils, the Lord of Kerak simply defied him. Ernoul's account here is muddled, though. For the year 1183 he tells what appears to be the identical story again, and both tales may reflect a later adventure of Reynald's with another caravan. If this caravan were captured in 1181, it must have fallen victim to Reynald's raid.

It is not even conclusive that Reynald actually broke the truce with Saladin in 1181. William of Tyre, usually scrupulous in these matters, wrote that Saladin himself was actually responsible for breaching the truce, when he illegally seized 1,600 passengers and the valuable cargo of a Frankish ship forced ashore by a storm in Egypt. William mentions reports of Reynald taking 'certain Arabs' prisoner and not releasing them at Saladin's demand, but he clearly did not see this as a breach of the king's truce with Saladin.

Whether Reynald violated the truce or not, Saladin waited for the agreement to expire before attacking the kingdom of Jerusalem. In May 1182 he marched from Egypt, heading for Syria. Thousands of civilians took the chance to travel with his army for safety – a sure sign of how effectively Reynald's activities had scared off normal caravan traffic. As Saladin approached Oultrejordan, Reynald persuaded King Baldwin to take the army to Kerak to block the sultan's advance. Raymond of Tripoli, never keen to help Reynald, disagreed, arguing that this would leave the north of the kingdom dangerously exposed. The Frankish host forced Saladin to skirt Oultrejordan, but Raymond's fears were realized when the forces of Damascus launched a raid through Galilee, sacking some villages and capturing the cliff fortress of the Cave de Sueth.

In July 1182, the sultan invaded Galilee with a great host. Led by King Baldwin IV and the True Cross, the army of Jerusalem marched to meet the invaders, mustering as usual by the ancient wells of Sephora. On 15 July, in heat so intense that many on both sides died of sunstroke, including one of the canons attending the True Cross, the Franks offered battle near the fort of Le Forbelet. Veteran Frankish soldiers said they had never seen such a large Muslim army, estimating the number at 20,000. With just 700 knights and an unknown number of sergeants, the Franks were severely outnumbered, but with their charismatic leper-king at their head, they were a determined, unified force and their internal rivalries were forgotten. It was a savage fight. The Franks suffered substantial casualties amongst the lower ranks, but only a few knights were killed. The Muslims fared worse and buried their dead after dark to hide their losses. Saladin was forced to retire across the Jordan 'with great anguish in his heart'.

Saladin then mounted a joint land and sea attack on Beirut, but was again driven off. Frustrated by the Franks on the field of battle, Saladin turned his attention back to his Muslim rivals. He made another attempt to subjugate the Zengids of Mosul. Although the Latin states were proving able to defend themselves, Saladin was contemptuous of their offensive potential. Pointedly he led his army eastwards across the Euphrates without bothering to conclude the normal truce with the Franks to protect his lands while away on campaign. This was even more humiliating for the Franks than the previous truce on equal terms, and was an ominous sign of their impotence.

In addition to his assessment of the Franks' weakness, Saladin knew they would be receiving no more help from the Byzantine Empire. In a great riot, the populace of Constantinople had risen against the Latins living in the city and massacred them all: men, women and children. The glamorous tyrant Andronicus Comnenos seized power, annihilating the pro-Frankish lobby at court. Beyond the strategic implications for the Franks, Reynald would personally have been appalled by what followed. Andronicus had Reynald's stepdaughter, the dowager empress Maria of Antioch, strangled. He added the sadistic twist of making her son, the emperor Alexius II, sign her death warrant. Soon afterwards Alexius was also murdered and Andronicus became sole emperor. The old lecher, who was aged about sixty-five, then married Alexius' widow, Agnes, daughter of King Louis VII of France. She was only twelve years old.

In 1185, the cruel Andronicus was overthrown in his turn, literally being torn apart by the mob and his remains tossed onto a dungheap to be eaten by dogs. His successor as emperor, Isaac II Angelos, was no more sympathetic to the Franks. Instead he opened friendly diplomatic relations with the ever more powerful Saladin. The Franks could no longer look to Byzantium for aid. From now on, crusader relations with the Greeks would degenerate into open conflict and eventually to the sack of Constantinople itself by the Fourth Crusade in 1204.

Desperate for aid against the mighty sultan, the Zengids in Mosul and Aleppo again cut deals with the Franks. Mosul agreed to an eleven-year truce, an annual tribute and the release of all Frankish prisoners, but Saladin's rivals could expect only scant assistance from the crusaders. Of all the Frankish leaders, only Reynald could be relied upon to truly challenge Saladin. And you could guarantee that he would do it in a dramatic and unique fashion. This time he excelled himself.

In the twelfth century there were thousands of tit-for-tat raids and skirmishes between Saracen and Frank. Most are forgotten or are mentioned as just another routine event. There were many truces breached, and most of these violations also passed without much comment. It is Reynald's raids, and Reynald's truce-breakings, that leave their imprint on history. The Prince of Kerak understood how to really *hurt* his enemy, and it is the unforgettable, dramatic nature of his violence that contributes to his image as somehow more savage and more bellicose than any of the other antagonists in these bloody wars.

The stage was set for the Lord of Kerak to unsettle once again the increasingly mighty sultan. For his next show, Reynald turned to a secret plan that he had nursed for a long while. Practical preparations had begun at least two years before, with the felling of great trees and the construction of a unique fleet of ships by the Dead Sea. Reynald was again taking aim at the Islamic holy places. It turns out that the Tayma raid served merely as a rehearsal, a reconnaissance in force for a campaign far more dramatic and, for the Muslims, even more appalling.

Reynald was about to do the unthinkable – something no other Christian leader had attempted before, or would dare to attempt again, something that would ignite forever the flame of jihad.

Port of Aydhab, Nubia, December 1182

Three strange ships came up steadily out of the east.

To the watchers on the desert shore it was clear that these were not the usual small *jilab* of the Red Sea, sewn together with coconut fibre and coated in shark-grease. These were lean ships of a different design, with ranks of oars beating, thrusting them towards the shore. And they were painted black as night.

Behind them came a straggling ragtag flotilla of assorted vessels.

In the boiling heat of the fly-blown, ramshackle port, 'brackish of water and flaming of air',[6] pilgrims bound for Mecca, merchants from India, Arabia and Ethiopia, paused in their haggling and looked on with growing surprise. Even the local tribesmen, the Beja, naked except for their loincloths, observed the approach of this menacing fleet with unease.

As the mysterious ships pulled up to the quay, they yielded up even stranger apparitions – white men.

These spectral figures exploded out of the galleys like the wrath of God. They were sheathed in iron, bearing the mark of the cross. Naked swords gleamed in their hands. They were crusaders. Pirates. And their leader was Reynald de Chatillon.

No white man had ever been seen in these lands before. Beja, Indian and Arab alike fled in terror as the demonic invaders hacked their way through the reed and coral huts, looting and killing. They plundered spices and incense from Asia and Yemen, cloths and provisions from Egypt. Some boats they seized as prizes, including a ship full of returning pilgrims. They torched the rest, along with great piles of food prepared on the beaches as supplies for the Holy Cities.

While they loaded their ships with vast quantities of pearls, cinnamon, pepper, frankincense and saffron, a raiding party struck out west across the desert, along the trade route to the cities of the Nile Valley. Out in the endless sands the Franks met a caravan coming from the town of Qus. They plundered the goods and killed the merchants, leaving their bones to whiten in the desert sun amongst the sodom-apple plants.

Through the smoke of burning goods and vessels, the black ships sailed into the east, leaving behind them death, ruin and devastation. The Frankish devils were heading out across the Red Sea, making for Arabia and the coast of the Hejaz, land of Islam's holiest sites – the city of the Kaaba, Mecca, and the city of the Prophet, Medina.

Reynald's most audacious and shocking campaign was under way.

Chapter 15

SEA WOLF

Have you not considered how your Lord dealt with the
  companions of the elephant?
Did He not make their plan into misguidance?
And He sent against them birds in flocks,
Striking them with stones of hard clay,
And He made them like eaten straw.

Quran, sura 105

Reynald's concept was one of remarkable temerity: to attack, by sea, the Hajj route and the Holy Cities of Islam. This is sacred ground, absolutely banned to non-Muslims even today. For infidel warriors to sully it would have been an indescribable sacrilege – as Reynald knew all too well.

The campaign began with an astonishing tactical coup, transporting a fleet of prefabricated warships to the Red Sea, where no Christian vessel had sailed in half a millennium since the foundation of Islam. Completed in great secrecy, it was a logistical feat of great complexity that took at least two years to prepare. Shipwrights had to be found, presumably in the coastal cities, and paid enough to lure them to

Oultrejordan. The ships were constructed from the timber of Moab and tested on the Dead Sea. The craft had to be modular enough to be dismantled, carried on camels to Aila at the head of the Red Sea, then reassembled and relaunched. Sailors had to be hired to crew the fleet, and Arab pilots were needed – men who knew the treacherous Red Sea shoals and reefs. Hundreds of mercenaries had to be recruited, men without fear, prepared to voyage into an alien and hostile sea. Deals had to be struck with the Bedouin to transport the ships south across the desert. To prevent the plan coming to the attention of Saladin's efficient espionage network, all involved had to be cowed and bribed to keep their mouths firmly shut.

Ernoul describes the project as one of exploration of the Red Sea, where 'flows a river of paradise':

> On the shores of this sea, Prince Reynald built five galleys. Once
> they were ready, he launched them on the sea and crewed them
> with knights and sergeants and provisions to find out what peoples
> lived on this sea. Once they were equipped, they set off on the
> high seas, but from the moment they left, not a thing has been
> heard of them, and nobody knows what became of them.[1]

But while geographical knowledge was of course useful, it is hard to picture Reynald leading a voyage of discovery in search of a mythical river, or to broaden the sum of human knowledge. Reynald was a man of his time, yes, but like the sixteenth-century conquistadors who took the New World for Spain, in reality he was driven to brave the unknown by more tangible motives. Bernard Hamilton suggests that Reynald's campaign was the southern thrust in a concerted Frankish attempt to undermine Saladin's latest attack on Mosul. While Reynald attacked in the Red Sea, there were simultaneous raids against Bosra by Count Raymond and against Damascus by King Baldwin.[2] Such a strategy may have helped justify the undertaking, but if these actions were coordinated, they had little effect. 'They take villages while we take cities,' commented Saladin of Baldwin's raid into the territory around Damascus.

The only one of these attacks that mattered – the only one that is remembered to this day – was Reynald's. The campaign certainly went beyond a mere raid, representing at the very least the next stage in the Lord of Kerak's systematic attempt to disrupt the Hajj and embarrass Saladin, while hitting at his empire's trade routes on land and sea.

In 1181, Reynald's raid towards Tayma had cut the overland caravan and Hajj trail from Syria and Egypt to the Hejaz. In 1182, Reynald transferred his attention to the sea-lanes. First the Muslim fort at Aila was overwhelmed. This would have brought some satisfaction to the Lord of Oultrejordan, as Aila was officially part of his fief. Also the garrison at Aila was a base for incursions against his territory. Reynald's galleys, painted an intimidating pirate black, were then reassembled on the Red Sea shore. Two ships stayed in the vicinity of Aila to blockade the nearby castle on the barren Ile de Graye. The other three galleys set off southwards down the narrow gulf between the rocky mountain walls of Sinai and Arabia. It is not clear whether Reynald stayed with the galleys in the Gulf of Aila or led the larger squadron southwards. Knowing Reynald, we can be sure that he was on board ship. He liked to lead from the front, in the thick of the action, and we cannot imagine him missing out on such an adventure, especially if it was the implementation of a long-gestated revenge.

The Red Sea, or the Sea of Qulzum to the Muslims, had long been free of Islam's enemies. As a consequence, and as Reynald well knew, there was no Muslim navy to resist his piracy; there had been no need for one for 500 years. As they sailed south unopposed, Reynald's buccaneers had the benefit of complete surprise. They took or sank Muslim merchantmen and pilgrim transports with impunity. At least sixteen

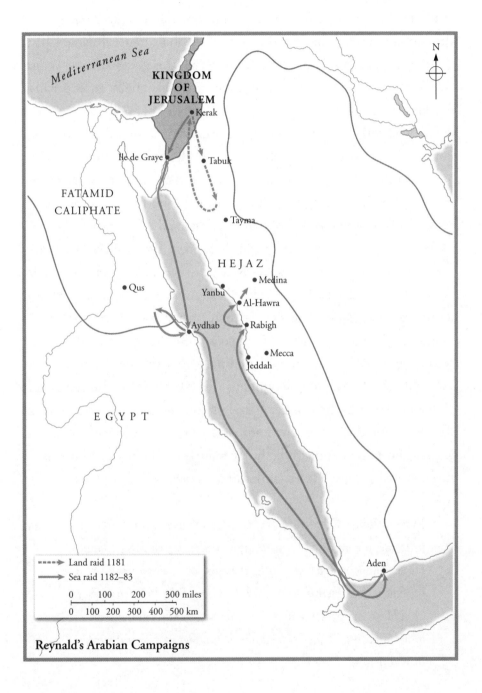

N

Mediterranean Sea

**KINGDOM
OF
JERUSALEM**

FATAMID
CALIPHATE

• Kerak

Ile de Graye •   • Tabuk

• Tayma

H E J A Z

• Qus

Yanbu   • Medina

• Al-Hawra

Aydhab   • Rabigh

• Mecca

Jeddah

E G Y P T

Aden

- - - ▸ Land raid 1181
——▸ Sea raid 1182–83

| 0 | 100 | 200 | 300 miles |

| 0 | 100 | 200 | 300 | 400 | 500 km |

Reynald's Arabian Campaigns

Muslim ships were destroyed or captured and added to the pirate fleet. A motley band of knights, sergeants, mercenaries and Arab renegades, the corsairs headed first for the port of Aydhab. Since Reynald had cut the road leading from Egypt across Sinai, this godforsaken spot on the desolate Nubian coast had become the major point of departure for Egyptians making their pilgrimage. From there the leaky *jilab*, overloaded with pilgrims, made the risky crossing to Jeddah, the nearest port to Mecca. With his fleet, Reynald curtailed this sea traffic as surely as he had the overland trail the year before. As well as the ships taken on the high seas, during the sack of Aydhab, the Franks pillaged two vessels packed with merchandise from Yemen and a ship full of pilgrims.

And Aydhab was just the beginning. From the Nubian coast the black ships sailed east across the Red Sea to Arabia, guided by their Arab pilots. Some said they sailed as far as Aden and the Indian Ocean, looting as they went. The Franks then turned back northwards and plundered the ports along the Hejaz coast from Rabigh up to al-Hawra, setting up a base onshore and raiding across the coastal strip and even into the surrounding mountains towards Medina. The campaign seemed to confirm the fear generated by the previous year's *razzia* that Reynald wanted to attack the tomb of the Prophet at Medina, perhaps with a view to removing his body. According to Ibn Jubayr, who passed through Aydhab just a few months after its sack by the crusaders:

> *Many infamous acts they committed, such as are unheard of in Islam, for no Rumi [Christian] had ever before come to that place. The worst, which shocks the ears for its impiousness and profanity, was their aim to enter the City of the Prophet – may God bless and preserve him – and remove him from the sacred tomb. This intent they spread abroad and let report of it run on their tongues.*[3]

The unlikely plan was apparently to rebury the Prophet Muhammad in Christian territory and make money out of the Muslim pilgrims who would then come to visit the site. Reynald almost certainly planned nothing of the sort (though, as Lord of Hebron, he knew the value of pilgrim traffic to the grave of Abraham). Still the rumours and the news of infidel troops so close to the Holy Sanctuaries horrified the Islamic world, arousing apocalyptic fears that, in the words of the Qadi Al-Fadil, 'The end of the world was nigh, that the portents were manifesting themselves and the earth was about to fall into darkness.'⁴

The attack recalled the 'Year of the Elephant' mentioned in the Quran, when in the sixth century AD, Abraha, the Christian ruler of Yemen, launched an assault on Mecca using war elephants. Earthly means of defence against Reynald's unimaginable attack appeared to be non-existent, so Muslims prayed for God's anger to fall upon Reynald's Frankish devils and thwart their plans, just as it had on Abraha.*

In Cairo the startled authorities responded swiftly. The experienced admiral Husam al-Din Lu'lu' ('Pearl') took a leaf out of Reynald's book and transported ships in sections to the Red Sea. The Egyptian fleet first attacked and defeated the galleys blockading the Ile de Graye. Some of the Franks escaped into the wild ravines and wadis of Sinai and tried to make their way back through the desert, pursued by the fickle and rapacious Bedouin.† Lu'lu' then sailed in search of the rest of Reynald's pirates, catching up with them on the coast of the Hejaz at al-Hawra. Lu'lu' found that most of the Franks had struck off along the trails leading across the mountains towards Medina, 'guided by Arabs more impious and hypocritical than they'.⁵

---

* Abraha's war elephants seemed irresistible as they approached Mecca, but Allah then sent birds to drive off the invaders by pelting them with pieces of baked clay. This story is an exegesis of Quranic sura 105.
† It is tempting to conjecture that one of these desperate Franks left behind the mysterious suit of crusader mail discovered in Sinai in the 1970s.

Requisitioning horses from the local tribes, Lu'lu' set off in desperate pursuit. His men attached purses of silver to their spears to win over the Bedouin guiding the Franks. In a bitterly earnest game of cat-and-mouse, the Muslims tracked and skirmished with the crusader raiding party through the desolate canyons and passes for five days. Eventually the Franks were cornered in a waterless valley just a day's march from Medina. There was a sharp battle, which the far more numerous Muslim forces won. Some of the raiders may have fled into the mountains, but about 170 survivors negotiated terms with Lu'Lu', surrendering on the promise that their lives would be spared. Lu'lu' later claimed that he killed or captured all of the Franks. To those who were taken, Saladin would show no mercy. His vizier, the Qadi Al-Fadil, quoted the Quran:

The Unbelievers will be
Led to Hell in crowds.[6]

Reynald had struck too close to the bone. He had again all too successfully succeeded in wounding Saladin's prestige, calling into question his credentials as protector of the Hajj. If it happened again, the sultan worried, 'tongues in the east and west would blame us'. He could not risk further embarrassment. The world had to be 'purged of their filth and the air of their breath'.[7] The sultan ordered all the prisoners to be killed. His brother, Al-Adil, the governor of Egypt, questioned this command. His view was that under Islamic law, because the prisoners had been given quarter, their lives were now protected. According to Imad al-Din, Saladin overruled Al-Adil, justifying his action on the basis that these infidels now knew the Red Sea shipping lanes and the routes to the Holy Cities. They must be beheaded to the last man, so that:

*There did not remain among them one sign of life, not even a
single man who could tell of the escapade, or guide others, or have
knowledge of the routes of the Red Sea, that inviolable barrier
between the infidels and the Holy City.*[8]

In any case, the sultan wrote to his brother:

*The judgement of God on men like this is not a problem for
scholars… let the decision to kill them be carried out… Their
attack was an unparalleled enormity in the history of Islam.*[9]

Reynald's outrageous act remains unique as the only attack by
non-believers on the Hejaz since the foundation of Islam. It is not
surprising that this harrowing and traumatizing event brought its
reaction in terms of jihad. More than 800 years later, the founder of
Al-Qaida, Usama Bin Laden, declared war on America and its allies
simply because of the presence of non-Muslim troops on Arabian soil.
Reynald's actual military threat to the Holy Places was sure to strike a
chord with Muslims everywhere, swelling the number of volunteers for
the jihad, and rousing passive and squabbling Islamic leaders to finally
unite against the Franks. The Zengid emirs, recently allied with the
crusaders, were ashamed to have allies who perpetrated such atrocities
against Islam.

Long before angry jihadists targeted the citizens of Chicago with
their cargo bombs in 2010, the first to suffer Muslim vengeance for
Reynald's raid were his captured pirates. Saladin's orders were carried
out in full. Two of the men were ritually sacrificed like animals, their
throats slit in front of crowds of pilgrims during the Hajj at Mecca.
The other raiders were publically beheaded in Cairo and other cities of
Saladin's dominions. Gruesomely, religious scholars acted as Saladin's
executioners. Their ineptitude with weapons prolonged the condemned

men's agonies. Ibn Jubayr saw some of the doomed Franks paraded through baying crowds in the streets of Alexandria, mounted on camels, 'facing the tails and surrounded by timbal and horn'. It was a spectacle to 'rend the heart with compassion and pity'.[10]

To Saladin's fury, the cursed Arnat, ringleader of the blasphemous raid, had escaped. If he had been with the lead flotilla at Rabigh, he must have escaped sometime before the final battle with Lu'Lu', perhaps even when the Egyptian ships appeared, or sometime during the chase through the mountains. Reynald was back in Palestine by March 1183.

In his rage, Saladin swore that if Arnat ever fell into his power, he would kill him with his own hand.

Kerak, Oultrejordan, 22 November 1183

The bells of Kerak's church rang out, fading in the winter air down the great canyon that led to the Dead Sea. With the peals mixed the notes of harp, lyre and tambourine.

Prince Reynald knew how to throw a party and had gathered musicians, singers, jugglers and dancers, the finest entertainers and wandering minstrels from all over the Levant, for the wedding of his stepson Humphrey of Toron to Princess Isabella of Jerusalem. It was the social event of the year, and Kerak was brimming with illustrious guests from the leading families of Outremer.

The fortress was also full of livestock and provisions, great stockpiles of weapons, armed men – and fear.

Clouds of dust on the horizon had signalled the approach of a vast army. Hardly had the wedding vows been uttered when, outside the walls, the Muslim host was shuffling into position. Saladin had come to take his revenge on Prince Arnat. The defiant Reynald, for his part, was not going to let anything interfere with the festivities.

In one of the quaint chivalrous episodes that mark the life of Saladin, Reynald's wife, Stephanie de Milly, sent messengers out to the sultan's tent; they took Saladin 'bread, wine, beef and lamb' from her son's wedding feast. The story goes that Stephanie reminded Saladin how he had carried her in his arms many times when he was a captive in the castle and she was a little girl. Saladin, moved by Stephanie's gesture (and presumably overlooking the faux pas of the wine, unwelcome to an observant Muslim), asked the messengers to point out the nuptial chambers of the happy couple. He then ordered his men to bombard the fortress, but to leave the newlyweds' tower unharmed.*

The initial assault was so ferocious that the fortified suburb was breached almost immediately. The citizens fled for the protection of the castle, Saladin's men hot on their heels, killing everyone they caught. A knight called Yvain bravely held the single, slender bridge across the fosse, fighting off all-comers. Thanks to him, many townspeople crowded across and squeezed through the citadel's only gate. Yvain, studded with arrows, was the last man in. The defenders dropped the portcullis and destroyed the bridge behind him.

That night, the castle, overflowing with non-combatants, shuddered as boulders launched by the sultan's siege engines began to hammer into the north wall. Reynald ordered the beacon on the highest turret to be lit, summoning help from Jerusalem.

* Bernard Hamilton archly points out that this 'chivalry' made good commercial sense; the sultan would have been wary of hurting the two most valuable potential prisoners in the castle.

Chapter 16

THE LION AND
THE WOLF

*When the wolf caught the scent of the lion, he took refuge in
his lair.*

Abu Shama

At the top of a great ravine leading down to the Devil's Sea, the fortress
of Kerak loomed above the King's Highway, the ancient road from
Damascus to Arabia. Climbing to the top of the mighty bastion where
the beacon burned, Reynald might just have been able to make out, on
a clear night, the answering beacon flaring on the heights of Jerusalem.

If relief came, it would take time, but Reynald did not panic. He
knew that Kerak would not succumb easily. Between the castle and the
walled *bourg* or suburb to the north lay a daunting fosse sixty feet deep,
hewn out of the solid rock. From the north wall, the castle stretched
southwards along a steep ridge, dominated by high ramparts. There was
no chance of being stormed from the east, where a smooth stone glacis

clad the hillside, sloping down to the highway; or from the west, where the ground plummeted away in a great canyon to the depression of the Dead Sea, twenty miles away and more than 4,000 feet down. On the south side there was the added protection of another great trench, used as a moat and reservoir by the castle. Within the massive walls, above ground and beneath, were level upon level of chambers, passageways, armouries, chapels, storerooms and great halls large enough to provision and stable an army. All the cattle and sheep of the region had been gathered together as well. Because there was no room in the castle, these had been herded into the deep ditches around the walls. The fortress was all but impregnable. According to the Muslim besiegers looking at it from outside the walls, it was a forbidding prospect: 'hard to climb and difficult to access from all sides' – 'perfectly fortified'.[1] But it had its weaknesses.

The storming of the fortified *bourg* was a dangerous development. If it fell, an attacker could position artillery within range of the defences on the only feasible line of approach – from the north. Reynald had been determined to defend the suburb, and had forbidden the citizens from moving their families or their belongings into the castle. Not only were many of the inhabitants trapped and killed outside the castle when the Saracens stormed the town, but all their goods and provisions were lost as well. Commentators criticized Reynald for this decision, which the *Estoire d'Eracles* says he made because he was so valiant.

Once the suburb fell, Saladin immediately built seven huge mangonels. These siege engines began lobbing great slabs of stone over and through the north wall. Along with a constant rain of thousands of arrows, the besiegers drove the defenders into hiding and smashed great gaps in the defences. The garrison put up a vigorous resistance, but the great throng of wedding guests, entertainers and other civilians hampered their efforts. Still no relief force came from Jerusalem. Under cover of their barrage, the Muslims climbed down into the ditch and helped themselves to the castle's beef – much to the defenders' annoyance. The bombardment was so effective that, after almost two weeks, 'neither trebuchet nor mangonel could achieve anything more'. The only barrier left was the redoubtable fosse.

Reynald could have been forgiven for fretting about the arrival of the relief, which had been delayed by political developments elsewhere. In his latest campaign against his Zengid foes, Saladin had again failed to capture Mosul, but he was steadily increasing his power. In mid-June 1183 came news the Franks had been dreading for the nine years since the death of Nur al-Din: Saladin had finally won control of Aleppo. He had taken it, relatively peacefully in the end, from the weak Zengid leader Imad al-Din, who accepted the meagre town of Sinjar in exchange. This coup completed Saladin's encirclement of the crusader states. His empire now stretched from Libya to Mesopotamia. He had united the vast manpower and wealth of Egypt with the great Syrian cities of Aleppo and Damascus. The Muslim powers bordering his lands owed him allegiance, and had promised to send troops to fight the jihad. The Sunni caliph in Baghdad provided him with spiritual legitimacy. Byzantium was no longer a threat. It only remained for the sultan to finish off the pesky Frankish presence – an alien enclave in the middle of his territories, and a blot on the face of Dar al-Islam. As Saladin wrote in a letter, 'Islam is now awake to drive away the phantom of unbelief.'[2]

First he settled affairs in the north. No doubt fully informed of Bohemond's negotiating position by his treacherous consort, Sybille, Saladin concluded a four-year truce with Antioch. Then he turned his attention southwards. He gathered a huge army and, in September, attacked the Kingdom of Jerusalem once more. On learning of Saladin's plans, the Franks (including Reynald and Raymond of Tripoli) had mustered at their favoured spot – the centrally located, well-protected and well-watered wells of Sephora, in Galilee. Their mobilization was highly effective, funded by a startling and highly suspect innovation

– an income tax. This was levied at 2 per cent on annual incomes of 100 bezants or more. Its promulgators naively hoped that this would be an emergency, one-off event and not a precedent for later generations. Forces marched to Sephora from all over the Latin East. The contingent from Oultrejordan was smaller than it should have been, however. Reynald's stepson, Humphrey of Toron, was riding to join the host with the troops of Kerak and Mont Real when Muslim troops ambushed them en route from Nablus. They lost many dead and about a hundred men were taken prisoner.

All told, the Franks awaited Saladin's invasion with a tremendous force of around 1,300 knights and 15,000 foot soldiers behind the True Cross. Aged men could not remember seeing an army so well equipped. It was the largest, costliest and best-armed host the Franks had put in the field since the Second Crusade. The fervent hope was that it would be used to deal Saladin a decisive blow. Unfortunately, its leader was not King Baldwin, or either of the most experienced and proven military leaders, Reynald or Raymond, both of them former regents. The army's general was Guy de Lusignan.

Earlier in the year, while Reynald was leading his raid on the Red Sea, the twenty-one-year-old leper-king had again fallen gravely ill. When he recovered from his fever, he was clearly incapable of governing. He was blind and his limbs were useless; the leprosy was rotting away his hands and feet. Lying sick in Nazareth, with Saladin's army advancing, King Baldwin had summoned his court and, in front of his mother, the patriarch and the barons of the realm, had appointed his brother-in-law Guy as regent of the kingdom. The nobles swore fealty to Guy, though many did so with great reluctance. The powerful faction led by Raymond and the Ibelins argued that Guy simply was not up to the job, and he was indeed an untried military commander. The chroniclers labour the fact that Guy was neither valiant (*preux*) nor wise (*sage*). In terms of chivalry, he was described in opposite terms to Reynald – he was just not an ideal knight. He was also, as William of Tyre repeatedly sniffed, 'indiscreet'. The bumptious new regent did not help his own cause by glorying a little too much in his promotion.

A few years later, at the siege of Acre in 1189, Guy would prove a brave and effective soldier, but in this bewildering first command he was incapable of uniting the army's competing factions. The campaign was dogged by logistical problems, quarrels, passivity and indecision. Guy moved the army forward to a base at the wells of Tubaniya, where arguments raged as to what strategy to adopt. Many wished to attack, but others pointed to the vastly more numerous Saracen forces waiting to encircle them and refused to fight. William of Tyre reported that 'Simple people without experience of the malice of the leaders'[3] could not understand why Guy did not attack. Some alleged cowardice amongst the leadership, others that Guy's political enemies – Raymond and his faction – refused to give battle precisely because the magnificent Frankish army was likely to win, in which case Guy would get the credit. In the face of Frankish reticence, Saladin made great efforts to provoke a pitched battle. He set up camp just a mile from the Frankish lines, made probing attacks and sent out raiding parties, which scorched the surrounding area. To the great consternation of the rank and file, who desperately wanted to get at the enemy, Guy stayed put.

After more than a week camped in the face of the Frankish force, Saladin realized that he would not be able to force a battle. His army was suffering from hunger and, as always, the more impatient contingents were proving challenging to keep in the field, especially as nothing was happening. He retired in frustration across the Jordan, turning his thoughts again towards his greatest enemy, Reynald de Chatillon. The Frankish army dispersed and Reynald soon sped off with a force of knights to Kerak. He was about to host a royal wedding and, according to his scouts who reported on Saladin's movements, he would have to withstand a siege as well.

The Franks' defensive strategy may have been the wisest course of action. It preserved their field-army intact, and Saladin's massive force had been forced to withdraw. It could have been seen as a victory for Guy, but in fact the regent was heavily criticized for not exploiting the mighty army at his disposal. He had simply been unable to work effectively with the other crusader leaders. His inactivity was viewed more as dithering indecision rather than as a decided strategy, and the muddled organization of the campaign also told against him. While hemmed in at Tubaniya, the army had almost run out of food, being rescued only by the 'miraculous' discovery that the wells were packed with fish.

Guy's performance had clearly not impressed King Baldwin IV, and the regent soon alienated his monarch further. Baldwin decided that the sea air was better for his health, so he asked Guy to give him the port of Tyre in exchange for Jerusalem. Guy refused. As regent, he may have had good reason to say no; Tyre, with its busy port and impenetrable castle on an isthmus, was the strongest refuge in the kingdom and far more valuable than Jerusalem as a source of revenue. But snubbing the sick king went down very badly. At the prompting of Guy's opponents, like Raymond of Tripoli, King Baldwin dismissed Guy from the regency and had his nephew Baldwin crowned as joint king. Unfortunately, this did not resolve succession issues; the leprous King Baldwin IV would not live much longer, and little King Baldwin V was only five years old.

Critically, Reynald was not present at this overthrow of his ally. He was trapped in his embattled fief, besieged by Saladin. When the relief force finally set off for Kerak, the leper-king himself was at its head.

At the approach of the Frankish army, Saladin was forced to raise the siege. From the ramparts of Kerak, the relieved defenders saw the Muslim troops pack up and leave, burning their siege engines behind them. Carried into the shattered fortress on a litter, the ailing King Baldwin provided Reynald with the funds and labour to patch up the damaged defences, while the detained wedding guests and entertainers at last moved on to their next engagements. Saladin marched back to Damascus, his troops raiding the territories around Nablus on the way. Once again he had nothing to show from a campaign against the polytheists.

In the summer of 1184 the sultan yet again summoned his troops to the jihad against Reynald. Forces came from Egypt, Damascus, Aleppo, Sinjar and Mosul. They surrounded Kerak on 23 August. According to Gregory the Priest, Reynald was prepared: he 'went onto the mountain and he entered Kerak and he made it exceedingly strong'.[4] But Saladin too was more prepared for this round of his struggle with the cursed Arnat. Determined to have his revenge, the sultan attacked with greater determination and ferocity. His men erected fourteen great mangonels to pummel the repaired defences. Backed by archers loosing thousands of arrows day and night, the bombardment was far more intense than the previous siege, as Abu Shama chronicled:

> The arrogant towers collapse... the stones fall in waves on the summit of the towers and on the head of the evildoers; they strike the battlements and those who defend them. They go straight to their aim, and in killing the Franks, prove to them that they follow a false route. Not one of them can show his face without getting an arrow in the eye... we hold the enemy by the throat... our machines destroy the buildings. The rampart opposite them collapses with its turrets and walls. Pillars and foundations are overturned. If it was not for the barrier of the ditch, it would be easy to invade the place... because it is not an ordinary ditch, but very wide and deep, a terrifying natural ravine with sheer precipices and dreadful chasms.[5]

Saladin had learned from the previous siege and set out immediately to fill the ditch between the suburb and the castle. At first the hail of missiles from inside the castle made this impossible, but the Muslims built covered towers, palisades and walkways under which they could approach the ditch without danger. According to Ernoul, Saladin sent out a summons to 'anyone who wanted to earn money, that for every basket full of earth, they would get one bezant'. This generous incentive lured plenty of enthusiastic volunteers and the ditch steadily filled around the clock, untroubled by the slings and arrows of the defenders:

> Our men do not fear to congregate under the walls of the fortress even in broad daylight, as they do in the courtyards of Damascus during the great feast days. They are sheltered from harm and know with certainty that victory is theirs.[6]

Reynald ordered the garrison to erect a mangonel to attack Saladin's siege engines, but the enemy's bombardment was too heavy and too accurate. The carpenters abandoned their work and the machine was destroyed. Saladin's army was on the verge of taking the city, and the Muslims knew it. Imad al-Din was certainly counting his chickens:

> If relief does not come soon, the city will be taken, because the top of the towers are broken off, the crenellations smashed, the curtain walls decapitated, the siege engines broken, the roofs disembowelled, the ramparts cracked, the murder holes perforated. Victory is as inevitable as a foot on a leg.[7]

The defenders watched the mounting pile of earth with trepidation. So shallow did the ditch become that a chained Muslim prisoner managed to escape unharmed by leaping from the castle walls into the fosse.* Reynald was no doubt aware of Saladin's vow to kill him if he

---

* This may be the source of Reynald's erroneous reputation for throwing prisoners over the ramparts.

was captured, so to him the inexorably growing mound filling the moat was as sure a sign of approaching doom as the advance of the vengeful Manuel through Cilicia in 1159. It was enough to oblige Reynald to hurry up the relief, as Ernoul relates:

> *When Prince Reynald who was in Kerak, saw how effectively*
> *they were filling the ditch, he ordered a sergeant to climb down the*
> *cliff and report to the King of Jerusalem on how badly the fortress*
> *was damaged and how the ditch was being filled.*[8]

As the besiegers prepared to cross the ditch and storm the castle, the army of Jerusalem finally approached. Saladin was again forced to retire empty-handed, though his troops crossed the Jordan and sacked the towns of Nablus and Jenin on the way back to Damascus.

Oultrejordan had some strategic value, but Saladin's focus on Kerak betrays his personal obsession with overcoming Arnat. Reynald's provocations of the sultan were proving much more than irresponsible adventures; they benefited the Latin states by diverting Saladin's efforts against the hated Prince of Kerak. The rising tide of Muslim power in the Levant was beating uselessly against the impervious walls of the great fortress of Moab.

This second relief of Kerak in 1184 was one of the last events recorded in the great history of William of Tyre. Not long afterwards the Archbishop died, excommunicate and in exile. With his political rivals in the ascendancy and the kingdom's leadership bitterly divided, William's last entries are very pessimistic:

> *We who used frequently to triumph over our enemies and bring*
> *home the palm of victory with glory, now in almost every conflict,*
> *being deprived of Divine grace, are the losers.*[9]

Still, despite the growing power of Saladin, the jihad was making little real progress. Outnumbered and surrounded, the Latin states were proving doughty opponents. Somehow the sultan needed to weaken them further before being able to try another decisive blow. Luckily, fate and the Franks themselves would do much of his work for him.

Ascalon, Kingdom of Jerusalem, December 1183

The towering walls of Ascalon were lined with curious townspeople. They stared, transfixed, at the sandy ground before the gatehouse, where a strange and excruciating scene was unfolding.

Below them their ruler, the diseased King of Jerusalem, lay on a litter, attended by all the leading barons of his realm. At his arrival the city gates had not been flung open to welcome the monarch. They had been shut in his face. Now the litter was carried forward towards the bolted gates.

Summoning all his strength, the king struck the gate with what remained of his decaying hand. He called on the Count of Jaffa and Ascalon, Guy de Lusignan, to come forth.

Frozen in place by fascination and fear, the onlookers knew that deep political divisions in the kingdom had led to this. The king and the Count of Jaffa had a deep and ever-worsening loathing for each other. So far had Guy fallen from grace that the king wished to exclude him from any chance of inheriting the throne.

Guy was not going to risk arrest, nor would he allow access to his wife, Princess Sybilla, who was closeted with him in Ascalon. He knew the king planned to separate them and annul their marriage.

The gate remained firmly shut.

Twice more the king beat upon the doors and called on Guy. Twice more there was no response.

The king collapsed back onto his litter, and his entourage turned away from the gate of Ascalon and rode slowly away northwards across the dunes. As soon as he arrived at Jaffa, Guy's other major possession, Baldwin seized the city from his rebellious brother-in-law.

With Guy and his clique out of favour, when the king finally weakened, it would be to Raymond of Tripoli that he would turn.

Reynald's greatest rival would finally win power.

Chapter 17

THE 'MANCHURIAN' REGENT

The most considerable among the accursed Franks is the accursed Count, the Lord of Tripoli and Tiberias... He is qualified to be king and is indeed a candidate for the office. He was a prisoner of Nur al-Din's... then ransomed himself by a payment of a great sum in the time of the first governorship of Saladin, to whom he admits his vassalage and emancipation.

Ibn Jubayr[1]

Poor Raymond... Made to commit acts too unspeakable to be cited here... by an enemy who had captured his mind and his soul...
Marco in *The Manchurian Candidate*[2]

King Baldwin IV did not long survive the superhuman effort of his struggle with his brother-in-law. In 1184 he received the shocking news that Guy had raided the Bedouin close to the Egyptian border. These nomads grazed their flocks under the king's protection. Attacking them not only alienated useful allies of the Franks, but was also a blatantly rebellious affront to the king. The distress of this news was too much for the young man and he fell mortally ill.

Baldwin was now clearly dying and was determined to make provision for the succession, without including Guy. He summoned all the nobles of the realm and turned back the clock to the beginning of his reign, reappointing Raymond of Tripoli as regent. It is interesting that he did not turn to Reynald here, perhaps because the Lord of Kerak was so absorbed in defending his fief from the constant attacks of Saladin; less likely perhaps because, eight years on from Mont Gisard, the warrior prince, now around sixty, was regarded as too old. It is possible that the king's dislike of Guy was so great that it extended to those who had supported him. We may also finally see Baldwin acting without the influence of his mother – Queen Agnes died around this time. Baldwin insisted that all the nobles again swear fealty to his nephew, Baldwin V, and to Raymond as regent. Apart from Guy de Lusignan, all the nobles obliged, even Reynald and Joscelin.

In the spring of 1185, the poor leper finally died. He was twenty-three years old. Despite his terrible disease he had bravely, and at the cost of great personal suffering, managed to maintain the kingdom intact against the menace of Saladin. Without his illness he might have been a great king. Only the example of his sacrifice and his royal charisma had kept the ambitious magnates of the kingdom from tearing it apart. On his death, the deep divisions that he bequeathed soon emerged. Reynald had been utterly loyal to the king throughout his reign, apart from a query over the doubtful episode of the caravan in 1182. After Baldwin's death, he continued to follow the leper-king's wishes, swearing to obey Count Raymond as regent. Many barons, though, including Reynald, remained very suspicious of Raymond; the count's royal ambitions were common knowledge. As Ibn Jubayr wrote of his travel through the Holy Land in autumn 1184, the 'shrewd and crafty' Raymond was 'qualified to be king and indeed is a candidate for the office'.[3] And according to Ibn al-Athir, 'The Franks had nobody more influential than him, none braver and more excellent in counsel… he was ambitious to be king.'[4]

Those magnates loyal to the legitimate royal line, like Reynald, could not countenance this outcome, so while they confirmed Raymond's regency for the next ten years, they bound it with onerous conditions. These included the unprecedented step of placing all the royal castles under control of the Military Orders and so beyond Raymond's reach. The most important and revealing clause mandated that the boy-king was not to be entrusted to his regent, but rather to the care of his great-uncle, the seneschal Joscelin of Courtenay. This would protect the young Baldwin V from any harm the regent might dream up. It also maintained the grip of the Courtenay faction on the crown itself. Raymond, however, was granted the valuable fief of Beirut, and at Baldwin V's crown-wearing ceremony in Jerusalem, the pre-eminence of the count's faction was driven home when the young king was carried into the Holy Sepulchre on the tall shoulders of Raymond's closest ally, Balian of Ibelin.

Raymond's most noteworthy act during his second regency was to negotiate a truce with Saladin. According to Ernoul, this was for four years. If true, this was a surprisingly long truce for the kingdom. Count Raymond is lauded for this agreement by the highly biased Ernoul, who claimed that the 'Count of Tripoli was much loved and honoured by the people of the land for the truce he made with the Saracens.'

Raymond's armistice helpfully covered a period of famine in the kingdom, but otherwise it was unfortunately timed for the Franks. At first it gave Saladin a free hand to campaign against his Zengid rivals in Mosul. Then, later in 1185, Saladin became very ill. He lay close to death for months and was not out of danger until spring 1186. His empire suffered the predictable unrest, including widespread strife between Turcoman nomads and the Kurds of Mesopotamia and Anatolia. At a time when they would normally have taken advantage of their enemy's indisposition to attack his leaderless lands, the Franks looked on impotently, held in check by the truce, or by Raymond's reluctance to attack, or both. Certainly in the light of Raymond's later behaviour with Saladin, it is worth raising the question of whether the count negotiated the truce on behalf of the Franks as a whole or with a view to maintaining his own authority for as long as possible; or, indeed, whether he was aware that a truce was in Saladin's interest.

In the 1962 film of *The Manchurian Candidate*, a prisoner of war, Raymond Shaw, is brainwashed by his captors during the Korean War. He returns to his country and becomes part of a plot to seize power. All the while he is secretly under the control of the enemy. Away from the realms of movie fiction, it is tempting to wonder just how far Raymond of Tripoli's long imprisonment affected his attitudes towards the crusaders' enemies and shaped his views on the future of the Christian states in the Levant. As the modern historian Zoé Oldenbourg wrote:

> *During his captivity, Raymond had learned other things besides*
> *the Holy Scriptures. He loved and understood the Moslem world,*
> *and perhaps even admired it.*[5]

Unfortunately, from the point of view of the crusader world, no Manchurian Candidate could have undermined Frankish strength as effectively as Raymond, who would later become – literally – a paid agent of Saladin. We are told that the count 'performed dishonourable acts to the cost of his own religion, in order to obtain gifts more easily'. And in a startling indication of how far Raymond had moved from the Christian fold, the Muslim historian Imad al-Din claimed that: 'The zeal of the count for the Muslims only grew, to the point where if he had not feared his co-religionaries, he would have embraced Islam.'[6]

Another unwanted side-effect of Raymond's truce, from the Franks' point of view, was that many crusading knights who had come to fight for the cross had to return home without striking a single blow against the Saracens. This not only wasted the latest crop of eager recruits, but was also damaging to the pipeline of fresh crusaders. Knights in Europe were reluctant to make the long voyage eastwards only to find the Latin states at peace with the heathen.

Safe from Frankish attacks during his illness, instead of suffering a break-up of his empire, Saladin actually saw his power grow. Most significantly, he received the homage of the last Zengid leader, Izz al-Din of Mosul. Izz al-Din promised obedience to Saladin and agreed to send troops for the Holy War when required. This submission confirmed Saladin's hegemony over Syria and northern Mesopotamia at the same time as his close brush with death reinforced his commitment to the jihad. Imad al-Din wrote of Saladin's malady: 'That sickness was sent by God to turn away sins… and to wake him from the sleep of forgetfulness.'[7]

While Saladin was ill, encouraged by Al-Fadil, he vowed to God that if he recovered he would never attack Muslims again, but would devote himself to the jihad. The sultan also promised once again that if he captured Reynald de Chatillon, he would kill him. The Qadi also got him to add Raymond of Tripoli, for good measure – whether friend or foe, to Saladin, Raymond was expendable. Thanks to the truce, the Franks had missed an opportunity to attack Saladin when he lay sick and helpless. By the time he recovered they were faced with a man who had reached a natural limit to his wars with his own faith and was fervently set on the annihilation of the polytheists.

In the late summer of 1186, while Saladin was still convalescing, the Kingdom of Jerusalem suffered another body blow. The young King Baldwin V died. He was still only eight years old. This brought Raymond's regency to an end, but the ambitious count was not keen to surrender power. He saw the chance to make a bid for the throne himself. The young king was to be buried in Jerusalem, and his mother Sybilla and her husband Guy went there immediately for the royal funeral. So too, from Kerak, did Reynald de Chatillon. His role was to prove critical to the succession struggle that was about to unfold. Rather than attend the funeral rites at Jerusalem, Raymond summoned a council of the barons in Nablus – a revealing location, as it was the power base of his Ibelin allies. Most of the leading nobles attended. Joscelin, the seneschal, remained on the coast to ensure control of the key port of Acre. He also seized the wealthy port of Beirut from Raymond. Critically, the other great magnate who definitely did not attend Raymond's council was Prince Reynald. The stage was set for a showdown between Raymond and his long-standing opponents.

Raymond had the majority of the barons on his side. At Nablus he also had Amalric's second daughter, Isabella, a potential heir to the throne, along with her husband, Humphrey of Toron. Raymond appealed to the web of oaths that the barons had sworn when he became regent. Some of these referred to a vague and unworkable scenario in which the next monarch of Jerusalem would be chosen by the Pope and a triumvirate of the King of England, the King of France and the German emperor. Actually this oath called for the crown to revert to 'the most rightful heirs' until such a process could be implemented. In the event, that is what happened. A successor was required immediately, so everyone simply ignored the more complex and unrealistic aspects of their oath, which might only have prolonged Raymond's regency.

The faction in Jerusalem held the trump cards. The count's old adversary, Prince Reynald, was one of these. He was the only man with the power, reputation and determination to stand up to Raymond. Patriarch Heraclius was on board as a long-time ally of the Courtenay faction and he provided critical Church support and spiritual authority. Also aligned with Raymond's opponents was the Master of the Temple, Gerard de Ridefort. Beyond any dynastic disagreements, there was 'malevolence and great strife' between Gerard and Raymond. This old feud dated back to the time when Gerard first arrived in Syria. He had been a knight-errant like Reynald and had served the Count of Tripoli as a mercenary. Raymond III had promised young Gerard the hand of the widowed heiress, Stephanie of Botron. But before the marriage could be finalized, a rich Pisan merchant called Plivain offered Raymond the lady's weight in gold if he could marry her instead. Raymond did not hesitate. He sold the heiress to Plivain. Soon afterwards Gerard joined the Order of the Temple and swore himself to celibacy. He never forgave Raymond, and in this succession dispute he gave full rein to his simmering hatred. Raymond's opponents also had possession of Jerusalem, the Holy Sepulchre and the royal regalia. Most importantly, they had the best claimant to the throne: the eldest daughter of King Amalric, sister of Baldwin IV and mother of the recently deceased Baldwin V, Princess Sybilla.

With so much at stake, events unfolded at a desperate pace. The barons at Nablus sent a delegation of bishops and nobles to Jerusalem to prevent the coronation of Sybilla. Reynald and his cohorts rejected their arguments. Aware that a military attack could come from Nablus at any time, Sybilla's supporters shut the gates of Jerusalem. It was a critical moment in the history of the kingdom. There was only a brief window in which to act.

At such a time Reynald de Chatillon could be relied upon to take the decisive step.

Hospital of the Order of St John, Jerusalem,
12 September 1186

The courtyard in St John's Hospital echoed to the strident sound of voices raised in anger. These were not just lay brothers squabbling. They were three of the most powerful men in Outremer. The Lord of Kerak and the Master of the Temple, Gerard de Ridefort, had found the Master of the Hospitallers, Roger de Moulins, hiding in his headquarters and they were now struggling with him over a key.

Not just any key.

The royal regalia of Jerusalem was kept locked in the *trésor* of the kingdom. Three keys were needed to open this vault. One was held by the Patriarch of Jerusalem, the second by the Master of the Templars, the third by the Master of the Hospitallers. Reynald and Gerard were demanding that third key.

The Master of the Hospitallers resisted as best he could, but few men could defy Reynald for any length of time. Thoroughly exasperated, Master Roger gave way and flung his key down into the courtyard. Reynald and Gerard retrieved it and, now with all three keys, proceeded to unlock the *trésor* and carry the royal crowns to Patriarch Heraclius, who awaited them in the Church of the Sepulchre.

There, in Christendom's Holy of Holies, glittering with gold in the light of a forest of candles, it was Reynald de Chatillon who took charge.

He rose to speak to the assembly of knights, church and civic leaders crowded into the building. Behind him on the altar sat the two crowns, destined for the next King and Queen of Jerusalem. As he stepped up into the chancel, Prince Reynald, Lord of Oultrejordan, onetime Prince of Antioch, was reaching the apogee of his career.

'Lords,' he said, loud and clear, looking down on the congregation, 'you know well that King Baldwin the Leper and his nephew, whom he had crowned, are dead. The kingdom has been left without an heir and without a ruler. Today, by your acclamation, we would crown Sybilla, who is here, for she is the daughter of King Amalric and sister of King Baldwin the Leper. She is the closest and the most rightful heir to the realm.'

With one voice, the congregation acclaimed Sybilla.

The Patriarch Heraclius solemnly placed the crown upon her head. She was now Queen of Jerusalem. Sybilla turned to her husband Guy, who knelt before her as she set the second crown upon his head.

Reynald de Chatillon was king-maker in Jerusalem in 1186. And his creation was King Guy I.

Chapter 18

KING-MAKER

The Patriarch, the Master of the Temple and Prince Reynald said that they were bound by no oath or faith. They would crown the lady Queen.

Ernoul

Watching from the congregation at the Holy Sepulchre that September day in 1186 was a spy.[1]

From Nablus, Raymond had sent a sergeant, disguised as a monk, to report on the situation in Jerusalem. Because the city gates were shut, the man had to enter by the postern of the Church of the Madeleine in the north wall. After the coronation, the spy slipped out of the city and returned to Nablus. The news that their anointed king was now Guy de Lusignan was greeted with dismay by the barons. Baldwin of Ibelin, who had wanted to marry Sybilla himself, was particularly disgusted. He swore that he would not serve under Guy, but would rather leave the kingdom, adding that Guy would not last a year as king.

The sheer speed of action by Reynald and Sybilla's party in Jerusalem had comprehensively outmanoeuvred the barons. Raymond had been outflanked, but he had one card left to play. He suggested crowning Reynald's stepson, Humphrey of Toron, as king in opposition to Guy. Like Guy, Humphrey's claim came through his wife; Isabella was the younger daughter of King Amalric and therefore had a claim almost as good as Sybilla's. The barons agreed. It was a fateful decision because, by setting up an anti-king, they were committing the country to civil war. However, they made a simple error, one that Reynald would never have made; they decided to crown Humphrey the next day.

The barons should not have given Humphrey time to think. Faced with the enormity of the decision, the young man realized he did not want to be king. Possibly this was due to his timid character; Humphrey was said to be 'more like a woman than a man, gentle in his dealings with a bad stammer'.[2] It may also have been due to the influence of his dominant, terrifying stepfather, Reynald de Chatillon. It is very likely that Reynald, for whom *loyauté* to the throne was always a cardinal virtue, would have sent a message to Humphrey in Nablus, reminding his stepson of the duty he owed to the rightful line and to the reigning monarch, whoever that might be. In this case, the galling fact was that the duly anointed king, to whom all loyal vassals owed allegiance, was now Guy de Lusignan. Humphrey may of course simply have rejected the crown to avoid plunging the country into a devastating conflict, one that would leave it at Saladin's mercy. Whatever his reasons, the unwilling pretender scurried to Jerusalem, apologized to his sister-in-law, Queen Sybilla, made his homage to King Guy and thus avoided his stepfather's wrath. Thanks to Humphrey's defection, the barons' revolt was aborted. The kingdom had been spared a disastrous civil war. The rebellious local nobility had only one viable alternative – submission. One by one the despondent barons made the journey to Jerusalem to do homage to the new king. Raymond, however, took refuge in Tiberias.

Guy was soon back to the old tricks he had tried as regent, favouring some of his Poitevin cronies over the native *Poulains*. When Guy became king, the Poitevins inflamed the locals' resentment by singing in the streets of Jerusalem:

> *Maugre li Pulain,*
> *Avrons nous roi Poitevin.*
>
> (In spite of the Poulains,
> We have a king who is Poitevin.)

According to the *Estoire d'Eracles*, 'This hatred and scorn gave rise to the loss of the kingdom of Jerusalem.'[3]

In late 1186 Guy held his first parliament. He summoned all the barons to assemble at the Church of the Holy Cross in Acre. The new king mounted the pulpit and harangued the congregation on how he had been crowned by the grace of God. The true power behind the throne, Reynald de Chatillon, stood prominently at his right hand as the barons swore fealty, one by one. And when it came to the turn of Baldwin of Ibelin to make his homage, it was Reynald who called him forth. Three times, in the king's name, Reynald summoned Baldwin to do his duty. Three times Baldwin refused. When the king called him in person, Baldwin still demurred, saying, 'My father never paid homage to your father, and I will not do so to you.'[4] Then he committed his lands to the care of his brother Balian and set off for Antioch with all his knights.

The arrival there of such a famed warrior and his powerful retinue was good news for Reynald's stepson, Bohemond III of Antioch. Prince Bohemond may also have relished helping out his stepfather's enemy:

> *When the prince of Antioch heard that Baldwin of Ibelin was*
> *coming to him with so many knights, he was delighted. He went*
> *to meet them and received them with great joy.*[5]

But Antioch's gain was Jerusalem's loss. The kingdom could not spare such an experienced leader and so many fighting men. By leaving with all his vassals, Baldwin was doing his best to make Guy's reign as short as the single year he had forecast, but any problems King Guy and his supporters had with Baldwin were nothing compared to the menace of Count Raymond.

In the most commonly accepted version of the crusader story, Raymond is a hero. He is one of the wise *Poulains* born and raised in Outremer who understood Muslims and was prepared to live amongst them. In the view of historians like Sir Steven Runciman, Raymond's faction was that of an assimilated local baronage pitted against aggressive, short-sighted and acquisitive newcomers like Reynald and Guy. This version clearly does not make sense because the Courtenays, one of the great native families of Outremer, were at the centre of opposition to Raymond. And by the 1180s Reynald had spent more than thirty years in the East – hardly a newcomer.

This traditional view of the factions in the crusader kingdom has mutated subtly over the years into a different caricature, reflecting modern preoccupations with international geopolitics, especially in reference to Middle Eastern conflicts such as those in Iraq, Afghanistan and the wider conflict with fundamentalist Islam, the 'War on Terror'. In this anachronistic view, Raymond's faction is vaguely understood as the more tolerant, understanding 'Doves'; Reynald's as the more aggressive 'Hawks', with Reynald cast as the Hawk par excellence and portrayed as the arrogant expatriate crushing the local Muslims under his colonialist Christian boot. Somehow Reynald's critics seem to believe that alliances such as those Raymond undertook with the Muslims offered an alternative future of accommodation for the Latin states in the Levant.

These views are of course misguided, relying on the naive idea that some sort of magical multicultural compact might have enabled Frank and Saracen to live together in harmony in the Promised Land.

The archetypal expression of this take on the factions of the Latin Kingdom is seen in Ridley Scott's film *Kingdom of Heaven*. In the movie, the Raymond character, 'Tiberias', is wise, tolerant, dovish, virtually a pacifist. He is a crusader version of how the saintly Saladin is portrayed in the same film. Both portraits of these ruthless men of violence are wildly inaccurate of course, but in likening Raymond to Saladin, Scott was closer to the truth than he might have realized. Because, after Guy's coronation, Raymond took the only route that still offered him a hope, however slim, of winning the throne. Perhaps it was a route to which he had been disposed ever since his captivity under Nur al-Din. Raymond had indeed 'gone native' to such an extent that he joined forces with the crusaders' greatest enemy. He still sought the kingship and, to get it, he cut a deal with Saladin. According to Saladin's secretary, Imad al-Din:

> The count put himself under the protection of the sultan and became one of his partisans. The sultan had welcomed him with kind words and, to encourage him, released some of his officers he had in captivity. The count sent detachments against the countries of the Franks that came back with booty and prisoners...[6]

One of the chroniclers who continued the work of William of Tyre[7] says that, after leaving Nablus in 1186, Count Raymond parleyed with Saladin's nephew. The count came to terms with the Muslims and became Saladin's vassal, paying homage to him for Tripoli. Ibn al-Athir recorded that Raymond asked Saladin for help in attaining his ambitions. Saladin accepted Raymond's allegiance and, in return, 'He guaranteed that he would make him independent leader of all the Franks.'[8]

Raymond's treason was a devastating blow to crusader unity.* The lord of Tiberias, greatest magnate of the Kingdom of Jerusalem, and the ruler of its Christian ally, the county of Tripoli, had defected to the enemy, with all his strength. Muslim observers such as Imad al-Din were well aware that the count's alliance with Saladin represented a dangerous weakening of the kingdom:

> *One of the events decreed by Providence in favour of Islam for the ruin of Unbelief was the following: The count of Tripoli desired to enjoy friendly relations with the sultan and resorted to an alliance with him against his fellow Christians.*[9]

Ensconced in his fortress town of Tiberias on its great lake, the Sea of Galilee, Raymond continued to refuse homage to Guy. Indeed, it would have been tricky for him to swear homage to Guy, since he had already done so to Saladin. The king assembled an army and moved into Raymond's fief, intending to bring him to heel. The count then took the extreme step of invoking his pact with Saladin. He put himself under the sultan's protection and Saladin dispatched Muslim cavalry, infantry and archers to garrison Tiberias against the king. Faced with Saladin's soldiers in a Frankish city and the prospect of a catastrophic civil war, Guy backed down.

Not only would such a conflict have been fatal for the realm, but it might also have violated the truce Guy himself had negotiated with Saladin after he had been crowned. Raymond's displacement as regent and his alliance with Saladin meant that the truce he had negotiated for the Kingdom of Jerusalem was void. With rampant factionalism racking the country, one of Guy's first acts as king – backed by leading advisers, including the Masters of the Temple and Hospital – had been

---

* Even Runciman, a staunch Raymondophile, admits that the count's actions were 'undoubtedly treasonable'.

to renegotiate the truce with Saladin; the kingdom was too fractured to risk a conflict with the sultan. The days of the Muslims paying for peace were long past. The Franks paid Saladin the swingeing price of 60,000 bezants for an armistice.

The peace was confirmed until the following Easter. That would fall on 5 April 1187. In theory, the kingdom could enjoy peace until then, unless something – or someone – got in the way.

The King's Highway, Oultrejordan, winter 1186–7

The grizzled veteran was back in his element. In full battle gear, Reynald de Chatillon sat on his warhorse, ready for action. Around him, in concealed positions flanking the highway, lurked his armed men – as many as he had been able to find at short notice. They lay in wait for a great prize.

Just a few days before, one of Reynald's spies had come to him in haste at Acre. Oultrejordan's early-warning system had detected a great caravan on its way from Cairo to Damascus. With the caravan marched a substantial military force. Their route would take them past Kerak. Reynald had mounted his horse without delay and ridden straight to his fief to prepare the ambush.

The magnificent caravan, a seemingly endless lines of beasts and their drivers, moved slowly into sight, camels swaying under their loads, columns of soldiers marching and riding alongside. Proceeding under the safety of the truce, they were completely unprepared when Reynald's men sprang the trap.

Without warning, the Franks swept down on their prey like wolves on the fold. They captured the caravan in its entirety. Overwhelming the troops, Reynald seized their weapons, beasts and merchandise and imprisoned them in the dungeons of Kerak.

When Saladin heard that Arnat had taken the caravan, he was beside himself with rage. The sultan protested to King Guy, demanding restitution. Guy in his turn asked Reynald to return the prisoners and the goods.

'I will return nothing,' answered the Prince of Kerak. 'I am lord in my lands, as you are in yours. I have no truce with the Saracens.'

To his Muslim prisoners, pleading to be released, Reynald was equally dismissive.

'Let your Muhammad set you free!' he said.[10]

Chapter 19

TRUCE-BREAKER

When there is peace on every hand, let there be a strip of war
    left for me.
Blight his eyes who parts me from it, although I may have
    begun it first!
Peace gives me no comfort; I agree with war,
For I neither hold nor believe any other law.

Bertran de Born

Perish the hands of Abu Lahab, and perish he!
His wealth avails him not, neither what he has earned;
He shall roast at a flaming fire.

Quran, sura 111

Unlike the questionable capture of the caravan back in 1182, there is no
doubt that Reynald attacked a caravan in the winter of 1186–7. Muslim
and Frankish writers alike record this. The taking of this caravan is one
of the great crimes laid at Reynald's door. Ernoul said it was the cause of
disaster for the Frankish kingdom. Posterity has long held the same view.

For Sir Steven Runciman it was 'impious brigandage... shameless... an outrage'.[1] But even if this action did break the truce, it is wrong to use it to brand Reynald as more violent or irresponsible than other leaders of the period. Many truces had been broken over the years: Baldwin I invaded Damascene territory in 1113; King Baldwin III did the same in 1164; King Amalric breached his oath by invading Egypt in 1168. Baldwin II was shocked that a Muslim 'knight' like the emir Toghtekin reneged on his promises, but he did. According to William of Tyre, even the usually honourable Saladin broke a truce when it suited him in 1181. Reynald's actions here have been magnified out of proportion. For instance, Ernoul spices up the story by incorrectly claiming that Saladin's sister was captured with this caravan. And of course Reynald did his image no favours with his vivid use of language to Christian and Muslim alike – 'I am lord in my lands, as you are in yours', 'Let your Muhammad set you free!' – these phrases that the chroniclers ascribe to Reynald have his typically expressive, memorable ring.

There are also other questions over this event, or at least over whether it was seen as a violation of the truce at the time. The Muslim chronicler Ibn al-Athir, for instance, does not say that Arnat breached any general truce, but rather that he had had arranged his own personal *aman*, or armistice, for himself and his family. Given the sworn enmity between Saladin and Reynald, this is highly unlikely. For the pro-Saladin historian Imad al-Din, Reynald's offence was the excessive tolls that he exacted on passing caravans. It appears that the sultan's anger with Reynald was as much about the constant problem he represented as about any particular incident.

After all, why would Reynald have attacked this caravan? Perhaps he was simply an inveterate brigand acting on irresistible impulse. But hundreds of tempting caravans had passed through his dominions unmolested over the years. The Seigneur of Oultrejordan earned a healthy profit from them through taxes – an expense greatly resented by the Muslims, but hardly a violation of the truce. During the 1180s, Muslim observers confirmed that caravans routinely passed through Frankish territory, paying tolls and customs duty, even when truces were not in place. Why would Reynald have jeopardized this perennial revenue stream for one rash attack?

The mention of the substantial military escort is a clue. In the early months of 1187 Saladin was known to be planning an attack on the kingdom. He was mustering his forces, apparently with the intention of resuming the jihad when the truce expired at Easter. Ibn al-Athir stresses that the caravan was 'accompanied by a good number of soldiers'.[2] Reynald may well have regarded this as a movement of troops rather than a merchant caravan. Imad al-Din wrote that the rich caravan was:

> escorted by a contingent of soldiers. He [Reynald] made them fall into a trap. He took them to Kerak. He took their mounts and equipment and inflicted on them the worst of punishments. The sultan then swore that he would have his life.[3]

However, under the terms of the truce, Reynald would have been within his rights to waylay a hostile military force moving through his territory. And he would have felt justified in rejecting calls for reimbursement. After Reynald captured the caravan, Imad al-Din records that Saladin sent Arnat a message, 'Blaming him for his conduct and reproaching him for his perfidy and pillage, but he simply became more obstinate and malicious.'[4]

It is clear, in the light of later events, that Saladin's propaganda needed to paint Reynald as a villain. Frankish writers like Ernoul were also seeking to shift the responsibility for subsequent disasters away from their patrons (in Ernoul's case, the Ibelin family and the man they followed, Raymond of Tripoli) and place the blame on Reynald. Ernoul's version mirrors his two previous confused accounts of Reynald's capture of caravans. In all three cases, Reynald rebuffs the monarch when he demands return of the goods and prisoners. In King Guy's case, he is hardly likely to have made such demands. Reynald was, after all, Guy's leading supporter. Any such requests would have been purely for show. Intriguingly, the *Latin Continuation of William of Tyre* records that Saladin asked Count Raymond to take up the question of restitution with Arnat. Unsurprisingly, Raymond got short shrift from the Lord of Kerak, and reported as much back to his master, the sultan.

Whatever the truth, Reynald had enraged Saladin once more, and again the sultan vowed to kill the Prince of Kerak. In any case the capture of the caravan was clearly not the real cause of the next stage in the Holy War. If Saladin did actually cite Reynald's actions to justify taking up jihad again, it was only as a pretext. As the modern biographers of Saladin, Malcolm Lyons and D. E. P Jackson, put it:

> *The seizure of the caravan may have envenomed Saladin's relations with Reynald, but it was obvious even without this that the Holy War was about to be resumed.*[5]

Saladin had completed his subjugation of the Zengid territories, and his illness had finally focused his commitment to the jihad. He would have attacked the Franks anyway. This view is supported by the fact that Saladin allowed the truce to expire before invading the kingdom. He clearly felt he had no good justification for breaking the truce himself, though Reynald's actions may have made him unwilling to renew it.

For the Franks, the portents of 1187 had not been good. As Saladin prepared his war there were prophecies of famine, earthquake and doom.[6] Meanwhile the kingdom was as divided as ever; its greatest vassal was in league with the enemy, and Saladin's 'knights, sergeants and bowman' still occupied Tiberias. Saladin had promised Raymond that if Guy 'attacked in the morning, rescue would come by evening. If he was attacked in the evening, he would be rescued in the morning.' Under the protection of the sultan, Raymond remained in flagrant rebellion against the king. It was as though the Franks had a death wish, as Ibn al-Athir recorded:

> *Thus their unity was disrupted and their cohesion broken. This was one of the most important factors that brought about the conquest of their territories and the liberation of Jerusalem.*[7]

All too aware of the Franks' divided state, Saladin mustered troops from all parts of his empire to fight the jihad. They came from Mosul, Harran, Edessa, Irbil and from all over Syria and Egypt. There were siege engineers from distant Khorasan and fervent volunteers from as far afield as Morocco. But it was not until after Easter and the expiry of the truce that Saladin moved into Frankish territory. In April 1187, the sultan's first attack was again aimed at his worst enemy. He moved his troops down into Oultrejordan and ravaged the lands around Kerak, cutting down 'crops, vines and olive trees'. The lion was yet again forcing the wolf back into his lair.

Meanwhile Saladin sent raiding parties into the kingdom, passing through the lands of his ally, Count Raymond, around Tiberias. Now Raymond's treachery went beyond undermining Frankish unity and had direct and devastating military impact. Fatally, he gave permission to Saladin's general, Kukburi, to lead a raid deep into Frankish territory. 'These troops left in the dead of night, sneaking through the gloom' and the count allowed them to pass unhindered through his fief of Galilee. But Galilee, as the frontier province, was normally the first barrier against Muslim incursion. The Frankish lands behind Galilee were unprepared for an attack. On 1 May 1187, when the Masters of the Temple and Hospital, who were at the nearby Templar fort of La Fève, heard that the Saracens had entered the kingdom and were ravaging the lands around Nazareth, they gathered all the knights they could find and marched to repel the invaders.

It was a potent strike force – about eighty Templars, ten Hospitallers and forty knights from the royal garrison at Nazareth. Near the wells of Cresson, they came upon the Saracens. The Muslim army was many times larger, perhaps 7,000 horse. According to Ibn al-Athir, the ensuing battle was one 'fit to turn black hair grey'. When the Marshal of the Temple, Jacques de Mailly, hesitated before charging the massed Turkish cavalry, his Master, Gerard de Ridefort, taunted him that he loved his blond locks too much to risk them. Jacques joined the other knights in a ferocious attack. The outnumbered Franks were all but annihilated, and Jacques de Mailly was beheaded. The Master of the Hospitallers was killed and all the royal knights captured. Only the badly wounded Master of the Temple and two other knights escaped. The Saracen raiders rode back across the Jordan dragging lines of yoked prisoners. The heads of the Frankish knights they skewered on their spear tips. The people of Tiberias could see their friends' heads bobbing on the Saracen lances as they passed.

The Muslims well understood the significance of the battle: Saladin rejoiced in the victory, which had dealt a body blow to the fighting strength of the kingdom. The Franks had lost an experienced senior commander in Roger de Moulins, and around 10 per cent of their knights – all of them among the best trained and most effective. 'It was a great triumph,' wrote Ibn al-Athir, 'for the Templars and the Hospitallers are the Franks' firebrands.'[8]

As soon as he heard of the victory at Cresson, Saladin raised the siege of Kerak and moved north to join the rest of his army, camped close to the Jordan River. It was an impressive host. Saladin had gathered chieftains and their warriors from all over the Near East. Imad al-Din was amazed. He had never seen such a powerful, well-armed force, 'so menacing for the infidels and so numerous'.[9] It was:

An imposing entourage of illustrious chiefs, in the middle of a
massive, well-equipped army, a legion of invincible lions... our
camp stretched for several leagues in all directions, covering the
hills and plains.[10]

Around 26 June 1187, Saladin led this monstrous force across the
Jordan and into crusader territory at the south end of the Sea of Galilee.
Imad al-Din described how 'The army, like the ocean, enveloped the
Lake of Tiberias, and the vast plains disappeared under the unfolding
tents.'[11]

Guy and Raymond had to settle their differences or the kingdom
faced certain destruction. The pro-Raymond Frankish sources claim that
King Guy reconsidered and decided to make his peace with Raymond.
Islamic historians reveal the real reasons behind the rapprochement:
Raymond had gone too far and had alienated many of his supporters.
They resented the alliance with Saladin, and blamed Raymond for
the disaster at Cresson.* The king sent a high-level delegation from
Jerusalem to Tiberias and censured Raymond for his actions. 'There
is no doubt that you have become a Muslim,' the delegation said,
'otherwise you could not have endured what the Muslims did to the
Templars and Hospitallers recently.'[12] Raymond's vassals agreed with
the royal embassy, warning the count that they would throw off their
allegiance unless he renounced his deal with Saladin. At the same
time the patriarch threatened to excommunicate Raymond and annul
his marriage. This was a potent threat – Raymond was only Prince of
Galilee through his wife. Annulment would cost him his fief. 'When
the Count saw the seriousness of his position,' the Muslim sources tell

---

* Attempting to exculpate Raymond, Ernoul spun a convoluted yarn about the
battle of Cresson. Effectively he said the Muslim cavalry were on a peaceful
sightseeing day-trip through Frankish territory and, if the foolish Templars had
let them pass, everything would have been fine. Bizarrely, many historians have
accepted this fable.

us, 'he was fearful, made excuses, renounced [his recent course] and repented.'[13]

Raymond offered his homage to King Guy. With the kingdom preparing to weather another great Saracen storm, Guy needed all his fighting strength. He was obliged to accept Raymond's apology. At a staged and, no doubt, stilted ceremony near the castle of St Job, he received Raymond's fealty and gave him the symbolic kiss of peace. In theory the kingdom's great powers were now reconciled, but the public agreement only papered over the bitter divisions. The wounds of the succession battle were still fresh and the feud between the main factions, based on resentments old and new, still ran deep. Reynald de Chatillon, for one, was not convinced by Raymond's show of remorse.

While Saladin's forces gathered, the Christian army mustered at Sephora as usual. The king issued the *arrière ban*, calling up all available men. He recruited visiting crusaders and hired as many mercenaries as he could. Those Templars and Hospitallers who had not been present at Cresson arrived in full strength, along with a contingent of knights from Antioch. The newly reconciled Count Raymond and his knights from Tripoli and Galilee were there, too. The True Cross trundled to Sephora from Jerusalem. Castles all over the land were emptied of their garrisons as the Franks assembled the biggest army in the history of the Kingdom of Jerusalem. This force offered a daunting challenge to their Muslim foes. 'Their flags fluttered in ranks,' wrote Imad al-Din, who accompanied Saladin on this campaign, 'their banners deployed on the walls of Sephora, knights and infantry, lancers and archers assembled in great numbers.'[14]

This army was paid for by treasure provided by Henry II of England, rather than by an income tax. He had donated the gold to help assuage his guilty conscience over the murder of his erstwhile friend and turbulent Archbishop of Canterbury, Thomas Becket. The fund was meant to cover Henry's costs if and when he came on crusade, but the kingdom's leaders judged that it was needed immediately.

Once again Guy de Lusignan was in charge of a mighty host, a colossal 1,200 knights and perhaps 18,000 infantry. Again he needed to overcome doubts, divisions and discord. The two great antagonists, Reynald and Raymond, still led their two hostile factions, and their differences threatened to crystallize at a time of utmost peril for the entire crusader venture in the East.

King Guy would have to find a way for them to work together, or even this great army risked disaster.

Wells of Sephora, Galilee, late June 1187

In the close summer night the encampment of the great Frankish army around Sephora sweated in a state of paralysis beneath the stars. Around them Saladin's hordes roamed unchecked, plundering and burning across Galilee. As night fell, the crusaders looked out on apocalyptic vision. All the countryside was aflame, 'like a sea of fire'.

In the great brocaded tent of King Guy the arguments raged. Reynald, as ever, was at the centre of the storm. He was probably now in his sixties, and most men of his generation were dead or decrepit. Not Reynald. Endowed with an iron constitution and a vigorous mind, the prince had not lost his leadership skills. He was still the insatiable, aggressive man of action. A lifetime of warfare had left him in no doubt as to what strategy should be adopted.

He urged Guy to seize the initiative and attack. Supported by the Master of the Temple and many others, Reynald counselled the king that he should not make the mistake he had made in 1183, sitting idly while Saladin ravaged and pillaged with impunity. Guy was new to the throne. He had to establish his authority.

Reynald's advice was simple: 'Chase Saladin from the realm,' he told the king, 'or your kingdom is lost.'

Predictably, the newly reconciled Raymond of Tripoli disagreed. As he had in 1183, when he undermined Guy's regency, he suggested a defensive strategy.

'Sire,' he said, 'I advise that you provide your cities and your castles with men, arms, provisions and anything else that is necessary... Once the heat of the summer has tired out Saladin's forces, we will fall on the rearguard of his army and inflict such damage that, if God pleases, the realm will enjoy complete peace.'

But Raymond's rivals had not forgotten, or forgiven, his pact with Saladin. And Reynald perhaps remembered even further back; his doubts about Raymond's sympathies may have arisen long before, in the prison pits under the white citadel of Aleppo. You can almost hear the snarl in Reynald's voice down the ages as he turned on Raymond: 'You can stop trying to make us frightened of the Muslims. There is no doubt that you are on their side and favour them, otherwise you would not have said this.'

Along with the Master of the Temple, whose old dislike of Raymond had become a burning hatred since the slaughter of his Templar brothers at Cresson, Reynald dismissed the count's advice as the words of Saladin in disguise.

'This counsel,' Prince Reynald said, 'is mixed with the hair of the wolf.'

'Tiberias is already as good as lost,' Raymond pleaded with the king. 'You must not move from here. Saladin has too many men.'

Reynald scoffed at this. The victor of Mont Gisard had no fear of superior numbers.

'They are indeed many,' he said, 'but the fire is not daunted by the size of the wood pile.'[15]

Chapter 20

APOCALYPSE

*About two years later, I passed by the site of the battle and saw
the ground covered with their bones, visible from afar, some of
them heaped up and others scattered about and this was apart
from those that torrents had swept away or wild beasts in those
thickets and hollows had taken.*

Ibn al-Athir[1]

The arguments for an immediate attack were forceful. It might have
appeared a riskier option, especially for the normally cautious Franks,
but there was much to be said for it. The crusader army would have
to face a numberless enemy, yes, but it had triumphed over great odds
before. A bold strike might even inspire the host to valiant deeds. An
attack could seize the initiative, win over Guy's doubters and perhaps
even weld together the disparate factions in his army. And Saladin's
men were not invincible. They had their fears and their doubts. Their
army had its factions and its weaknesses. As Baha al-Din recorded,
Saladin's nervous host was far from believing that an easy victory was
at hand:

The Muslims were well aware that behind them was the Jordan
and before them enemy territory and that there was nothing to
save them but God Almighty.[2]

But as the councils succeeded one another at Sephora, Guy paid heed to Count Raymond's advice. The king waited. This was a hard strategy for Guy to carry off. It might have been tempting to wait at his safe, well-watered base until Saladin withdrew, but, as Prince Reynald and the Master of the Temple had reminded him, Guy was under great pressure to act. Even if his inaction at the wells of Tubaniya four years before had been militarily excusable, it had been a political disaster so seismic that it had cost him the regency. As a new king, a repeat fiasco would leave him irrevocably weakened. Furthermore, this great army had been hired at vast cost, emptying the coffers of the kingdom, including the hoard supplied by Henry of England. Not to exploit such a host would be a sin.

While he hesitated, Saladin's men ravaged the countryside, burning crops, sacking villages and looting the great monastery on Mount Tabor. For a week the Franks watched patiently from their base, immobile under their tents. Then Saladin forced Guy's hand. On 2 July 1187, the sultan took the risk of splitting his army. He led a substantial force to besiege Tiberias. This might have been the best opportunity for the Franks to engage the invaders in a pitched battle – Reynald had exploited such a dispersed force to defeat Saladin in 1177 – but the sultan had judged his current opponent well. Guy and his army were rooted in their reactive strategy.

If Tiberias held out, the Franks still had a number of options, including the tempting prospect of pinning the besieging force against the town. But, shockingly, within just an hour of the first, ferocious assault, Tiberias fell. Despite ample warning, and despite his own recommended strategy of defending the fortified places, Raymond had pitifully failed to garrison the city. It did not help that the Muslim forces knew its defences intimately. Thanks to Raymond's alliance with Saladin, they had manned the walls of Tiberias until just a few weeks before. The same troops now turned on their erstwhile allies and sacked the town without mercy, killing, pillaging and enslaving. Raymond's wife and children held out in the citadel. They sent the news to the king, just fifteen miles away at Sephora, begging for relief. The rank and file of the crusader army were infuriated by the news and cried out for the host to 'go and rescue the ladies of Tiberias'.[3]

The story given in some of the sources is that, despite the pleas of his family and the destruction of his fief, Raymond argued against going to the relief of Tiberias. It is hard to believe that any leader in that position, let alone a knight like Raymond, would abandon his family and his vassals to annihilation or enslavement. Other sources paint a more likely picture, with the *Latin Continuation of William of Tyre* recording that Count Raymond begged the king to go to the aid of his city.

With Tiberias captured and its citadel besieged, King Guy could no longer remain inert. Finally the trumpets sounded and the great crusader army heaved into motion around the True Cross. It was an awesome sight to their Muslim foes. The Frankish host was like a range of mountains on the move, a succession of billowing waves of shining steel and coloured banners, with the holy, golden cross shining at its centre. But Guy had not decided on attack. He had chosen a third option – a fighting march to the relief of Tiberias. Presumably Reynald would have supported this option over complete passivity, but it was still not the pitched battle that he had argued for from the beginning of Saladin's invasion. By waiting until Saladin had captured Tiberias, the Franks had handed him a great prize, a boost in morale and the initiative. Saladin had chosen the battleground.

The marching battle was one the crusaders employed successfully on many occasions. The tactic gave the Franks the option of engaging directly, if the chance arose. If it did not, they could simply carry on marching. The typical formation was for the infantry and archers to form a protective curtain around their most potent weapon, the mounted knights. The crusaders proved time and again that, if they maintained this formation, the Muslims could not beat them. They could march all day under the rain of arrows from the Turkish horse archers. The Frankish coats of mail were superior to the Muslim armour and were worn doubled, by those who could afford it. Inside, they were padded with thick jerkins. The crusaders would be so peppered with arrows after a day's march that they were often described as 'hedgehogs'.

Baldwin III had marched for days across the bare desert during his retreat from Bosra in 1147. On that occasion the host had also been tortured by thirst and by the attacks of a far more numerous Muslim army. Under the undisputed leadership of King Baldwin, the Franks had held together and survived. In 1191, Richard the Lionheart would fight marching battles day after day against Saladin during the Third Crusade, with notable success.

Through the sweltering 3 July the tactic proved itself again. Amidst clouds of dust and a constant storm of arrows that darkened the sky, the Franks marched steadily towards Tiberias. Despite the heat and Saladin's vast host, the Franks were able to beat off any number of Muslim attacks, to the great frustration of their enemies, as the eyewitness Imad al-Din reported:

> *The burning heat of the dog days beat down on these men encased*
> *in steel. The blazing sky inflamed their fury. One after another*
> *the cavalry sorties succeeded each other amid the shimmering*
> *haze of heat… Despite the terrible thirst that devoured them, they*
> *remained patient, stoic, arrogant, persisting in their attacks like*
> *dogs.*[4]

After some hard fighting, rather than directly attacking the Saracens or pressing on to the lake and the relief of Tiberias, Guy called a halt. The Franks made camp by the hamlet of Meskanah.[5] It lay on the barren plain below the Horns of Hattin, a bare, rocky outcrop with two low summits on either side of a saddle. The *Estoire d'Eracles* says the decision to stop was made on the advice of the Count of Tripoli. 'The king accepted this advice, but it was bad advice. If the Christians had pressed home the attack, they would have defeated the Turks.'[6]

Others claimed the halt was Guy's idea, perhaps forced by Saladin launching a massive attack against the Templar rearguard. Either way, the decision was not a helpful one. In the 1183 campaign, the inexperienced Guy had failed to organize food supplies. In 1187, logistics again proved his Achilles heel, but this time the shortage was even more critical – water. The night was baking hot, and water at the Meskanah campsite was in short supply. A large pool held some dregs of the winter rains and there were huge rock cisterns cut into the hills, but the thirsty army exhausted these overnight. Meanwhile the Muslims surrounded the Franks so tightly that 'not a cat could have escaped'. The two armies were close enough to chat from their campfires across no-man's-land.

Rumour in the Frankish camp turned to bad omens, and a story spread among the men about an old Saracen woman whom some sergeants in the rearguard had met on her donkey earlier in the day. Believing her to be a witch, they had tried to burn her alive and then finished her off with a hatchet in the head, but it was thought that the curse she had set upon the army had not been lifted. In the baleful darkness, pierced by the constant Muslim chants of 'God is Great', doubts and dissension bubbled over. In the night a native Frankish knight went to the king and urged him to fight. This would finally erase the resentment between Guy's retainers from Poitou and the *Poulains*. 'Sire,' he said, 'now is the time for you to make the *Poulains* with their beards dear to the men of your country.'

While hostility simmered between the local Franks and the king's Poitevin entourage, some went further in undermining the Frankish cause. A band of five knights went over to the sultan. Significantly, they came from the retinue of the Count of Tripoli. The *Estoire d'Eracles* accuses them of converting to Islam and urging Saladin to attack the crusaders: 'Lord, what are you waiting for? Fall upon them. They can do no more. They are as good as dead.'[7]

This defection and the insight it gave into the Christians' vulnerable state gave Saladin and his men extra confidence. The Muslims and Franks had been equally tired that night after the first day's fighting. Saladin's biographer, Baha al-Din, said that both sides:

> Had spent the night in arms, expecting his adversary at every moment, though too weak through tiredness to stand up and unable through fatigue to crawl, let alone run.[8]

Overnight the Muslims became eager to attack the Franks, though the day before they had been fearful of them. The next day would be a fight to the death.

In the morning, both armies knew that 'whichever was broken' would be destroyed. When the Franks resumed their march, the Saracens redoubled their attacks, loosing arrows like swarms of locusts. The fighting was fierce, but the Franks held their formation. Guy's men were now under attack from all sides. The sheer numbers of the Muslim army were terrifying. Morale was precarious. Perhaps some of the less-committed divisions, such as those of Raymond of Tripoli and Balian of Ibelin, were already murmuring about escape. At some stage during the day the king decided that he had listened to Raymond enough. Guy turned to Reynald de Chatillon for counsel. The old warrior gave the advice you might expect, as one of William of Tyre's continuators records:

> *When the king saw the torments that were afflicting his army, he*
> *called the master of the Temple and Prince Reynald and asked*
> *their advice. They counseled him to join battle with the Saracens.*[9]

Reynald advised the king to attack. Finally the mighty host would take the fight to Saladin. Reynald's veteran hand was once again at the helm of the royal army. But this was not the inspired band of warriors that he led to victory at Mont Gisard, or even the disciplined, united corps with which the leper-king had won the day at Le Forbelet in 1182. Quarrelling commanders bedevilled this hapless army, and morale was sabotaged by suspicion, doubt and treachery.

Under the relentless Muslim attacks, the showers of arrows obscuring the sky and the strength-sapping heat, Frankish morale began to crack. Discipline stretched to breaking point. The infantry and cavalry became separated. Without their screen of footmen, the precious warhorses were more vulnerable to Turkish arrows. Some of the foot soldiers struck out pell-mell towards the distant Sea of Galilee, desperate for water, and were cut down. Some disheartened infantrymen began to surrender, listless with dehydration. The Muslims set fire to the brush, and the breeze fanned the flames and smoke towards the Franks, roasting horses and exacerbating their thirst.

Even now, all was not lost, but as the battle turned against the Franks, they suffered a catastrophic blow. At the worst possible moment, predictably but tragically, the crusader army snapped along factional lines. While Reynald de Chatillon stood and fought loyally beside the king, Raymond of Tripoli, the greatest magnate of the kingdom, with all his surviving knights – perhaps 200 horse – fled the field. The suicidal political divisions in the kingdom had delivered their *coup de grâce*. Frankish and Muslim sources alike described this moment:

The Count of Tripoli charged down the slope at the Saracens in
the valley. And when the Saracens saw them charging they parted,
making way for them as was their custom. As soon as the Count
had passed through, the Saracens closed ranks again and attacked
the King.[10]

The Count was a clever and shrewd leader of theirs. He saw that the signs of defeat were already upon his co-religionists and no notion of aiding his fellows stopped him thinking about himself, so he fled at the beginning of the engagement before it grew fierce…[11]

To the Christians, Raymond's desertion was cowardice or treachery, or both. According to the *Chronicle of the Third Crusade*, written not long after Hattin, Raymond:

actually intended to betray his people, as he had agreed with
Saladin… right at the moment of engagement, the aforesaid count
of Tripoli fell back and feigned flight. It was rumoured that he did
this in order to break up our formation and that he had agreed to
abandon his own people, to strike fear into those whom he should
have assisted, while arousing the enemy's courage.[12]

Conveniently, the troops of Guy's other opponents, Balian of Ibelin, and the knights of Antioch, also somehow found the means to escape the battle. The chronicle of Abu Shama states clearly that it was Raymond and the 'chiefs of his faction' who fled the field.

The desertion crippled the Frankish army, but they did not give up. In Abu Shama we read of how the Franks were at first downhearted, but quickly 'they regained courage; far from surrender, they held firm in their positions and even returned to the attack. They charged and penetrated our ranks.'[13]

Now missing many of their best knights, the Franks still pushed forward as far as the Horns of Hattin. Some of the infantry had already scaled the outcrop. There, behind the ruins of an ancient wall, they set up defensive lines and found some respite from the Saracen arrows. The Frankish high command also clambered up the hill and Guy ordered the royal tent to be pitched on the summit. From the hill they could see down to the Sea of Galilee, glimmering far below like a mirage. Coiling all around their position, in clouds of dust, boiled the hordes of innumerable Turkish horsemen, in a constant Brownian motion of whirling attacks and retreats. And always the dark clouds of arrows surging up and then swooping down into the Frankish ranks, like 'flocks of starlings'. The hard-pressed defensive lines were pushed back perilously close to the True Cross. One of its attendants, the Bishop of Acre, was killed. The Saracens began to sense victory.

In the throbbing heat of 4 July in Palestine, atop of one of the Horns of Hattin, Reynald and the most renowned knights of the kingdom gathered around their bewildered king and planned their next move – a charge against Saladin's centre. The charge was the Franks' most fearsome weapon. To opponents it seemed that a mounted mailed knight could 'drive a hole through the walls of Babylon'.[14] In close formation, wedged together so tightly that some horses might even be lifted off the ground, the charge, with its cutting edge of couched lances, could prove unstoppable. Reynald had advised attack from the start and knew that, if delivered against the centre, where Saladin sat surrounded by his high command and his Mamluk bodyguard, a successful onslaught could still turn the battle. This was the advice given to the king by a certain John, a knight who had served in the Muslim armies. But it might just as easily have been Reynald's hand behind this throw of the dice. At Mont Gisard ten years before, Reynald had sent his charge straight at the elite troops around Saladin. Then the Muslim formation had been pierced and Saladin had only just escaped with his life. Now, from the saddle of the Horns of Hattin, with all the ferocity they could muster, the Franks delivered their massed charge into the heart of the Muslim lines.

Saladin's son, Al-Afdal, was on the receiving end of the terrifying attack of this armoured juggernaut. Ibn al-Athir recorded his story:

> I was alongside my father in that battle… When the king of the Franks was on the hill with that band, they made a formidable charge against the Muslims facing them, so that they drove them back to my father. I looked towards him and he was overcome with grief and his complexion pale.[15]

The Muslims managed to beat off the attack and pushed the crusaders back up the Horns. Critically, the Franks lacked the knights of Tripoli and the other deserters, but even so the first well-directed onslaught came remarkably close to success. Undeterred by their repulse, Reynald, the king and the surviving knights broke off from the mêlée, re-formed their ranks and aimed another charge right at the spot where Saladin sat beside his son: 'The Franks rallied and charged again like the first time and drove the Muslims back to my father.'[16] This charge, like the first, 'almost drove the Muslims from their positions, despite their numbers'.[17]

This was the Franks' final effort. Again it came tantalizingly close to success, so close as to suggest that such an aggressive tactic might have succeeded earlier. Perhaps if these charges had been delivered on fresher horses, with more confident, more eager riders; perhaps if they had included the Templar and Hospitaller knights who had been lost at Cresson; or perhaps if they had been delivered with the full weight of the Frankish army that day – including the knights of Tripoli, of the Ibelins and of Antioch – then such a charge might have had enough momentum to crack the formations around Saladin and put his army to flight. But the 130 elite knights who fought at Cresson were slaves or headless corpses. More than 200 knights had fled with Raymond and his allies. The remaining force was not quite enough.

For both Muslim and Christian commentators, one moment above all others had signalled the outcome of the battle – the desertion of Count Raymond. Ibn al-Athir wrote: 'When the Count fled, their spirits collapsed and they were near to surrendering.'[18] According to Michael the Syrian, 'after the departure of the Count the Franks were like unto men who had lost all hope'. The *Old French Continuation of William of Tyre* agrees that, after Raymond's troops had left the field:

> *The anger of God was so great against the Christian host because of their sins that Saladin vanquished them quickly. Between the hours of terce and nones [9 a.m. and 3 p.m.] he won the entire field.*[19]

It is a striking fact – one that is notably glossed over in modern descriptions of the battle of Hattin – that the only units to escape the ensuing carnage were those of Raymond of Tripoli, Balian of Ibelin and the knights of Antioch. In other words, precisely the forces most opposed to Guy's faction, to its strategy and to its most powerful member, Reynald de Chatillon. This may just be coincidence, but it is more likely to have been deliberate, malicious betrayal. Perhaps the explanation is simply that escape from the fight was much easier for those whose hearts were not truly in it. Whatever the reason for their flight, by the time the True Cross fell, all of Reynald's leading political rivals and their knights were long gone.

Since his youth in Burgundy, Reynald de Chatillon had launched countless charges at the enemy. In tournaments he had jousted with rival Franks. In battle, Armenians, Turks, Byzantines and Arabs had all suffered the thrusts of his lance. The second great Frankish charge at Hattin was Reynald's last. After their attacks had been repulsed, their horses killed or exhausted, Prince Reynald and the other Frankish knights threw down their lances and dismounted. They then fought it out on foot with sword and mace, defending the twin hilltops of Hattin against the tightening noose of the Muslim army. Eventually, late in the battle, the holy 'life-giving' True Cross was overwhelmed. The uncharismatic King Guy inspired little or no allegiance, so the True Cross was the only symbol holding the hard-pressed crusader forces together. With its fall, morale collapsed, as Imad al-Din and Ibn al-Athir respectively observed:

> *The capture of this cross was more important to them than the capture of their king... for the cross they sacrifice their lives, from it they expect salvation... The loss of this cross was a catastrophe that destroyed their courage more than their casualties or the fall of the fortress [Tiberias].*[20]

The seizure of it [the True Cross] was one of their greatest misfortunes, after which they were sure they were doomed to death and destruction.[21]

The end came quickly after that. The mighty Frankish army – the greatest they had ever put into the field – was utterly wiped out. Muslim troops swarmed up the Horns of Hattin, encircling the dwindling knot of warriors around the king's tent, as Frankish resistance finally ebbed. Saladin's son described the moment of victory:

> *I again shouted, 'We have beaten them!' but my father rounded on me and said, 'Be quiet! We have not beaten them until that tent falls.' As he was speaking to me, the tent fell. The sultan dismounted, prostrated himself in thanks to God Almighty and wept for joy.*[22]

With the fall of the royal tent, the king and all the Frankish leaders were taken prisoner. Reynald de Chatillon was captured by a squire of the emir Ibrahim al-Mihrani and was once more in the grip of the Muslims. In 1161, as a valuable hostage, the Prince of Antioch's chances of survival had been pretty high.

This time it was different.

Horns of Hattin, Galilee, 4 July 1187

In front of his tent the victorious sultan surveyed his greatest prizes, lined up for his review. Dusty, bloodied and exhausted, parched with thirst, the mightiest knights of the Latin East stood in humiliated defeat before Saladin.

Saladin courteously invited the Frankish leaders, King Guy and Prince Reynald, to sit. Then he passed Guy a cup of iced water.

'Drink,' he said.

The king drank, then handed the cup to Reynald, who drank in his turn.

Saladin said sharply, 'You are the one giving him the drink. Not with my permission did this man drink and so gain my safe-conduct.'

Saladin then went to inspect his army.

Returning later in the evening, the sultan summoned just the king and Prince Reynald. The king sat outside in the vestibule of the tent, while Saladin had Reynald de Chatillon brought before him in the inner sanctum.

'Prince Arnat,' said Saladin, 'how many times have you sworn an oath and then violated it, or signed agreements that you have ignored?'

'I did nothing more than kings are accustomed to do,' replied Reynald.

'By your law,' asked Saladin, 'if you held me captive, as I do you, what would you do?'

'So help me God,' said Reynald, 'I would cut off your head.'

'Pig,' responded the sultan, 'you are my prisoner and still you answer me with such arrogance!'

Saladin then made an offer, which Reynald had to refuse: abjure Christianity and embrace Islam. Reynald knew this would save his life, but there was no chance that the old crusader would take that way out.

The last words of Reynald de Chatillon were a defiant refusal to renounce his faith.

Saladin drew his sword and struck Reynald where the shoulder meets the neck, almost severing his arm. Reynald fell, his wound spurting blood.

Saladin's Mamluks dragged him into the vestibule and decapitated him.

Chapter 21

THE ULTIMATE CRUSADER

I [Saladin] made a vow to sever the head of the prince, Lord of Kerak, this felon, this King of the Infidels, this fugitive from hell. As soon as he came before my eyes, I cut his throat.

Saladin

His loss was the greatest blow suffered by the unbelievers.

Saladin[1]

Now Reynald was an old man who was experienced in wars, and there was no limit to his strength and courage, and he was held in great fear by the Arabs.

Gregory the Priest

The headless corpse of Reynald de Chatillon slumped in the dust in front of a terrified Guy de Lusignan. Saladin calmed the king down. 'Do not worry,' he said, 'princes do not kill princes, but this man transgressed all boundaries.' According to the *Estoire d'Eracles*, Saladin then sprinkled some of Reynald's blood on his head to signify that he had fulfilled his oath of vengeance. He ordered Reynald's body to be dragged through the dust in Damascus and his head to be displayed there, and in the other cities of Islam.

The version of Reynald's death outlined above blends together a number of the multiple eyewitness and second-hand accounts[2] that make it one of the best-attested death scenes of the Middle Ages. As with any event, details of what happened on 4 July 1187 vary between reports: in some versions Reynald is killed immediately after the battle, not called back later; in one, he refuses to drink the sherbet passed to him by Guy, saying to the sultan, 'If it pleases God I will never eat nor drink anything of yours'; in others, it is Saladin himself who chops off Reynald's head. As an example, Gregory the Priest's version goes as follows:

> *Saladin paid honour to Guy, and made him to sit by his side; and*
> *he also made Reynald to be seated. Then Guy, because he was*
> *burnt up with thirst, demanded water as soon as he sat down,*
> *and Saladin commanded and they gave him water which had been*
> *cooled by snow to drink. And when he had drunk one half of it he*
> *gave the other half to Reynald and he drank. Then Saladin said,*
> *'It is not right for you to give him drink without my command.'*
> *And Guy said unto the Sultan, 'Thirst is death; do not put him*
> *to death with two deaths. Defeat is murder; therefore do not*
> *murder him twice.' And his words pleased the Sultan, and he was*
> *prepared to spare the life of Reynald, if the nobles had not urged*
> *him to kill him. And they said unto him, 'This man is not fit to*
> *live. For behold, he hath sworn the oath [of fealty] several times,*
> *and hath lied'... an hour later he sent and had Reynald brought to*
> *him by himself; and he drew his sword and he killed him with his*
> *own hands.*[3]

A more hyperbolic account is that of Peter of Blois. His version is steeped in religious rhetoric and is based, he claims, on reports from eyewitnesses, including the constable, Amalric de Lusignan:

> *The servants of Satan, swift to spill blood, hung on the words*
> *of the tyrant [Saladin] and that son of eternal death pronounced*
> *sentence of death on the sons and heirs of heavenly life, saying*
> *'This man [Reynald], who has dared to blaspheme against the*
> *glory of my majesty, I will kill with my own hand; the others*
> *will be taken from here and all who do not deny Christ will be*
> *executed.'*
>
> *But when the tempestuous whirlwind broke upon the prince*
> *it was clear what sort of man he was: his face did not pale, his*
> *blood did not freeze, his hair did not stand on end, his voice did*
> *not stick in his throat, his body did not tremble, nor was his mind*
> *disturbed; his intellect and memory were not affected but, intrepid*
> *and serene, he lost none of his customary dignity.*
>
> *The most illustrious prince was thrown to the ground and,*
> *while he lay supine with his eyes raised and fixed on heaven, the*
> *tyrant, with his right foot on Reynald's sacred chest, thrust his*
> *sword into his throat as he spoke the name of Christ that was*
> *always in his heart and on his tongue.*[4]

The killing of Reynald was a remarkable event, and is the only example during the crusades of a ruler openly executing such a prominent enemy. While princes died in the heat of battle, and rulers like Saladin were targeted with assassination attempts, executing the opposition's leaders was unheard of, as Saladin himself confirmed with his comment 'A prince does not kill a prince.' Muslim historians were as amazed as the Franks, and Saladin's propagandists went to great lengths to justify it.

Imad al-Din was fascinated by the killing, which he witnessed. He 'did not cease to investigate the reason for it' until he learned of the oath that the Qadi al-Fadil had made Saladin swear back in 1186, when the sultan was still severely ill. Islamic law holds that prisoners who surrender should be spared. It is in this context of subsequent justifications of the cold-blooded murder of Reynald that the stories about his wicked truce violations and oath-breaking emerge.

Christian historians certainly saw much more behind Reynald's death than truce-breaking. For Michael the Syrian, Reynald was killed through fear and envy of his notable qualities:

> Now Reynald was an old man who was experienced in wars, and there was no limit to his strength and courage, and he was held in great fear by the Arabs.[5]

And the anonymous Frankish chronicler of the Third Crusade wrote that:

> The tyrant [Saladin] either because of his fury or deferring to the excellence of such a great man, cut off the distinguished and aged head with his own hand.[6]

If there was any doubt about the fear and awe Reynald inspired in his Muslim foe, Saladin himself dispelled it. After the battle of Hattin he wrote to the caliph in Baghdad that he had:

> Sworn to shed the blood of the tyrant of Kerak, a man who afflicted the lands of Islam with death and captivity and who had fought previous battles [with the Muslims]... His loss was the greatest blow suffered by the unbelievers.[7]

The sultan himself confirmed what Reynald's story makes clear: the Lord of Kerak was the most effective enemy of the Muslims in the Levant and the most prominent Frankish leader. According to a man who should know, of all the blows dealt to the Franks at Hattin – the massacre of their fighting strength, the capture of King Guy himself – the greatest single blow to the crusader cause was the death of Reynald de Chatillon. As Saladin repeatedly states in his letters of this period, Reynald was the real 'King of the Infidels'.

The victors revelled in the death of their most-hated enemy. One of Imad al-Din's poems runs:

> Noble and pure sword, which cut the head of the Prince and
>   struck the most infamous of the unbelievers!
> His head when falling was bathed in its own blood, like a frog
>   diving into a swamp.
> Troubled by his perfidy, he lashed out like a wild beast, but to
>   the assaults of a traitor, death is the only response.[8]

Saladin killed Reynald partly out of revenge – revenge for the depredations he had made on caravans; revenge for his blasphemous, humiliating attacks on the holy cities and the Hajj routes; revenge as well, perhaps, for the devastating defeat at Mont Gisard, which had smarted with the sultan for more than a decade. Above all, Saladin killed Reynald because he was too dangerous to keep alive. The other leaders could profitably be spared and ransomed. Reynald had to die.

Similarly, in a massacre of nightmarish barbarity, Saladin ordered the death of all the Templar and Hospitaller knights in captivity. This was not because they had violated any oaths, but just as Reynald was the most dangerous and resolute of the Frankish leaders, so the knights of the Military Orders were the Franks' most effective soldiers. As Ibn al-Athir explains:

He singled these out for execution because they were the fiercest
fighters of all the Franks. He wished the Muslims to be rid of their
wickedness.[9]

Christian writers understood this too, explaining that Saladin
'decided to have them utterly exterminated because he knew that they
surpassed all others in battle'.[10] These helpless, shackled prisoners were
slaughtered in another of Saladin's sadistic free-for-alls. Every one of
the warrior monks was scrupulously offered his life if he converted to
Islam, but very few took that option. Blades were then handed to the
Sufis, Qadis and other Islamic cadres who marched with the jihad. Imad
al-Din watched as they rolled up their sleeves and ineptly set about
their gruesome task:

The swords of some of them cut perfectly, they were congratulated;
the blades of others were clumsy and blunt, they were excused;
others were simply ridiculous and they had to be replaced.[11]

Saladin, Imad al-Din tells us, watched the gory spectacle with a
beaming face. The sultan was surprised by the extent of his triumph,
which was unprecedented and complete:

God, the Almighty and Glorious had given the sultan the royalty
and power to achieve what no other king had been able to
achieve… Never, since the Franks occupied the Syrian littoral,
had the Muslims slaked their thirst for vengeance as they did on
the day of Hattin.[12]

Seeing the number of dead, you would not believe that there could
be any prisoners. Seeing the prisoners, you could not believe that
anyone could have been killed.[13]

To commemorate his extraordinary victory, Saladin built a mosque on top of one of the Horns of Hattin.

The battle was indeed a catastrophe for the Kingdom of Jerusalem. The strategy of engaging Saladin in a decisive confrontation, which Reynald had advocated, had failed disastrously. So many men were killed that the plain was carpeted with their corpses. According to the ecstatic Imad al-Din:

> The dead were left abandoned in the ravines and on the hills...
> and their stench was the perfume of glory... the fate inflicted
> on their chiefs taught me a wise lesson: I saw heads flung far
> from their lifeless bodies, eyes crushed in their sockets. I saw
> dirt-covered bodies from which the beauty had been torn by
> the talons of birds of prey, their members sliced off in combat
> and scattered in the dust, naked, ripped, shredded, quartered,
> skulls crushed, throats gashed, ribs broken, heads cut off, feet
> amputated, noses mutilated...[14]

There were many thousands of prisoners too, tied together and led away in droves. Of the proud Frankish nobles there remained:

> Only arrogant lords caught like beasts, only fettered chiefs led on
> a leash, kings reduced to servitude, evildoers unmasked, free men
> reduced to slavery, impostors delivered to the righteous.[15]

There was not enough tent rope to secure them all. So common were Frankish slaves after the battle that a whole family was sold for the price of a pair of sandals.*

---

* This deal was a conscious act of propaganda aimed at posterity: a Muslim fakir (holy man) made the sale deliberately so that people in later years would say, 'There were so many Christian captives that you could buy them for a pair of sandals.' It worked.

There they were, humiliated these insolent ones, naked these
rebels, captive these possessors of thrones. They stumbled, these
egotists. Counts were nothing more than hunted game, knights
became food for wild beasts, precious existences were sold for a
small sum.[16]

The booty, the prisoners and disembodied heads by the bushel were
paraded through Damascus, along with Reynald's remains and the
True Cross, desecrated and brought in upside-down. The Templars
and Hospitallers who had been taken as captives to Damascus were
beheaded in the streets.

Ironically, the vast treasure donated by Henry II had proved to be
a fatal gift. It was only this great wealth that had enabled Guy to hire
soldiers out of all the castles. Fortresses and cities across the kingdom
had been emptied as volunteers signed up, eager for a bit of extra pay.
After Hattin, weakened garrisons across the land, with no relieving
army on the horizon, surrendered one by one. The citadel of Tiberias
capitulated the day after the battle. Nazareth, Haifa and Caesarea were
taken soon afterwards and their populations killed or enslaved. The
great port of Acre surrendered without a fight. Jaffa resisted and was
taken by storm, with great slaughter. Jerusalem, under the command of
Balian of Ibelin, fought fiercely, but eventually the defenders negotiated
terms. Saladin reclaimed the city for Islam on 2 October 1187.

Reynald's last defeat had cost Christendom the Holy City and the
entire Kingdom of Jerusalem. His generalship and aggressive stance may
well have postponed the doom of the Latin Kingdom in the years before
Hattin, but as the power behind the throne of Jerusalem when it fell,
Reynald must bear some responsibility for the catastrophe. However,
growing Islamic power in the region spelled the end of the crusader
states sooner or later. And while Reynald did make mistakes, they are
not the ones traditionally ascribed to him – that he broke truces or was

too aggressive, or too uncomprehending of the realities of the East. No, Reynald's true failure was his inability to reconcile or decisively defeat Raymond of Tripoli and his party. Perhaps for the good of the kingdom he should have stepped back and let his rivals take control, but the same could be said of Raymond.

When Raymond made his show of contrition and rejoined Frankish ranks just before Hattin, Reynald could not bring himself to forgive and forget. He remained openly suspicious and hostile. This antagonism may well have contributed to the terrible defeat, but when you look at Count Raymond's actions before and during the battle, you can't help wondering if Reynald was right all along. In the final reckoning, it was Raymond who lusted after the throne; Raymond who rebelled and allied with Saladin; Raymond who deserted the crusader army at a critical point and condemned it to defeat.

Ever since Urban's speech at Clermont in 1095, the crusading movement had been driven by the goal of capturing and defending Christianity's holiest places. Their loss was the ultimate calamity. Just as the sack of Edessa some forty years before had led to the Second Crusade and spurred Reynald to take the cross, so the fall of Jerusalem shocked and horrified Christendom, inspiring a revival of crusading zeal. Launched in 1189, the Third Crusade was led by the greatest rulers in Western Europe: Emperor Frederick Barbarossa of Germany, King Philip of France and the indomitable Plantagenet King of England, Richard the Lionheart.

With rumours of a new crusade on the horizon, the elated but exhausted Saladin made strenuous efforts to evict the dogged remnants of the Frankish colonies. Soon only a few isolated outposts remained in Frankish hands: on the coast, Tyre, protected by its isthmus, and the city of Antioch, most of whose men had not been at Hattin. Raymond did manage to secure the port of Tripoli, and in the mountains of the county not even Saladin dared challenge the mighty *Krak des Chevaliers*.

In Oultrejordan, Reynald's citadels of Kerak and Mont Real also held out.

Here we see the shadow that Reynald continued to cast on events after his death. Unlike the rest of the kingdom's barons, Reynald had left his castles well manned enough to withstand a siege. He had also left them motivated to resist, despite their hopeless situation. The defenders were reduced to eating cats and dogs, but even when the Lady of Oultrejordan, Stephanie de Milly, asked the garrison of Kerak to surrender (Saladin had promised to release her son, Humphrey, in return), they refused. Only starvation eventually obliged Kerak to surrender in November 1188. Mont Real held out even longer, not yielding until May 1189. On both occasions the defenders were allowed to leave unmolested and made their way to Frankish territory at Tyre.

When the main contingents of the Third Crusade finally arrived in Outremer in 1191, the Emperor Frederick had drowned on the way and King Philip of France proved weak and quarrelsome. Richard the Lionheart was the crusade's true leader and it was he who fought a titanic struggle with Saladin for the Holy Land. The Franks reconquered much of the littoral, where they would rule for another hundred years, but despite defeating Saladin in a series of battles, Richard could not take Jerusalem. Every subsequent crusade in the East would have the recapture of Jerusalem as its goal, but apart from a short interlude in the thirteenth century,* Jerusalem would remain in Muslim hands until the British, under General Allenby, took the city from the dying Ottoman Empire during the First World War.

Raymond III did not survive to greet the Third Crusade. Initially he might have given thanks for his escape from Hattin and taken some satisfaction at the downfall of his rivals, but he soon changed his mind, as the enormity of what he had done sank in. Whether it was

---

* The mercurial Emperor Frederick II regained Jerusalem through negotiation in 1229. The Christians retained the city until 1244, when it fell to the Khwarazmians.

due to calculated treachery or simple cowardice, Raymond was bitterly aware of the impact his desertion had on the outcome of the battle. He may have also regretted the relentless ambition that had led him into alliances with the enemy and had fatally undermined the unity of the Frankish kingdom. Count Raymond of Tripoli died just months after Hattin – of guilt and shame, it was said.

It is odd, given Raymond's alliance with the Franks' greatest enemy, Saladin, that modern historians have focused the blame on Reynald for the loss of the Kingdom of Jerusalem. Abd al-Rahman Azzam's view is typical: 'It can be fairly said that it would have been better for the fate of the Latin Kingdom had he remained in a dungeon in Aleppo.'[17]

For Zoé Oldenbourg, if Reynald had been 'Saladin's paid agent', he could not have been more effective in precipitating Frankish problems. In fact Reynald fought tirelessly and loyally to maintain the Latin Kingdom, while it was Raymond of Tripoli who did more than anyone to destroy it, actually becoming in the process a 'paid agent' of Saladin.

Raymond's ally, Balian of Ibelin – called cruel, fickle and faithless by one chronicler of the Third Crusade – continued to play a controversial role amongst the Franks of Outremer. He remained a determined critic of Guy de Lusignan and became a supporter of Guy's rival, Conrad of Montferrat, for the throne. In 1191 Conrad replaced Guy, who was compensated with the island of Cyprus. There he became the first of a Lusignan dynasty that would last almost three centuries.

In the years after Hattin, Reynald de Chatillon's family maintained his legacy of crusading zeal. When Saladin attacked Tripoli in 1188, new crusaders from the West appeared to reinforce the city. Ironically, given Reynald's feud with the Count of Tripoli, one of these crusaders was the Burgundian noble Hervé de Donzy, probably Reynald's nephew. Among the defenders he was 'before them in renown' and 'he lent timely assistance to the land'.[18] Later, Hervé was to be found fighting at Acre as well. In the next century, Reynald's grandson, King Andrew II of Hungary, sustained the crusading tradition. He was one of the leaders of the Fifth Crusade in 1213. Perhaps he had been brought up on heroic tales of his crusading forebear.

Two years after Reynald's death, when King Richard I was riding to Vézelay to launch his crusade, he made a stop at Donzy. Was this a call of respect on the family of Reynald de Chatillon? Certainly, while Richard was entertained in Donzy, the memory of the great warrior would have been toasted. It is very possible that his epic deeds were sung.

Modern writers have tended to forget just how heroic Reynald's reputation once was. Zoé Oldenbourg claims that, when he died, Reynald 'made his solemn entry into the pantheon of hell, from which it occurred to no Latin historian to rescue him'. This was not the case. Reynald's memory was very much alive for the chroniclers of the Third Crusade, such as the anonymous author of the *Itinerarium Perigrinorum* and his main source, the crusader prose-poet Ambroise, who wrote of Reynald's 'great excellence'. Other surviving tributes to Reynald include that of the monk Robert of Auxerre, who called Reynald, 'A man of wise counsel and good sense, lover of honesty, brave fighter against the Turks and loyal defender of the Christians.'[19]

Reynald even had a would-be hagiographer, the prominent cleric Peter of Blois, Archdeacon of Bath, who served at the Norman court in Sicily and at the Plantagenet court in England. Peter's tract is called *Passio Reginaldi Principis olim Antiocheni*, 'The Passion of Reynald, one-time Prince of Antioch'. Written in 1188, the work was aimed at encouraging men to join the Third Crusade. It portrayed Reynald's execution by Saladin as the 'passion' of a holy martyr.

At the time, the fate of Reynald, the Templars and the Hospitallers after Hattin was commonly seen as martyrdom. All of them bravely refused to abjure their faith, and the Templars are depicted as competing with each other to be the first to seek glorious death. After the mass murder, it was believed that 'A ray of celestial light shone down clearly on the bodies of the holy martyrs during the three following nights as they lay unburied.'[20]

The *Passio Reginaldi*, focusing on Reynald, goes even further, providing an example of how 'The sacrifice demanded of the faithful soldier of Christ is distilled into a vision of glory.'[21] According to Peter of Blois, Reynald's life was not one of brutality, greed and selfish indulgence, but of saintly moderation and Christian virtue:

> For he was most strenuous in arms, most firm in faith in Christ, most serene of face, full of reverence in his actions, patient in hope, profuse in his charity.[22]

Reynald's death was holy and heroic: not only did he resist conversion to Islam, but, in the face of doom, he attempted to convert Saladin to Christianity! 'If you believe in him [Jesus],' Peter of Blois has Reynald tell Saladin, 'you can avoid the tortures of eternal damnation which you know are prepared for you.'[23]

As a member of Henry II's entourage around the time of Reynald's death, Peter was in touch with Henry's queen, Eleanor of Aquitaine, and later became her secretary. It is tempting to conjecture that Eleanor remembered Reynald from the days of the Second Crusade half a century before. Perhaps Peter heard some (no doubt embroidered) stories from the queen, reminiscing about the handsome young knight she might have laughed with in her youth, in that heyday of courtly love. Maybe this is the source of Peter's (highly unlikely) romantic tale that the youthful Reynald abandoned a wealthy fiancée in favour of the crusade.

Reynald, the embodiment of the traditional crusading spirit, was a hero famous all over Europe and, if posterity had turned out differently, he might well have ended up a saint, rather than a villain. During the Third Crusade the chances of a St Reynald looked good – his reputation had the sympathy of the great King Richard himself. When he arrived in

Outremer, Richard embraced Reynald's faction and backed the claim of Guy de Lusignan to the disputed crown of Jerusalem. But Richard's rival on crusade, King Philip of France, espoused the party led by Reynald's bitter enemy, Balian of Ibelin, and supported Conrad of Montferrat for the throne. Back in Europe after the crusade, the differences between Philip Augustus and the Plantagenet kings of England flared into open war. After the death of the invincible Richard, Philip overcame his weaker brother, the ill-fated King John. The historian Joel Gourdon sees this defeat of Reynald's Plantagenet sympathizers as a turning point for Reynald's reputation.[24]

The most common way in which Christian contemporaries understood the loss of Jerusalem was as God's punishment on the Franks of Outremer for their evil deeds. This made it hard for any of the Frankish leaders to win too holy a reputation. Then there was the prevalence of Reynald's critics, like William of Tyre and Ernoul, in mapping out crusader history. There was also the idealization in the West of Saladin as a chivalric hero. All this – and the need for a simple storyline for the crusader adventure – helped to cast Reynald as the scapegoat and relegate him to the lower levels of hell.

In more recent times, Reynald's reputation has suffered even further. His resolute and belligerent opposition to Saladin has not sat well in an age riddled with guilt over colonialism and doubts over Western military interventions in the Middle East.

Reynald was certainly no saint, but neither was he a cruel, irredeemable villain. He was a man brought up to kill, and who did so with devotion and skill, usually – though often tenuously – in the name of God. He could be reckless, brutal, vengeful and rapacious. In his youth the ambitious knight-errant with the swan emblem was romantic. Throughout his life he thrived on wealth, luxury and glory. He was extreme in his passions, both in sinning and repenting. He loved the grand gesture.

He was not inferior to Raymond of Poitiers as Prince of Antioch, nor was he unadapted and uncomprehending as the leading lay power in the Kingdom of Jerusalem. He dedicated his life to the crusader cause, and was unswerving in his commitment to his monarch and to the interests of the families and fiefdoms he acquired. He was the leader of one of the factions guilty of ripping the kingdom apart, but that faction was defined more by its loyal opposition to the excessive ambition and treachery of Raymond of Tripoli than by anything else. Reynald almost certainly did, like many others, break truces, though these breaches appear to have been as much for the good of the Kingdom of Jerusalem as for his own gain.

Reynald was a twelfth-century man imbued with the energetic, adventurous spirit of the time. He was at the cutting edge of that outward-looking, expansionist society. As much as, if not more than, the great creators, inventors and thinkers of Christendom, it was the crude adventurers and fighting men like Reynald who, through the deep wounds they inflicted on Islam in the crusading period, laid the foundations for Western supremacy and turned the tide of history. In doing so, Reynald attacked Islam in a way so traumatizing that it fanned the flames of jihad and still antagonizes some Muslims to this day.

The sheer ambition and graphic nature of his excesses peeled away the veneer of the chivalric ideal. He could be considered, persuasive and diplomatic in the loftiest circles, charismatic enough to make a king. In the chivalrous parlance of the time, he was a *preudhomme*, wise, courteous, noble and steadfast. Above all he was loyal, he was brave and he was a soldier, well versed in war.

Reynald de Chatillon was a knight.

Reynald de Chatillon was a crusader.

ENDNOTES

Introduction: A Monstrous Unbeliever

1 Imad al-Din (1125–1201) was a contemporary of Reynald de Chatillon and a bureaucrat in the service of Reynald's bitter enemies, Nur al-Din and Saladin. Imad al-Din's views are preserved here in the chronicle of Abu Shama, *The Book of the Two Gardens*, in *Receuil des Historiens des Croisades, Historiens Orientaux*, Vol. 4, Part 1, pp.258–9.

2 The name on the address was actually 'Reynald Krak', taken from Reynald's fortress of Kerak (or Krak). A second bomb was sent by UPS and addressed to Diego Deza, whom AQAP accused of 'the extermination and expulsion of the Muslim presence on the Iberian Peninsula'. Deza was Grand Inquisitor of Spain in the early sixteenth century and an assiduous persecutor of Muslims. Luckily, thanks to some brave and brilliant Saudi undercover work, both bombs were intercepted before they exploded.

3 *Inspire* magazine (November 2010), p.7

4 Amin Maalouf, *The Crusades Through Arab Eyes* (1983), p.186

5 Ibid.

6 Zoé Oldenbourg, *The Crusades* (1965), p.345, and Sir Steven Runciman, *A History of the Crusades*, Vol. 2 (Cambridge, 1951), p.186. Sir Steven's misreading of Reynald does not detract from the fact that his magnificent work is still the best overview of the crusades in English and remains the canonical text.

7 See especially the remarkable, scholarly work of Bernard Hamilton in his article 'Elephant of Christ', in *Studies in Church History*, Vol. 15 (Oxford, 1978), and his book, *The Leper King and His Heirs* (Cambridge, 2000).

8 The source for this is Matthew Teller, *Rough Guide to Jordan* (2009), p.243. Other examples include the travel blog www.raesevelt.com/2011/11/karak. html.

9 Atlas Tours website, www.atlastours.net/jordan/kerak.html

10 *Crusades*, BBC TV series (1995), presented by medieval scholar and Monty Python comedian Terry Jones

11 *Kingdom of Heaven*, released in 2005, directed by Ridley Scott, starring Orlando Bloom as the crusader lord (and rival of Reynald) Balian of Ibelin, and the glorious Eva Green as Princess Sybilla

12 Odo of Deuil, *The Journey of Louis VII to the East*, ed. and trans. Virginia Gingerick Berry (New York, 1948), p.9

13 Letter from Bernard of Clairvaux to Pope Eugenius III, collected in J. P. Migne (ed.), *Patrologia Latina*, Vol. 182, letter no. 247, trans. in Runciman, op. cit., p.254

1 Dead Man Walking

1 Most in-depth discussion of Reynald's ancestry is in Jean Richard, *Aux origines d'un grand lignage, des Palladii a Renaud de Chatillon*, in *Media in Francia, Recueil de mélanges offert à Karl Ferdinand Werner* (Hérault, 1969), pp.409–18.

2 The point about the expansion of Christendom is brilliantly made by Jonathan Phillips in his book *The Second Crusade* (2007).

3 William of Malmesbury, *Gesta Regum Anglorum*, ed. and trans. R. A. B. Mynors, R. M. Thomson and M. Winterbottom (Oxford, 1998–9), Vol. 1, p.655

4 Nersēs Šnorhali, *Lament over Edessa*, trans. T. M. Van Lint, in *East and West in the Crusader States*, ed. K. Ciggar and H. Teule (Leuven, 1999), p.74

5 Papal Bull *Quantum Praedecessores*, trans. Jonathan Riley-Smith, in J. Riley-Smith, *The Crusades: A History* (London, 2014), p.149

6 Orderic Vitalis (X, 19), trans. Thomas Forester

7 Usama Ibn Munqidh, *An Arab-Syrian Gentleman and Warrior in the Period of the Crusades, Memoirs of Usama Ibn-Munqidh*, trans. Philip K. Hitti (New York, 1929), p.115

8 Fulcher of Chartres, *Historia Hierosolymitana Gesta Francorum Peregrinantium*, trans. August C. Krey, *The First Crusade: The Accounts of Eyewitnesses and Participants* (Princeton, 1921), p.281

9 Ibid.

10 C. Oulmont, *Les Débats du clerc et du chevalier* (Paris, 1911), p.113

11 Peter of Blois, *Passio Reginaldi Principis Olim Antiocheni*, trans. Bill Newton, *The Passion of Reynald, One-time Prince of Antioch* (2015)

12 *Les Chansons de croisade avec leurs melodies*, ed. J. Beier and P. Aubry (Paris, 1909), pp.8–11, trans. M. Routledge, quoted in Jonathan Phillips, op. cit.

13 Guibert of Nogent, *The Deeds of God Through the Franks*, quoted in M. Keen, *Chivalry* (New Haven and London, 1984), p.48

14 Fulcher of Chartres, *A History of the Expedition to Jerusalem, 1095–1127*, trans. Francis Rita Ryan, ed. Harold S. Fink (Knoxville, 1969)

15 Bernard of Clairvaux, *Epistolae*, in *Sancti Bernardi Opera*, ed. J. Leclerq and H. Rochais (Rome, 1955–77), trans. B. S. James, *The Letters of Saint Bernard of Clairvaux* (Stroud, 1977), p.462

16 Bertan de Born, 'A War Song for the Count of Toulouse', from Barbara Smythe, trans., *The Trobador Poets, Selections from the Poems of Eight Trobadors translated from the Provençal with Introduction and Notes* (London and New York, 1911), pp.70–94

17 Cover blurb on Usama Ibn Munqidh, trans. Hitti, op. cit.

18 Usama Ibn Munqidh, trans. Hitti, op. cit., p.191

19 Usama Ibn Munqidh, trans. Hitti, op. cit., p.174

20 Roger of Hoveden, *Chronica*, ed. W. Stubbs (London, 1885), Vol. II, pp.166–7; translation cited in M. Keen, op. cit., p.88

21 St Augustine of Hippo, *City of God*

22 John of Salisbury, *Policraticus*, trans. John Dickinson (New York, 1927), Book 6, Chapter VIII

23 St Bernard of Clairvaux, *In Praise of the New Knighthood*, in *The Cistercian Fathers Series: Number Nineteen, The Works of Bernard of Clairvaux: Volume Seven, Treatises III*, trans. Conrad Greenia (Kalamazoo, MI, 1977)

24 Ibid.

25 Guibert of Nogent, quoted in Keen, op. cit., pp.48–9

26 Aymar de Pegulhan, quoted by S. Painter, *French Chivalry* (Baltimore, 1940), p.87

2 The Wild East

1 Fulcher of Chartres, trans. Ryan, op. cit., Book III

2 Ibn al-Athir, *Al-Kamil fi'l-Tarikh*, in Donald S. Richards, *The Chronicle of Ibn al-Athir for the Crusading Period* (2007), Part 2, p.40

3 Ibn Jubayr, *Travels*, trans. R. Broadhurst (London, 1952), p.318

4 *The Letters of Bernard of Clairvaux*, trans. B. S. James (Stroud, 1998), p.462

3 Knight-errant

1 John Kinnamos, *Deeds of John and Manuel Comnenus*, trans. Charles M. Brand (New York, 1976). Kinnamos was writing after the sack of Constantinople by the Fourth Crusade in 1204, so his assessment of crusading motives is somewhat coloured by hindsight. However, this deeply suspicious view was already present amongst the Byzantines at the time of the Second Crusade.

2 Odo of Deuil, trans. Virginia Gingerick Berry, op. cit., p.63

3 Gregory Bar Hebraeus ('Gregory the Priest'), *Chronography*, trans. E. A. Wallis Budge (London, 1932), Book X

4 William of Tyre, *A History of Deeds Done Beyond the Sea*, trans. E. A. Babcock and A. C. Krey (New York, 1943), Book XVI, Chapter XXVII

5 William of Tyre, trans. Babcock and Krey, op. cit., Book XIV, Chapter XXI

6 Kinnamos, trans. Brand, op. cit.

7 Nicetas Choniates, *O City of Byzantium, Annals of Niketas Choniatēs*, trans. Harry J. Margoulias (1984), p.62

8 Gregory the Priest, *Chronography*, Book X

9 Ibn al-Qalanisi, *Chronicle*, in *The Damascus Chronicle of the Crusades*, trans. H. A. Gibb (London, 1932)

10 Ibn Jubayr, trans. Broadhurst, op. cit., p.320

11 Usama Ibn Munqidh, trans. Hitti, op. cit., pp.140–1

12 The main guide for this short discussion of chivalry is the classic *Chivalry* (1984), by the late, great Maurice Keen

13 Peter of Blois, trans. Newton, op. cit.

14 William of Tyre, trans. Babcock and Krey, op. cit., Book XVII, Chapter IX

15 Ibid.

16 Michael the Syrian, *Chronicle of Michael the Great, Patriarch of the Syrians*

17 William of Tyre, trans. Babcock and Krey, op. cit., Book XVII, Chapter IX

18 Ibid.
19 Ibid.

4 Arriviste

1 William of Tyre, trans. Babcock and Krey, op. cit., Book XVII, Chapter XVIII
2 William of Tyre, trans. Babcock and Krey, op. cit., Book XVII, Chapter X
3 *William of Tyre, History of Deeds Done Beyond the Sea*, trans. M. Guizot (Paris, 1824), p.50
4 Kinnamos, trans. Brand, op. cit.
5 William of Tyre, trans. Babcock and Krey, op. cit., Book XVII, Chapter XVIII
6 Ibn al-Athir, trans. Richards, op. cit., Part 2, p.31
7 William of Tyre, trans. Babcock and Krey, op. cit., Book XVII, Chapter XVIII
8 Ibid.
9 William of Tyre, trans. Babcock and Krey, op. cit., Book XVII, Chapter XXVI
10 William of Tyre, trans. Babcock and Krey, op. cit., Book XVII, Chapter XXI
11 *Old French Version of William of Tyre, 'Estoire d'Eracles'*, Book XVII, Chapter XXVI
12 J. Richard, op. cit.
13 William of Tyre, trans. Babcock and Krey, op. cit., Book XVII, Chapter XXVI
14 *Estoire d'Eracles*, quoted in Pierre Aubé, *Un Croisé contre Saladin* (Paris, 2007), p.56
15 William of Tyre, trans. Babcock and Krey, op. cit., Book XVII, Chapter XXVI
16 *Estoire d'Eracles*, Book XVII, Chapter XXVI

5 Diabolic Daring

1 William of Tyre, trans. Babcock and Krey, op. cit., Book XVII, Chapter XVIII
2 William of Tyre, trans. Babcock and Krey, op. cit., Book XVIII, Chapter I
3 Ibid.
4 William of Tyre, trans. Babcock and Krey, op. cit., Book XV, Chapter XVII
5 Jonathan Phillips, *Holy Warriors* (London, 2009), p.107
6 For example, in his tract *The Passion of Reynald, One-time Prince of Antioch*, Peter of Blois says that Reynald speaks Arabic.
7 Ibn Jubayr, trans. Broadhurst, op. cit., p.322
8 Ibn Jubayr, trans. Broadhurst, op. cit., p.317
9 Ernoul, *Chronique d'Ernoul et Bernard le Tesorier*, Chapter IV
10 Ibn al-Qalanisi, trans. Gibb, op. cit.
11 R. C. Smail, *Crusading Warfare 1097–1193* (Cambridge, 1956), p.18
12 Usama Ibn Munqidh, trans. Hitti, op. cit., p.42

6 A Violent Sinner

1 William of Tyre, trans. Babcock and Krey, op. cit., Book XVIII, Chapter X
2 Ibid.
3 Ibid.
4 William of Tyre and Gregory the Priest both think Reynald defeated Thoros. Michael the Syrian, who was biased towards Thoros, claimed the Armenian

won. Reynald's victory is more likely, especially as the castles he demanded were restored to the Templars.

5 William of Tyre, trans. Babcock and Krey, op. cit., Book XVIII, Chapter X
6 Kinnamos, trans. Brand, op. cit.
7 William of Tyre, trans. Babcock and Krey, op. cit., Book XVIII, Chapter X
8 Ibid.
9 Ibid.
10 Ibid.
11 William of Tyre, trans. Babcock and Krey, op. cit., Book XVIII, Chapter XXIII

7 Guardian of the Land

1 William of Tyre, trans. Babcock and Krey, op. cit., Book XVIII, Chapter XVII
2 William of Tyre, trans. Babcock and Krey, op. cit., Book XVII, Chapter XXVI
3 *Eracles*, op. cit., Book XVIII, Chapter XVII
4 William of Tyre, trans. Babcock and Krey, op. cit., Book XVIII, Chapter XVII
5 Ibn al-Athir, trans. Richards, op. cit., p.87
6 Ibn al-Athir, trans. Richards, op. cit., p.89
7 William of Tyre, trans. Babcock and Krey, op. cit., Book XVIII, Chapter XVIII
8 Ibid.
9 Runciman, op. cit., Vol. II, p.349
10 William of Tyre, trans. Babcock and Krey, op. cit., Book XVII, Chapter VII
11 William of Tyre, trans. Babcock and Krey, op. cit., Book XVII, Chapter XIX
12 Abu Shama, op. cit., Part 1, p.96
13 Latin and Greek historians alike draw attention to the shame of Reynald's short tunic and sleeves. Long tunics and sleeves were fashionable and the mark of a knight. St Bernard, in his Epistle on the New Knighthood, criticized vain knights for tripping themselves up with 'long and full tunics', and for burying their 'tender, delicate hands in big cumbersome sleeves'.

8 Imperial Vassal

1 William of Tyre, trans. Babcock and Krey, op. cit., Book XVIII, Chapter XXIII
2 Kinnamos, trans. Brand, op. cit.
3 William of Tyre, trans. Babcock and Krey, op. cit., Book XVIII, Chapter XXIII
4 Choniates, trans. Margoulias, op. cit.
5 Ibid.
6 Ibid.
7 Ibid., p.62
8 Ibn al-Qalanisi, trans. Gibb, op. cit.
9 Aubé, op. cit., p.101
10 Choniates, trans. Brand, op. cit.
11 William of Tyre, trans. Babcock and Krey, op. cit., Book XVIII, Chapter XXXI
12 Choniates, trans. Brand, op. cit.
13 Michael the Syrian, op. cit.

9 In the Power of Nur al-Din

1 Usama Ibn Munqidh, trans. Hitti, op. cit., p.150
2 Abu Shama, op. cit., Part 1, p.89
3 William of Tyre, trans. Babcock and Krey, op. cit., Book XX, Chapter XVIII
4 Accounts of the 1170 earthquake from William of Tyre, Michael the Syrian, Gregory the Priest, all op. cit.

10 Years of Darkness

1 Nicholas N. Ambraseys, *The 12th century seismic paroxysm in the Middle East: a historical perspective*, in *Annals of Geophysics*, Vol. 47, No. 2/3 (April/June 2004)
2 Fulcher of Chartres, trans. Ryan, op. cit.
3 Ibn Khaldun, *Muqaddima*, trans. F. Rosenthal (New York, 1958), quoted in Carole Hillenbrand, 'On the Captivity of Reynald de Chatillon', in *Texts, Documents and Artefacts: Islamic Studies in Honour of D. S. Richards*, ed. Chase F. Robinson (Leiden, 2003)
4 William of Tyre, trans. Babcock and Krey, op. cit., Book XVIII, Chapter XXXIV
5 Brian Keenan, *An Evil Cradling* (London, 1993), p.103
6 Edna J. Hunter, 'The Vietnam POW Veteran; Immediate and Long-Term Effects of Captivity', in *Stress Disorders among Vietnam Veterans*, ed. Charles R. Figley (1978)
7 This is Yvonne Friedman's point in *Encounter Between Enemies, Captivity and Ransom in the Latin Kingdom of Jerusalem* (Leiden, 2002), pp.180–1
8 Hillenbrand, op. cit.
9 This is the view of, for instance, the leading modern historian of the Latin Kingdom, Joshua Prawer, in *The Crusaders' Kingdom* (New York, 1972), p.71
10 William of Tyre, trans. Babcock and Krey, op. cit., Book XX, Chapter XXVIII
11 '*Un peu de lettres*', quoted in Gustave Schlumberger, *Renaud de Châtillon* (Paris, 1898), p.158
12 Ibn al-Athir, trans. Richards, op. cit., p.221
13 Ibid.

11 Phoenix

1 Peter of Blois, trans. Newton, op. cit.
2 William of Tyre, trans. Babcock and Krey, op. cit., Book XX, Chapter XI
3 Ibid.
4 William of Tyre, trans. Babcock and Krey, op. cit., Book XXI, Chapter I
5 Ibn al-Athir, trans. Richards, op. cit., p.234
6 Reynald's part in this embassy was cleverly detected by Professor Bernard Hamilton in *The Leper King and His Heirs*, p.111
7 Choniates, op. cit.
8 Ernoul, op. cit., Chapter IV
9 List of knights' service by John of Ibelin, from *Livre de Jean d'Ibelin*, in *Receuil des Historiens des Croisades, Historiens Occidentaux*, Vol. 1., pp.422–6

10 Hamilton, *Leper King*, p.118
11 William of Tyre, *History*, quoted in Joel Gourdon, *Le Cygne et l'Elephant* (Paris, 2001), p.121
12 William of Tyre, *History*, quoted in Hamilton, *Leper King*, p.118
13 William of Tyre, *History*, quoted in Hamilton, *Leper King*, p.128
14 William of Tyre, trans. Babcock and Krey, op. cit., Book XXI, Chapter XX
15 Abu Shama, op. cit., and Michael the Syrian, op. cit.

12 Hero

1 Bertran de Born, trans. Smythe, op. cit., p.90
2 William of Tyre, trans. Babcock and Krey, op. cit., Book XXI, Chapter XXIV
3 Ernoul, op. cit., Chapter VII
4 Baha al-Din, *The Rare and Excellent History of Saladin*, trans. D. S. Richards (2002), p.54
5 Michael the Syrian, op. cit.

13 Lord of *La Grande Berrie*

1 Ibn Battuta, *Travels in Asia and Africa 1325–1354* (London, 1929), p.72
2 Prawer, op. cit., p.395
3 Imad al-Din in Abu Shama, op. cit., p.259
4 Baha al-Din, trans. Richards, op. cit., p.48
5 Ibid.
6 Hamilton, *Leper King*, p.141
7 Quoted in Hamilton, *Leper King*, p.140
8 William of Tyre, *History*, quoted in Hamilton, *Leper King*, p.151
9 William of Tyre, *History*, quoted in Hamilton, *Leper King*, p.152
10 William of Tyre, trans. Babcock and Krey, op. cit., Book XXI, Chapter IV
11 Ernoul, op. cit., Chapter VIII
12 Abu Shama, op. cit.
13 William of Tyre, trans. Babcock and Krey, op. cit., Book XXII, Chapter VI

14 Desert Raider

1 Ibn Battuta, op. cit., p.72
2 Hamilton, *Leper King*, p.171
3 Ibn al-Athir, trans. Richards, op. cit., p.276
4 Baha al-Din, quoted in Abu Shama, op. cit.
5 Ibn Jubayr, trans. Broadhurst, op. cit.
6 Ibid.

15 Sea Wolf

1 Ernoul, op. cit., Chapter VII
2 Hamilton, 'Elephant of Christ'
3 Ibn Jubayr, trans. Broadhurst, op. cit.
4 Letter from the Qadi Al-Fadil to the caliph in Baghdad, quoted in Abu Shama, op. cit., p.233

5 Letter from the Qadi al-Fadil to Baghdad, in Abu Shama, op. cit., p.234
6 Quran, sura 39, verse 71
7 Letter of Saladin, quoted in M. C. Lyons and D. E. P. Jackson, *Saladin, The Politics of Holy War* (Cambridge, 1982), p.187
8 Imad al-Din, quoted in Schlumberger, op. cit., pp.280–1
9 Letter from the sultan, quoted in Lyons and Jackson, op. cit., p.187
10 Ibn Jubayr, trans. Broadhurst, op. cit.

16 The Lion and the Wolf

1 Letter of Qadi Al-Fadil, in Abu Shama, op. cit., p.253
2 Letter to the Emir Toghtekin, quoted in Lyons and Jackson, op. cit., p.202
3 William of Tyre, *History*, quoted in Lyons and Jackson, op. cit., p.207
4 Gregory the Priest, op. cit.
5 Abu Shama, op. cit., pp.252–4
6 Letter of Imad al-Din, in Abu Shama, op. cit., p.255
7 Ibid.
8 Ernoul, op. cit., Chapter IX
9 William of Tyre, *History*, quoted in Hamilton, *Leper King*, p.199

17 The 'Manchurian' Regent

1 Ibn Jubayr, trans. Broadhurst, op. cit., p.324
2 G. Axelrod (screenplay), *The Manchurian Candidate* (1962)
3 Ibn Jubayr, trans. Broadhurst, op. cit., p.324
4 Ibn al-Athir, trans. Richards, op. cit., p.315
5 Oldenbourg, op. cit., p.404
6 Imad al-Din, in Abu Shama, op. cit., p.258
7 Imad al-Din, in Abu Shama, quoted in Lyons and Jackson, op. cit., p.241

18 King-maker

1 Main sources for Sybilla's coronation as described on previous pages and here: Ernoul, op. cit., Chapter XI, and *Estoire d'Eracles*, Chapter XVII. Reynald's speech in the Holy Sepulchre is in *Estoire d'Eracles*, Chapter XVII.
2 Anonymous, *Itinerarium Perigrinorum et Gesta Regis Ricardi, Chronicle of the Third Crusade*, trans. Helen J. Nicholson (2001), p.122
3 *Old French Continuation of William of Tyre*, trans. Peter Edbury, *The Conquest of Jerusalem and the Third Crusade* (Farnham, 1996), p.46
4 *Latin Continuation of William of Tyre*, quoted in Hamilton, *Leper King*, p.223
5 Ernoul, op. cit., Chapter XI
6 Imad al-Din, in Abu Shama, op. cit., p.258
7 *The Latin Continuation of William of Tyre*
8 Ibn al-Athir, trans. Richards, op. cit., p.316
9 Imad al-Din, in Abu Shama, op. cit., p.257
10 References for Reynald's statements: Ernoul, op. cit, and Baha al-Din in Abu Shama, op. cit., p.280

19 Truce-breaker

1 Runciman, op. cit., Vol. II, pp.450, 459
2 Ibn al-Athir, trans. Richards, op. cit., p.316
3 Imad al-Din, in Abu Shama, op. cit., p.259
4 Ibid.
5 Lyons and Jackson, op. cit., p.248
6 *Itinerarium Perigrinorum*, trans. Nicholson, op. cit., p.23
7 Ibn al-Athir, trans. Richards, op. cit., p.316
8 Ibn al-Athir, trans. Richards, op. cit., p.319
9 Imad al-Din, in Abu Shama, op. cit., p.263
10 Imad al-Din, in Abu Shama, op. cit., pp.261–3
11 Imad al-Din, in Abu Shama, op. cit., p.263
12 Ibn al-Athir, trans. Richards, op. cit.
13 Ibn al-Athir, trans. Richards, op. cit.
14 Imad al-Din, in Abu Shama, op. cit.
15 References for these statements: *Old French Continuation of William of Tyre*, Chapter XXXII; Ibn al-Athir, *Al-Kamil fi'l Tarikh*

20 Apocalypse

1 Ibn al-Athir, trans. Richards, op. cit., p.324
2 Baha al-Din, trans. Richards, op. cit., p.73
3 *Old French Continuation*, Chapter XXXIII
4 Imad al-Din, in Abu Shama, op. cit., p.267
5 This stop was identified in the best account of the battle – the scholarly and objective account by B. Z. Kedar, 'The Battle of Hattin Revisited', in *The Horns of Hattin*, Proceedings for the Second Conference of the Society for the Study of the Crusades and the Latin East (1987)
6 *Estoire d'Eracles*, Chapter XL
7 *Estoire d'Eracles*, Chapter XLI
8 Baha al-Din, trans. Richards, op. cit., p.73
9 *Old French Continuation*, trans. Edbury, op. cit., p.46
10 *Estoire d'Eracles*, Chapter XLI
11 Baha al-Din, trans. Richards, op. cit., p.74
12 *Itinerarium Perigrinorum*, trans. Nicholson, op. cit., p.32
13 Imad al-Din, in Abu Shama, op. cit., p.270
14 Anna Comnena, *Alexiad*
15 Ibn al-Athir, trans. Richards, op. cit., p.323
16 Ibid.
17 Ibid.
18 Ibn al-Athir, trans. Richards, op. cit., p.322
19 *Old French Continuation*, trans. Edbury, op. cit., p.47
20 Imad al-Din, in Abu Shama, op. cit., p.274
21 Ibn al-Athir, trans. Richards, op. cit., p.323
22 Ibid.

21 The Ultimate Crusader

1 *Diwan rasai'il al-Katib al-Isfahani*, MS. Nuri Osmaniye (Istanbul), No. 3745, quoted in Lyons and Jackson, op. cit., p.264
2 Including: *Old French Continuation*, trans. Edbury, op. cit., p.48; Baha al-Din, trans. Richards, op. cit., pp.38, 75; Ibn al-Athir, trans. Richards, op. cit., pp.323–4
3 Gregory the Priest, op. cit., Chapter X
4 Peter of Blois, trans. Newton, op. cit.
5 Michael the Syrian, op. cit.
6 *Itinerarium Perigrinorum*, trans. Nicholson, op. cit., p.34
7 *Diwan rasai'il al-Katib al-Isfahani*, MS. Nuri Osmaniye (Istanbul), No. 3745, quoted in Lyons and Jackson, op. cit., p.264
8 Imad al-Din, in Abu Shama, op. cit., p.290
9 Ibn al-Athir, trans. Richards, op. cit., p.324
10 *Itinerarium Perigrinorum*, trans. Nicholson, op. cit., p.34
11 Imad al-Din, in Abu Shama, op. cit. p.271
12 Ibid.
13 Imad al-Din, in Abu Shama, op. cit. p.272
14 Imad al-Din, in Abu Shama, op. cit. p.273
15 Ibid.
16 Ibid.
17 Abdul Rahman Azzam, *Saladin* (London, 2009), p.113
18 *Itinerarium Perigrinorum*, trans. Nicholson, op. cit., p.44
19 Quoted in Gourdon, op. cit., p.231
20 *Itinerarium Perigrinorum*, trans. Nicholson, op. cit., p.34
21 Christopher Tyerman, *God's War, A New History of the Crusades* (London, 2006)
22 Peter of Blois, trans. Newton, op. cit.
23 Peter of Blois, trans. Newton, op. cit.
24 Gourdon, op. cit., p.232

SELECT BIBLIOGRAPHY

Medieval sources

Abu Shama, *The Book of the Two Gardens*, in *Receuil des Historiens des Croisades, Historiens Orientaux*, Vol. 4 Baha al-Din, *The Rare and Excellent History of Saladin*, trans. D. S. Richards (2002)

Bernard of Clairvaux, Epistle on the New Knighthood

Bertran de Born, in Barbara Smythe, trans., *The Trobador Poets, Selections from the Poems of Eight Trobadors translated from the Provençal with Introduction and Notes* (London and New York, 1911)

Nicetas Choniates, *O City of Byzantium, Annals of Niketas Choniatēs*, trans. Harry J. Margoulias (1984)

Chronicle of the Third Crusade, trans. Helen J. Nicholson (2001)

Anna Comnena, *Alexiad*

De Expugnatione Terrae Sanctum per Saladinum

Ernoul, *Chronique d'Ernoul et Bernard le Tesorier*

Estoire d'Eracles

Fulcher of Chartres, *Historia Hierosolymitana Gesta Francorum Peregrinantium*, trans. August C. Krey, *The First Crusade: The Accounts of Eyewitnesses and Participants* (Princeton, 1921)

Gregory Bar Hebraeus ('Gregory the Priest'), *Chronography*, trans. E. A. Wallis Budge (London, 1932)

Guibert of Nogent, *The Deeds of God Through the Franks*

Ibn al-Athir, *Al-Kamil fi'l-Tarikh*, in Donald S. Richards, *The Chronicle of Ibn al-Athir for the Crusading Period* (2007)

Ibn Battuta, *Travels in Asia and Africa 1325–1354* (London, 1929)

Ibn Jubayr, *Travels*, trans. R. Broadhurst (London, 1952)

Ibn al-Qalanisi, *Chronicle*, in *The Damascus Chronicle of the Crusades*, trans. H. A. Gibb (London, 1932)

John Kinnamos, *Deeds of John and Manuel Comnenus*, trans. Charles M. Brand (New York, 1976)

John of Ibelin, *Livre de Jean d'Ibelin*, in *Receuil des Historiens des Croisades, Historiens Occidentaux*, Vol. 1

John of Salisbury, *Policraticus*, trans. John Dickinson (New York, 1927)

Michael the Syrian, *Chronicle of Michael the Great, Patriarch of the Syrians*

Odo of Deuil, *The Journey of Louis VII to the East*, ed. and trans. Virginia Gingerick Berry (New York, 1948)

Old French Continuation of William of Tyre, trans. Peter Edbury, *The Conquest of Jerusalem and the Third Crusade* (Farnham, 1996)

Peter of Blois, *Passio Reginaldi Principis Olim Antiocheni*, trans. Bill Newton, *The Passion of Reynald, One-time Prince of Antioch* (2015)

Roger of Hoveden, *Chronica*, ed. W. Stubbs (London, 1885)

Sempad the Constable, *Chronicle*

Usama Ibn Munqidh, *An Arab-Syrian Gentleman and Warrior in the Period of the Crusades, Memoirs of Usama Ibn-Munqidh*, trans. Philip K. Hitti (New York, 1929)

William of Malmesbury, *Gesta Regum Anglorum*, ed. and trans. R. A. B. Mynors, R. M. Thomson and M. Winterbottom (Oxford, 1998–9)

William of Tyre, *A History of Deeds Done Beyond the Sea*, trans. E. A. Babcock and A. C. Krey (New York, 1943)

Modern/secondary sources

Asbridge, Thomas, *The Crusades* (London, 2010)

Aubé, P., *Un Croisé contre Saladin* (Paris, 2007)

Azzam, A. R., *Saladin* (London, 2009)

Brundage, James, *Crusades, a Documentary History* (Milwaukee, 1962)

Clermont-Ganneau, C. S., 'Mont Gisart et Tell El-Djezer', in *Receuil d'Archéologie Orientale* (Paris, 1888)

Cobb, Paul M., *Infidel Dogs: Hunting Crusaders with Usama ibn Munqidh*, Notre Dame University History Faculty Colloquium (2004)

Edbury, Peter, *The Conquest of Jerusalem and the Third Crusade* (Farnham, 1996)

Gourdon, J., *Le Cygne et l'Elephant* (Paris, 2001)

Hamilton, B., 'Elephant of Christ', in *Studies in Church History*, Vol. 15 (Oxford, 1978)

Hamilton, B., *The Leper King and His Heirs* (Cambridge, 2000)

Hillenbrand, C., 'On the Captivity of Reynald de Chatillon', in *Texts, Documents and Artefacts: Islamic Studies in Honour of D. S. Richards*, ed. Chase F. Robinson (Leiden, 2003)

Hunter, E. J., 'The Vietnam POW Veteran; Immediate and Long-Term Effects of Captivity', in *Stress Disorders among Vietnam Veterans*, ed. Charles R. Figley (1978)

Inspire magazine

Kedar, B., 'The Battle of Hattin Revisited', in *The Horns of Hattin*, Proceedings for the Second Conference of the Society for the Study of the Crusades and the Latin East (1987)

Keen, M., *Chivalry* (New Haven and London, 1984)

Keenan, B., *An Evil Cradling* (London, 1993)

Kennedy, H., *Crusader Castles* (Cambridge, 1994)

Kingdom of Heaven (film), directed by Ridley Scott (2005)

Krey, A. C., *The First Crusade: The Accounts of Eyewitnesses and Participants* (Princeton, 1921)

La Viere Leiser, Gary, 'The Crusader Raid in the Red Sea in 578/1182–83', in *Journal of the American Research Center in Egypt*, Vol. 14 (1977), pp.87–100

Lawrence, T. E., *Crusader Castles* (1936)

Lawrence, T. E., *Seven Pillars of Wisdom* (1922)

Lewis, B., *The Assassins* (London, 1967)

Lyons, M. C., and Jackson, D. E. P., *Saladin, The Politics of Holy War* (Cambridge, 1982)

Maalouf, A., *The Crusades Through Arab Eyes* (1983)

McCarthy, J. and Morrell, J., *Some Other Rainbow*

Mallett, A., 'A Trip down the Red Sea with Reynald of Châtillon', in *Journal of the Royal Asiatic Society of Great Britain and Ireland* (Third Series), 18 (2008), pp.141–53

Nicolle, D., *Crusader Castles in the Holy Land 1097–1192* (2004)

Nicolle, D., *Medieval Warfare Sourcebook* (1997)

Nissenbaum, A. et al., *Dead Sea Asphalt from the Excavations in Tel Arad and Small Tel Malhata* (1984)

Norwich, J. J., *Byzantium, the Decline and Fall* (1989)

Oulmont, C., *Les Débats du clerc et du chevalier* (Paris, 1911)

Parry, J. J., *The Art of Courtly Love* (1941)

Phillips, J., *Holy Warriors* (2009)

Phillips, J., *The Second Crusade* (2007)

Prawer, J., *The Crusaders' Kingdom* (New York, 1972)

Richard, J., 'Aux origines d'un grand lignage, des Palladii à Renaud de Chatillon', in *Media in Francia, Recueil de mélanges offert à Karl Ferdinand Werner* (Hérault, 1969)

Runciman, Sir S., *A History of the Crusades*, 3 vols (Cambridge, 1951)

Schlumberger, G. L., *Renaud de Chatillon* (Paris, 1898)

Smail, R. C., *The Crusaders* (1973)

Smail, R. C., *Crusading Warfare 1097–1193* (Cambridge, 1956)

Timewatch – The Crusaders' Lost Fort (BBC TV programme)

Tyerman, Christopher, *God's War, A New History of the Crusades* (London, 2006)

Weir, A., *Eleanor of Aquitaine* (1999)

ACKNOWLEDGEMENTS

The seeds of *God's Wolf* were sown by the inspirational history department at Sherborne School. With Jerry Barker we re-enacted AD 43 at Maiden Castle and glimpsed the Dark Age warrior Arthur on Bokerley Dyke and South Cadbury ('which is Camelot'). Huw Ridgeway and Giles 'Doc' Mercer then kindled an enduring fascination for the twelfth century and the crusades.

At Oxford I would like to thank Alan Jones for teaching me Arabic, and D. S. Richards for his patient tutorials on the Seljuk period and latterly for his masterly translations of Baha al-Din and Ibn al-Athir. I was especially fortunate to be taught history – and how to do history – by the late, much missed Patricia Crone, the world's most acute and brilliant historical mind, who read this book early on and provided great encouragement.

I am grateful to Professor Carole Hillenbrand who generously read a draft and made helpful suggestions, as did Julian Ellison, Robert Twigger, and the ever supportive Hoss and Hass Amini. Bill Newton provided an invaluable, vibrant translation of the *Passio Reginaldi* by Peter of Blois – the first time it has appeared in print in English. Thanks as well to Stephanie Cabot, to my determined and perceptive agent, Julian Alexander, and to James Nightingale and the creative, professional team at Atlantic – it has been fun! Of course any errors in fact or interpretation are my own.

Finally, a profound thank you to the constantly amazing Tannaz Lee, who among many other wonderful traits, tolerates her husband's 'obsession with old walls'.

INDEX

A NOTE ABOUT
THE AUTHOR

Jeffrey Lee has a First in Arabic and Islamic History from Oxford and, as an award-winning broadcast journalist, he has produced and reported on news and current affairs in more than thirty countries. He lives in London.